Eleanor
Countess of Desmond

Eleanor
Countess of Desmond

Anne Chambers

Gill & Macmillan

Gill & Macmillan Ltd
Hume Avenue, Park West, Dublin 12
with associated companies throughout the world
www.gillmacmillan.ie

© Anne Chambers 1986, 2000, 2011
978 07171 4828 8

Index compiled by Helen Litton
Typography design by Make Communication
Print origination by Síofra Murphy
Printed by GraphyCems, Spain

This book is typeset in Linotype Minion and Neue Helvetica.

5 4 3 2 1

Contents

Chronology

Prologue

Out of every corner of the woods and glens they came creeping forth upon their hands for their legs could not bear them, they looked like anatomies of death, they spoke like ghosts, crying out of their graves, they did eat the dead carrions, happy where they could find them, yea, and one another soon after, insomuch as the very carcasses they spared not to scrape out of their graves and if they found a plot of watercresses or shamrocks, there they flocked as to a feast for a time, yet not able long to continue there withal, that in short space there were none almost left, and a most populous and plentiful country suddenly left void of man or beast.

EDMUND SPENSER

Edmund Spenser's horrific account of starvation, cannibalism and decay described the state of the most fertile province of Ireland in 1582. The celebrated poet and civil servant bore witness to the dreadful spectacle that appalled his eyes and compelled his stern Elizabethan heart to cry out in pity.

A once rich province, the size of modern Holland, Munster lay devastated. Lush green pasturelands were torched to a blackened heath, devoid of crops or animals. Famine stalked rampant through the vales and over the gently sloping hills. Among the smouldering remains the skeletal figures of the surviving peasantry foraged in vain. The castles and keeps of the local aristocracy lay in ruins, open to the unrelenting icy rain that hissed in vengeance on the smoking embers. The people were scattered and hid like wild beasts in the fortresses of Munster's rugged mountain ranges and in her great, dark forests and wild glens. They peered silently through the bare branches and waited. They awaited the return of the great overlord their master to whom, by tradition as ancient as the vast oak forests that sheltered them, they had given their absolute allegiance. They waited for him to lead them once more into battle in the bloody and futile war that for over three years had raged and ravaged the countryside.

But the great overlord shared the same fate as his clansmen. Askeaton castle, the mighty pile on the banks of the River Deel, the symbol of his family's once proud and powerful heritage, lay in ruins. A company of English horse was stabled in its great banqueting hall. Its lord was hunted like a wild animal over the despoiled estates of his Munster lordship. From the lowly wattle huts of his kern, from cold mountain caves to the ruined fortresses of his ancestors, through the marshy recesses of the Glen of Aherlow, into the dark forest of Kylemore and across the tortuous mountain passes to the west, Garrett FitzGerald, the fourteenth earl of the ancient and noble House of Desmond, fled for his life.

He had many impediments in his headlong flight. His once populous army had vanished, decimated more by famine and fear than by actual engagement with the enemy. His erstwhile allies had, one by one, forsaken him. Every friend had become a potential foe as the price on his head increased. His inheritance of over a half million acres of land in Munster provided the incentive and the scent to the eager English greyhounds who leaped from the slips in pursuit. But perhaps the greatest impediment to his safety stemmed from his own physical disabilities. His body had succumbed to the effects of palsy and the Irish ague, the result of lengthy periods of imprisonment and deprivation, aggravated by the dampness that oozed up from the marshes and bogs and by the rain that dripped incessantly from the bushes and undergrowth in which he hid, or from the sodden thatch of the kerns' cabins when he managed a fitful night's respite from the elements and the enemy. Yet despite these overwhelming liabilities, the earl had one remaining asset—his countess, Eleanor.

By 1582 Garrett and Eleanor had been married for seventeen years. It had, at first sight, seemed an unlikely match—the pale, proud Geraldine widower and the lively young girl from the rival Butler family. But Eleanor had soon proved her worth by bringing to the marriage certain qualities—coolness, prudence, pragmatism, skill in diplomacy, and an instinctive grasp of political realities—which might offset the less balanced traits of her husband. For the earl's outlook was rooted firmly in the feudal tradition of a bygone era from which he derived his jealously-guarded status as the absolute ruler of a territory larger than that of any other magnate in either England or Ireland. His pride and vanity and his aristocratic temperament made it impossible for him to come to terms with the challenges of a new age, typified by the Tudor monarchy, with its commitment to progress, reform, modernisation and the establishment of strong, central government. Such ideals were anathema to the autocratic Earl of Desmond, and were bitterly resented by him as an intolerable affront to his ancient and customary rights, powers and privileges. His diehard attitude set him inevitably on a collision course with the relentless forces of change; and the struggle, if he persisted in it, could have only one outcome. His young wife, with her greater intelligence and political awareness, perceived the likely trend of future events and determined to do everything in her power to safeguard her husband's interests and try to make him adapt to the unfamiliar new power structure in Munster. And even if Garrett himself was doomed to destruction, Eleanor saw it as her duty to ensure the preservation of his earldom for their son and heir.

With great skill and courage, the capable and strong-willed countess set about her difficult task. She first sought to act as a moderating influence on her volatile and headstrong husband. Where he threatened and raged against his English opponents, she counselled caution and diplomacy. Where he engaged in wild schemes or contemplated treasonable conspiracies, she conducted negotiations on his behalf with government officials. Where he took reckless and precipitate action, she moved swiftly to defuse the dangerous situation. On numerous occasions she mitigated the ill effects of his irresponsible and, at times, irrational behaviour. Eleanor had also to contend with threats from other quarters. Ruthless Tudor administrators intent on the 'pacification' of Ireland; rapacious English soldiers and government officials; neighbouring lords, envious of the earl's vast domain; power-hungry rivals from within his own family—all these desired Garrett's downfall and hoped to profit from the confiscation of his estates.

The precarious political state of affairs in Munster was further complicated by the intrusion of a new ideological dimension arising from developments in international politics. On the one hand, a group of Catholic zealots were attempting to use Munster as a cockpit from which to launch a crusade, with papal and continental backing, against the 'heretical' English Queen, while on the other, the fanatical Puritan officers of the English army were remorselessly determined to stamp out every vestige of papal influence. Finally, there was the age-old problem posed by the multitude of undisciplined, idle swordsmen who surrounded the earl and whose only trade was war and rapine. There was no future for such men in the new Ireland that was slowly and painfully coming into being; the archaic world of these Gaelic and gaelicised clansmen was already doomed, and if their hereditary overlord, the Earl of Desmond, allowed his interests to be identified with theirs, then his fate too was sealed.

Eleanor's efforts in the face of such opposition made many demands on her varied abilities and on her courage. It was she who single-handedly administered the Desmond estates and revenues during her husband's long absence in England. It was she who loyally shared his years of sordid captivity, nursed him through his illnesses, and petitioned for his release. It was she who kept a close watch on the devious activities of his enemies in Munster and on the even more sinister machinations of certain of his own kinsmen and followers. It was she who conducted important negotiations with successive governors and central and provincial administrators. Her concern for the future of the earldom of Desmond led her to confront the Queen of England and to maintain contact with her over the years by means of astutely worded diplomatic missives. The cold hostility initially displayed by the unfriendly sovereign was gradually replaced by a grudging respect for the Irish countess. In her endeavours to save the Desmond inheritance from confiscation and dismemberment, there was no one, English or Irish, who played a significant role in the affairs of Ireland with whom Eleanor did not confer.

And now, even after her husband had been proclaimed a traitor and a rebel, she refused to give up hope. Her home had been destroyed, her children scattered, her husband hunted as a fugitive, forced to seek refuge in remote forests and glens. Now once again, as the harsh winter weather penetrated the densely wooded Glen of Aherlow in the early weeks of 1582, she shared the misery and humiliation of his furtive existence—now cowering beneath a thick mass of under-growth, where the exhausted earl had collapsed, while a scouting party of English soldiers from the garrison at Kilmallock scoured the area in search of them; now swiftly mounting her horse and decoying the soldiers on a mad chase further and further away from her husband's place of refuge; now wearily returning to nurse the ailing and semi-crippled earl; now composing a letter to the Privy Council; now dashing off northwards to intercede with the Lord Deputy or one of his officials; now suddenly reappearing with news of the approach of another posse of soldiers; now hurrying with Garrett from one wretched hiding-place to another.

The life of Eleanor Butler FitzGerald, Countess of Desmond is testimony to the struggle of a courageous, spirited, enduring and gritty woman who refused to abandon hope in the face of an inexorable fate which sucked more powerful than she into its maw. And while it may appear that she failed ultimately in her goal to save her husband, her family, her home and her inheritance, her failure is heroic, her path towards it a triumph of the human spirit. One can only stand and applaud in amazement and admiration this forgotten heroine of the Tudor wars in Ireland.

While Eleanor may have lived 500 years ago, the personal trauma she experienced by the violent and systematic destruction of the fabric of her native society and way of life has reverberation and relevance today. Women in Bosnia, Somalia, Iraq, Afghanistan, Palestine and elsewhere, the mothers, wives, grandmothers, widows, sisters and daughters of the indigenous populations, have lived and continue to live through political, military and social upheaval, their lives torn asunder by forces, both foreign and local, over which they have little control. And yet despite such insurmountable odds, in the midst of such a hostile environment, these unsung heroines continue to protect, nurture and provide for their families and keep hope alive.

And it is to these brave women this book is dedicated.

Chapter 1
The Baron's Daughter

Sometime let gorgeous Tragedy
In sceptred pall come sweeping by,
Presenting Thebes, or Pelops' line.
Or the tale of Troy divine.

MILTON, 'IL PENSEROSO'

Eleanor Butler was born at Kiltinan castle, near Fethard, County Tipperary, about the year 1545. She was the second daughter of Edmund Butler, Lord Baron of Dunboyne. Her mother was Cecilia (Síle), daughter of Cormac Oge MacCarthy, Lord of Muskerry, County Cork, and widow of Sir Cormac MacCarthy Reagh. Eleanor had eight brothers, James, John, Piers, Richard, William, Thomas, Nicholas and Walter, and three sisters, Ellis, Katherine and Joan. Kiltinan castle was the principal seat of the family. At the time of Eleanor's birth, her father also possessed the castles of Dangan, Boytonrath, Grange, Ballygellward, Grallagh, Moygarth, Tyrnwyane, Cashel and Fethard.

Her father's title 'Dunboyne' denoted the family's association with Dunboyne, County Meath. The connection can be traced back to the Norman invasion of the twelfth century. In 1172 Hugh de Lacy was granted the lordship of Meath. On his subjugation of the local Gaelic clans he granted the manors of Dunboyne and Moynett to one of his followers, William le Petit. William's line continued until the reign of Henry III, when the sole heiress, Synolda, married Thomas Butler (le Botiller), third son of Theobald Butler, lord of the territory of Ormond in Munster. By this marriage Thomas Butler became the Baron of Dunboyne and removed his residence to County Meath.

The title, however, was not officially sanctioned until 1541, when Eleanor's father was formally created Baron of Dunboyne by royal patent of King Henry VIII.

The Dunboyne Butlers' re-connection with their Munster origins began in the fourteenth century, when Peter, second Lord Dunboyne, married the daughter and heiress of John de Bermingham, lord of Kiltinan and Knockgraffon, County Tipperary. The de Bermingham family had long been settled in County Galway, but one of their house had married the daughter of Philip of Worcester, the original grantee of the Kiltinan properties. The de Berminghams maintained their interest in Kiltinan until the mid-fifteenth century, preferring to base their claim, not on the feudal law of their ancestors, but on the more ancient Gaelic code, whereby property was retained by a family's more powerful members without much regard for proximity of blood or inheritance. In view of Peter's marriage, his grandson, Edmund, fourth Lord Dunboyne, staked his claim to Kiltinan by right of his de Bermingham grandmother. But the de Berminghams by 1410 had granted the castle to the third Earl of Ormond's illegitimate son, Thomas Butler, Prior of Kilmainham, in an attempt to circumvent the claims of the Dunboynes. The fourth Earl of Ormond, as overlord of the area, decided that only a duel could cut through the tangled legal web over ownership of Kiltinan. Consequently in the spring of 1420 Edmund Butler of Dunboyne fought a desperate duel to the death with the prior's son, also named Edmund. But Dunboyne was fatally wounded, and the prior's son won a brief respite for his family. The prior's descendants continued to hold Kiltinan until 1452, when the scales of justice were finally balanced. An interest in the property was conveyed to another Edmund Butler of Dunboyne, nephew of the duellist, and the Dunboynes finally entered into their rightful inheritance, albeit one and a half centuries late.

The rock fortress of Kiltinan castle stands in an imposing and picturesque location in the shadow of Slievenamon, some five kilometres from Fethard, County Tipperary. It is strategically situated above a steep ravine overlooking the Glashawley river, a tributary of the Suir. It commands a fine view over the rich pasturelands of the Suir valley sweeping away to the south and to the Comeragh and Knockmealdown mountains beyond. A remarkable geographical feature associated with Kiltinan is the 'roaring spring', where an opening in the rocks leads to an underground river from which a spring emerges; an internal waterfall or cascade is thought by geologists to be responsible for the roaring sound. Described as 'the castle and dwelling-house of the Lord of Dunboyne',[1] it was built towards the end of the twelfth century.

In Eleanor's time Kiltinan was a formidable structure of considerable size. It comprised a large quadrangular courtyard bounded by four towers, one of which was circular; they were built of limestone and sand mortar. The remains of the circular tower, its walls some seven feet thick, can still be seen today. Two of the square towers were subsequently incorporated into the manor house which still occupies the same site and which has recently been magnificently restored and renovated by its more recent owners. Kiltinan is now in the ownership of composer Sir Andrew and Lady Lloyd Webber.

The roadway to Kiltinan castle in Eleanor's time would have swept up to the great arched gateway, flanked on either side by two three-storeyed towers, rising high above the curtain walls which linked the towers one to the other. The spacious courtyard was a hive of activity as the guard, servants and labourers of the baron went about their allotted duties for the defence and maintenance of the castle and its inhabitants. High on the wall-walk, inside the parapet, sentries kept a watchful eye on the surrounding countryside. In the courtyard water was drawn in iron-bound wooden pails from the underground Glashawley spring. Wood was cut and stacked ready for use in the kitchen and to warm the great hall and living quarters. At one end of the courtyard the baron's horses were maintained by the grooms and horseboys, while in an adjoining shed the castle's smith pounded the red-hot iron into shape, pointed the lances and swords and riveted the armour for the baron's cavalry. A fire glowed in the centre of the yard around which armed men hunkered and awaited the baron's orders. Through the gateway, carts laden with sacks of barley and wheat, vegetables and poultry, butter and cheese, wood and straw, the obligatory payment in kind of the tenants to the lord of the manor, trundled over the cobblestones.

Inside the castle the narrow corridors and the stone spiral stairways leading to the upper apartments were dark and gloomy. Shafts of light filtered through the defensive slit windows and the musket and archery loops. Dark corridors ran along the inside of the outer walls, with doors leading into various chambers. On the second level an arched opening from the stairway led into the principal chamber of the castle, the great hall, a lofty room, running the entire length of the castle, its ceiling spanned by great oak beams, the walls lime-washed, and the limestone floor polished to a sheen. Light poured into the chamber through wide, arched windows set in deep embrasures, with stone window seats covered with cushions. From the windows there was an all-encompassing view of the rolling Tipperary pasturelands. A table, richly carved of solid oak, dominated the top of the room, flanked by two iron candlestands. The walls were dotted with iron brackets to support the large tallow candles used to light the room. Off one end of the great hall was the baron's kitchen, buttery and pantry where the servants prepared the food and drink for his table. When the baron entertained his neighbours and friends or received a visit from his overlord, trestle tables were set up within the hall to accommodate his guests.

The bedchambers on the next level were small square rooms, each dominated by a four-poster bed with a canopy of strong damask or rich velvet. By modern standards the rooms were spartan and, apart from the bedstead, furnishings consisted of a linen box, a cupboard containing a water ewer and basin, and a press for clothes. Adjacent to the lord's bedchamber was his private chapel, elaborately decorated with fine plasterwork and a window of stained glass. Life in such sixteenth-century castles was both cramped and chilly. Their primary function was defensive. They had been built in the twelfth century by the Normans to hold the land they had conquered and, in the changes undertaken by their descendants, the defensive aspect of their design was carefully preserved.

In Eleanor's day a medieval village, also of Norman origin, flourished outside Kiltinan castle. The village consisted of a street of cottages and craft workshops with lanes between the houses leading off into the surrounding countryside. The village craftsmen and workers supplied the castle with their wares and services. A few kilometres south of the castle stood the important medieval town of Fethard. It had been created an archepiscopal borough by letters patent of King John and had been a busy market town for many centuries. In 1553, on petition of the burgesses and commonalty of the town, a new charter ordained that the borough should become a corporate body with the same privileges and liberties as Kilkenny. The charter was subsequently confirmed by James 1 in 1608.

Together with his administrative and military powers as seneschal of the area, Eleanor's father was also a substantial landowner. He received specific rents and services from those who held lands under him. As was the custom, he either leased out land, usually for a period of twenty-one years, for a fixed rent, or let it on a share-cropping basis, providing the tenant with either one-third or a half of the seed for the consideration of what was known as the 'third sheaf'. His tenants, especially the more substantial, further sublet the land to others.

Lower in status than the tenanted classes in both the Gaelic and Anglo-Norman lordships was the great mass of land cultivators, herders and labourers, referred to collectively as 'churls'. Neither owning land, or stock, and not allowed to bear arms, they were dependent on their masters. Together with the 'third sheaf', the tenants provided obligatory labour for the cultivation and harvesting of the baron's crops. There was a greater emphasis on tillage within his lordship than in Gaelic-held areas, with crops such as wheat, rye and barley as well as vegetables cultivated. Pigs and sheep were also reared and, in common with most of his contemporaries, the baron maintained a stud, Ireland being noted then as now for its 'great breeds of horses'.[2] Falconry and hunting were the main outdoor recreations; chess, dice and backgammon helped while away the long winter evenings.

Eleanor's childhood and girlhood were spent mainly at her father's castle of Kiltinan, where she grew up in an environment influenced by the two principal traditions that dominated sixteenth-century Ireland: the old Gaelic civilisation, which, after the reversal it had encountered in the twelfth century, had over the succeeding centuries staged a gradual but steady recovery; and the feudal tradition of the Anglo-Norman settlers, which had succumbed in varying degrees to the resurgent Gaelic culture. The Butlers were among the original Anglo-Norman invaders but, like their FitzGerald and de Burgo fellow-conquerors, they had, through proximity with their Gaelic neighbours and especially through centuries of intermarriage with the Gaelic aristocracy, become gaelicised, to varying degrees. Eleanor's mother was a MacCarthy, and she had previously been married to Cormac MacCarthy Reagh, by whom she had one son and four daughters. One of Eleanor's half-sisters was in turn married to John Butler of Kilcash, and another was the wife of James FitzGerald of Decies, County Waterford. The incidence of intermarriage between those of Anglo-Norman descent and the Gaelic aristocracy was high, and most of the great dynastic families of both groups were blood-related. This feature also led to many incidents of incestuous marriage; Eleanor's own father had a daughter (later married to Seán an tSléibhe O'Carroll) by his half-sister, who later married Sir Piers Butler of Cahir. Eleanor's uncle Peter Butler was married to Honora, the daughter of James FitzGerald, eleventh Earl of Desmond. Her aunt Joan Butler had married Roland Eustace, Viscount Baltinglass, while another aunt, Ellen, married David Roche, Viscount Fermoy, thus linking her family with many prominent houses both Gaelic and gaelicised.

The Dunboyne Butlers were a cadet branch of one of the great dynastic families of Ireland, the Butlers of Ormond, over whom the Earl of Ormond was the titular head. The earls of Ormond enjoyed palatine jurisdiction over their estates in County Tipperary, which made them very powerful indeed. This privilege, given them by the English Crown, endowed them with the power to establish courts of law, administer justice and appoint court officers, 'thus ensuring that it was they rather than the King who were the ultimate arbitrators'.[3] The earls of Ormond owed theoretical allegiance to the Crown, but they jealously guarded their independence. While they administered their vast estates by right of feudal law, the indigenous Gaelic law had, over the centuries, infiltrated, and by the middle of the sixteenth century many Gaelic customs and practices were prevalent in Ormond.

The Gaelic or Brehon legal and social system was distinct to Ireland and had evolved over the centuries from its Celtic origins. It was geared to an agrarian economy and society. Gaelic society comprised septs or 'nations' of independent chieftaincies, and was based on the concept of a patrilineal 'descent group forming a definite corporate entity with political and legal functions'.[4] The existence of so many independent entities, each ruled by a chieftain that 'maketh war and peace for himself . . . and obeyeth to no other person . . . except only to such persons as may subdue him by the sword',[5] gave rise to much tribal warfare and unrest. It was also to irk the pride of the Tudor monarchs who, in the early years of their rule, had extinguished similar independent posturings among the English nobility, and who, more recently, in 1537, had inflicted a ruthless chastisement on the powerful House of Kildare when it had shown an inclination towards independence.

The clan was the centre-point of the Gaelic system and set it apart. The leader or chieftain of the clan was elected by the ruling sept instead of succeeding by right of primogeniture as was the English custom. The tenure of land also differed from the English practice. It was conducted according to a complicated system of land distribution whereby, on the death of a landholder, the land was shared out among the ruling or landholding members of the ruling family. The chieftain retained a life interest only in the clan land and could not bequeath it to his son. Although a woman could purchase and inherit land in her own right, she was prohibited from disposing of it outside the clan. The wealth of the clan was measured not in the extent of its territory but in the number of cattle it possessed. Cattle were the principal symbol of wealth and often the cause of disputes. The power of the chieftain was measured by the number of his followers. Each chieftain accordingly strove to have as many armed men in his company as he could afford. Similarly, it was important for the chieftain to maintain a large workforce of servants and labourers for the more servile work of tending and protecting the cattle herds, tilling the soil, and providing sustenance and accommodation for his band of warriors.

The chieftain was also in receipt of certain dues and services exacted, often by force, from client chieftains. Under various laws he had the right to a wide range of privileges, such as free entertainment for himself and his extensive household, specific provisions for his horses and hounds, and the right to his clients' attendance with a fixed number of armed men whenever he summoned a hosting. The whole system of sustenance for the lord became known as 'coyne and livery' and was, in effect, the basis of Gaelic authority. By the middle of the sixteenth century, many of these practices had also been adopted by the Anglo-Norman lords.

Fosterage played an important role in Gaelic society. The sons of chieftains were fostered, usually in the household of a dependent chief, who considered it an honour and a social and political bond between the two families. The system found little favour with the English administration, but fosterage survived, was widely practised and, in the course of time, had penetrated Anglo-Norman society also.

Like their Anglo-Norman counterparts, Gaelic chieftains adopted stone castles as places of dwelling and protection. In large banqueting halls, attached to the main tower, they held court and entertained lavishly. Every chieftain of note had his 'brehon' or judge who interpreted and administered the law within his territory. He also had a bard (*ollamh dána*), who enjoyed a special status in the chief's household and whose basic duty was 'the eulogy of the great and glorification of their deeds'.[6]

The chieftain employed three groups of fighting men. The first was the cavalry, recruited from within the ranks of the ruling sept or the more prosperous elements of the landowning class. Then came the galloglass (*gallóglaigh*, 'foreign warriors'), the heavy infantry of the chieftain's army, being selected men of great stature and strength, armed with long sword and battle-axe. Originally from Scotland, some had settled in Ireland, where they were given tracts of land in payment for their services as a standing army for the Gaelic chieftains and Anglo-Norman lords who could afford to employ them. The Butlers' traditional galloglass were the MacSweeneys. The third category of fighting men were the kern (*certhearnigh*); skilled in the use of bows and arrows and darts, they were the lightly-armed foot-soldiers of the chieftain's army.

Most of the Anglo-Irish lords and the Gaelic chieftains, despite the Reformation in England, still adhered to the old religion. But Catholicism in Gaelic Ireland differed from that practised on the continent. The sweeping reforms of the preceding centuries had, by and large, failed to apply in Ireland. A pattern of hereditary clergy had evolved where members of a particular family were invested with positions of high office in the church. Many of the bishops and clergy were married or maintained concubines. 'In no field of life was Ireland's apartness from the mainstream of Christian European society so marked as in that of marriage. Throughout the medieval period, and down to the end of the old order in 1603, what could be called Celtic secular marriage remained the norm in Ireland and Christian matrimony was no more than the rare exception grafted on to this system.'[7] There was also a high incidence of divorce, which was a legal right and could be invoked by either spouse. Plurality of marriages, many within the restricted degrees of consanguinity, as well as trial marriages, were common within both the Gaelic and the gaelicised lordships. Offspring born outside wedlock were not penalised in their rights of either succession or land tenure. Conn Bacach O'Neill, first Earl of Tyrone, stoutly declared that he was a man 'that never refused no child that any woman named to be his'.[8]

Thus Eleanor grew up in a society which, while it adhered in many ways to its Anglo-Norman origins, had also absorbed into its social and political structures many of the trappings of the Gaelic world that surrounded it. Her Gaelic mother would have further strengthened this development in the house of the Dunboyne Butlers. Their overlord the Earl of Ormond was, however, a loyal supporter of the Tudor monarchs and the least gaelicised of the Anglo-Norman lords in Ireland. Eleanor's father, together with his brother Peter, had served under the Earl of Ormond in the army of Henry VIII in France. They had seen action at the sieges of Montreuil and Boulogne. After the inexplicable death by poison of the earl in London in 1546, his son Thomas, known as Black Tom, then just fifteen years old, was brought up in the new Protestant religion at Court, as a friend and classmate of the young future king, Edward VI, and the future queen, Elizabeth I. Black Tom was to remain at court for many years before he entered into his inheritance in Ireland. During his absence Eleanor's father was placed in charge of the earl's forces in Ormond to repel the increasingly frequent raids of the neighbouring O'Carrolls of Ely. He was appointed Seneschal of the Liberty of Tipperary, an office held by each successive baron since 1295. Duties involved the stewardship of the earl's domains, the exaction and collection of his rents, dues and services, and the administration of his palatine court at Clonmel. Kiltinan bustled with activity during the early years of Eleanor's childhood.

Life for the daughter of a nobleman in the sixteenth century had its set pattern and its responsibilities. From the day of her birth Eleanor was groomed as a potential wife for some Anglo-Norman lord or Gaelic chieftain. Provided their credentials and assets were acceptable to her father and an agreement was reached on a suitable dowry, Eleanor would be given in marriage to the most suitable applicant. Political and financial considerations tended to dictate the matrimonial lot of women in the higher echelons of Gaelic and Anglo-Irish society. It was usual for girls to marry at the comparatively early age of fifteen or sixteen. Given in marriage to one of her own class, Eleanor would eventually become chatelaine of her own castle. With the privilege went the responsibility to oversee the upkeep and maintenance of her husband's castles: food and furnishings bought, stored and replaced; servants hired, fired and trained; banquets organised to impress a neighbour or to honour an overlord; household linens, utensils and liveries selected and accounted for.

To efficiently administer a large mansion with servants and retainers, to entertain and converse diplomatically with both friend and foe of her husband, involved a level of political and social awareness. In preparation for her exacting future role, Eleanor received some formal education, and English and Gaelic tutors taught her to converse ably in both English and Irish. She learned to write in both languages, and she became a prolific letter-writer, able to express herself succinctly and well, with an intelligent turn of phrase and a political insight that denoted an informed and comprehending mind. She was an able horsewoman, a skill that was to stand to her many times in the course of her traumatic life. Gaelic Ireland is often inaccurately depicted as having been a totally male-dominated society where women fulfilled a mainly subservient role, confined to domestic duties of housekeeping and child-rearing, and rarely becoming involved in the political turmoil of the times. On the contrary, there are many examples of women, mainly in the higher orders of both Gaelic and gaelicised society, who were actively involved in politics, not only in a supportive or advisory capacity to their husbands, but also as strong-willed and independent participants in their own right. Eleanor was to become a prime example of this little-acknowledged fact.

It was reputed that she was tall in stature, with light brown hair. On special or formal occasions she dressed in the current fashion of the day, in gowns of taffeta, velvet or fine cambric, edged with lace, as befitted her station. Her wardrobe might be purchased in Dublin, which tended to follow English fashion, or bought from the travelling merchants, who brought with them the fashions and fabrics of the continent, imported through the ports of Waterford, Cork and Kinsale. The native Irish attire of the time, a linen or fine woollen smock reaching to the ankles, with long wide sleeves falling in folds at either side, over which was worn a sleeveless dress with a laced bodice, dyed saffron or russet, might well have been worn by Síle MacCarthy's daughter on less auspicious occasions. The great Irish mantle of warm wool, with its thickly fringed collar, was worn by the upper classes of both cultures.

Travel was a difficult and hazardous undertaking in sixteenth-century Ireland, owing to the absence of a developed road system and also to the unsettled state of the country. But journeys, however hazardous, had to be undertaken as business was contracted, military campaigns conducted and social visits made. Such social occasions were marked by banquets, often lasting several days, when family, relatives, friends and foes, converged on Kiltinan. In the great hall the baron's chief steward conducted each guest to his allotted place in strict order according to social and political status. On the trestle tables joints of beef, mutton, venison, poultry and game, boiled or spit-roasted, were laid. Wheaten bread and oatcakes were in plentiful supply, as were vegetables such as cabbage, onion, leek and watercress. Wines from France and Spain, imported through Youghal or Waterford, native aqua vitae (*uisce beatha*), ale and mead, 'the dainty drink of nobles',[9] accompanied the plentiful helpings. Gaelic chieftains in their tight worsted trews and short quilted jackets of fine leather, their hair falling around their shoulders, mingled with the lords of the Pale, clad in doublet and hose. The long hall, warmed by a glowing brazier in the centre and lit by the flickering torches on the wall brackets, reverberated with a mixture of English and Gaelic tongues. A bard rose and sang the praises of Eleanor's father and his house, while her mother's MacCarthy origins were equally lauded. A verse extolling the baron's hospitality and the beauty of his wife and daughters followed. Games of cards, dice and backgammon were played and, as the night wore on, the bids became more reckless, and many a horse, jewelled dagger, silver plate, herd of cattle or tract of land changed hands. The harp and the pipes were played for the dancers, whose capering shadows cast silhouettes on the stone walls.

Eleanor's childhood, however, was not all feasting and revelry. Her early years were disturbed by a bitter feud between her father and her uncle which drove a wedge, not only between the brothers, but between her father and his great overlord, the Earl of Ormond. The feud had its origins in 1524 when Eleanor's grandfather, Sir James Butler, concluded a family settlement of his estate, bequeathing the greater portion to his eldest son, Edmund, Eleanor's father. He also directed that his second son, Peter, was to receive the castle and estate of Grallagh, while Thomas, his youngest son, was to inherit Boytonrath and other lands near Cashel. Edmund was Peter's overlord to whom he owed allegiance and, among other things, a 'suit and service of six footmen and one horseman'.[10] Despite their initial co-operation, on their return from the wars in France, a growing enmity developed between the brothers over possession of the Grallagh estate. Edmund claimed that the estate was entailed on the barons of Dunboyne and that his father had no right to bequeath it to Peter, who, he contended, had merely a life interest in the property. The quarrel became further aggravated by the personal animosity that arose between Eleanor's mother and Peter's wife, Honora, daughter of James FitzGerald, the Earl of Desmond. Their mutual dislike may have stemmed from the ancient animosity that existed between the MacCarthys and the earls of Desmond. Whether for this reason or for something of a more personal nature, the two ladies goaded their respective spouses against each other, as each plotted her own husband's triumph. As the feud between the brothers intensified it led to the formation of political affiliations and alliances that were eventually to have repercussions on Eleanor's future.

Her father filed a suit against his brother in the Court of Chancery. But on the advice of his cousin, Black Tom, who had recently returned from England to enter into his estates and title as Earl of Ormond, Peter refused to appear before the court. Ill-feeling already existed between Eleanor's father and the new Earl of Ormond, largely as a result of a dispute concerning the validity of the palatine rights pertaining to the earldom. The earl considered that Edmund had further rebuffed his authority by failing to submit his suit against his brother to his palatine court for his judgment. The Court of Chancery found in Edmund's favour and ordered Peter to restore the disputed Grallagh estate. On the advice of Black Tom, however, Peter refused to comply with the court order. The dispute continued to rage for many years. The legal battle culminated in attacks and reprisals by both brothers on each other and drove an ever-widening wedge, not merely between Edmund and his brother, but with his overlord the Earl of Ormond as well. Eleanor and her family were affected both politically and socially by the baron's estrangement from the Earl of Ormond. They experienced a sense of isolation as the other tributary lords of Ormond were reluctant to defy their powerful overlord and openly fraternise with the Dunboynes. Few invitations were extended to them to the earl's court at Clonmel or Kilkenny. The isolation of the Dunboynes left them open to exploitation in the climate of political discord and intrigue which characterised sixteenth-century Munster. In these circumstances it was inevitable that the family would become involved in the long-standing and more intense feud that existed between the Houses of Ormond and Desmond. While the dispute between Eleanor's father and uncle was to continue unabated until their deaths, when Grallagh was finally restored to the Dunboyne estate, it was to pale into insignificance in comparison to the age-old Desmond–Ormond feud which was about to erupt anew and engulf Eleanor and all Munster in its spreading flames.

The Butlers' loyalty to the English Crown was well-established before their arrival in Ireland. Theobald, the founder of the family, was created Chief Butler, one of the hereditary offices of state, by King Henry II. Theobald and his descendants were granted the lucrative prisage of wines, the right to one-tenth of the cargo of any wine ship that broke bulk in Ireland. This privilege was held by the family until, by an act of parliament in 1810, it was finally restored to the Crown. From this hereditary honour came the family name of Butler. The Butler lordship in Ireland comprised the northern half of County Tipperary, including the disputed overlordship of the old Gaelic kingdom of Ely O'Carroll. Successive Butler lords consolidated their positions over the succeeding decades. They upheld the Crown's interests in the newly-conquered territories and were amply rewarded. In 1315 Edward II gave Edmund Butler the castles and manors of Carrickmagriffon and Roscrea and conferred on him the earldom of Carrick. Edmund's son James married the niece of Edward III. In 1328 he was created Earl of Ormond and was granted the palatine liberties of Tipperary. In 1392 the third Earl of Ormond acquired the town of Kilkenny, which eventually became the principal seat of the family.

Cheek by jowl with the expanding Butler lordship were the lordships of two other Anglo-Norman dynasts. To the north-east the FitzGeralds of Kildare had prospered, while to the west the FitzGeralds of Desmond had carved out a vast estate at the expense of the native Irish chieftains. It was perhaps inevitable that the ambitions of these great Anglo-Norman families would conflict as they vied with each other for power, land and royal favours.

The ancestors of the FitzGeralds, or, as they became known in Ireland, the Geraldines, were also among the Norman conquerors who invaded Ireland. Their background in England, however, differed greatly from that of the Butlers. Their origins were in the wild marcher lands between England and Wales. After the Norman conquest of England their Italian progenitor Gheraldino was initially granted the lordship of Windsor. From there they advanced into Celtic Wales, where they acquired further lands, both by military and matrimonial means. In 1095 Gerald, the grandson of the original Gheraldino, married the beautiful and notorious Princess Nesta, daughter of the

King of South Wales, and built Carew castle on the lands granted to him in right of his wife. This Gerald was the progenitor of the Geraldines or FitzGeralds of Ireland. He died in 1135, leaving three sons, Maurice, William and David, afterwards Bishop of St Davids. Together with Nesta's son by her second marriage, Robert FitzStephen, and her illegitimate offspring by a previous liaison with King Henry I, this turbulent brood became a source of constant strife. In the border areas of the Welsh marches they conducted private wars of retribution without the slightest regard for the sovereignty of the English monarch who, in any event, was powerless to control them. It was an able and wily king who could devise the means to rid his kingdom of such independently-minded barons.

An invitation from the Gaelic King of Leinster, Dermot MacMurrough, provided him with the opportunity. At the forefront of the Norman invasion of Ireland was Maurice, son of Gerald of Wales. In return for his services Maurice was granted land in what is now County Kildare and built a strong fortress at Maynooth. The FitzGeralds of Kildare were descended from Maurice's eldest son, Gerald, and they eventually became powerful overlords of the greater part of Leinster. The FitzGeralds of Munster descended from his youngest son, Thomas. In 1329 Thomas's great-great-grandson Maurice was created first Earl of Desmond by Edward III and, similar to the Earl of Ormond, was granted the county of Kerry as an hereditary palatine liberty. Both he and his successors extended their power until eventually they claimed the overlordship of a vast area which stretched from north Limerick to Youghal and from Dingle in Kerry to the ancient Gaelic kingdom of the Decies in Waterford.

In the course of time all three houses, partly by reason of their close association and intermarriage with the neighbouring Gaelic aristocracy and partly because of their isolation from their English origins, become gaelicised. Of the three, the Desmonds could be said to have become the most gaelicised. Despite their English titles and honours, they were, true to their Geraldine tradition, outspoken champions of practical independence from the English Crown. In this they tended to have the moral support of their fellow-Geraldines, the Kildares. In 1345, for example, Maurice of Desmond flaunting his power over the Gaelic and gaelicised lords of Munster convened his own parliament in Callan, County Kilkenny. Thereafter the Munster Geraldines tended to withdraw into their remote domains, and in defiance of England gradually became indistinguishable in tongue, dress and custom from their Gaelic neighbours. Enmity arose between them and their less gaelicised neighbours, the Butlers of Ormond. Their dynastic quarrels were further heightened when each took different sides in the Wars of the Roses in England, fought between the Houses of York and Lancaster, until, finally, the antagonism between the Houses of Ormond and Desmond became entangled in the wider net of political conflict in England.

The Duke of York was the absentee viceroy of Ireland, but his ambitions soared to more exalted office—the Crown of England. After his defeat at the battle of Ludford Bridge and his subsequent conviction for treason, he was replaced as viceroy of Ireland by the Earl of Ormond. York escaped to Ireland and, aided and abetted by the Geraldines, made plans to invade England. In the event York was killed at the battle of Wakefield in 1460, but his ambitions were later realised by his son, who in 1461 was crowned King Edward iv. One of the first casualties of the Yorkist triumph was the Earl of Ormond, who was promptly executed. His brother and heir, Sir John Butler, in an attempt to revitalise the Lancastrian cause in Ireland, rallied his supporters but was defeated at Pilltown by James, the seventh Earl of Desmond. While this incident was, from the Geraldines' point of view, merely another chapter in the Desmond–Ormond feud, the victory was rewarded by a grateful Yorkist king, who had Desmond's son and successor, Thomas, confirmed as chief governor of Ireland in 1463.

But despite his apparent Yorkist leanings, the new Earl of Desmond remained independent and as gaelicised as his forebears and attempted to extend Gaelic law and custom into the English Pale. Soon the usually peaceful Pale was aflame. Desmond was speedily replaced by Sir John Tiptoft, who, without apparent royal consent, had Desmond beheaded at Drogheda. The effect on the country was instantaneous. Riots and uprisings erupted throughout Munster and Leinster; the dead earl's brother with a great army burned and pillaged the Pale. The imprisoned Earl of Kildare was released to calm the situation. Tiptoft was recalled, and the King proclaimed his disapproval of the Earl of Desmond's execution.

The execution of the earl was the final straw that broke the back of the uneasy alliance between the House of Desmond and the Crown of England. In the succeeding decades the Geraldines of Desmond withdrew from all contact with the Crown and its administration in

Dublin. They turned their backs on their English origins in favour of their adopted Gaelic world, which welcomed them as the premier buffer between it and the English Crown. Their great rivals, the earls of Ormond, continued to hold for the Crown, and many of the succeeding earls spent much of their time at the English court. Now in the second half of the sixteenth century the long-standing feud between both houses had come to rest in the hands of two volatile young heirs—Black Tom, tenth Earl of Ormond and Garrett FitzGerald, fourteenth Earl of Desmond, each eager to uphold the honour of his house by the destruction of the other.

Secure in Kiltinan, surrounded by her large family, Eleanor took little notice of the gathering storm-clouds. Her main preoccupation was that of any young eligible woman: she patiently plied her needle or read her verse and waited and wondered about her marriage prospects. What dashing lord or handsome chieftain would come to Kiltinan to seek her hand? Or would she instead become the prize in some political or financial deal, a sop to placate some ageing, lascivious noble? Fate was often known to deal a cruel hand in the matrimonial stakes. But whatever her thoughts, little could she have realised how inextricably her future would become entangled in the Ormond–Desmond feud which would hurl her into the very eye of the impending storm.

Chapter 2

The Feud

Two households, both alike in dignity,
In fair Verona, where we lay our scene,
From ancient grudge break to new mutiny,
Where civil blood makes civil hands unclean.

SHAKESPEARE, *ROMEO AND JULIET*, I, i

In 1558 the daughter of Anne Boleyn and Henry VIII ascended the throne of England. Deemed illegitimate by some of her subjects, God's appointed sovereign majesty by others, the twenty-six-year-old, slight, pale-faced woman determinedly grasped the sceptre of state, aware of the doubts and of the awesome task that she faced. Since the death of her father over a decade earlier, her inherited kingdom had floundered like a rudderless galleon. She had inherited a throne 'humiliated in war, paralysed by ineptitude and sinking into spiritual and financial bankruptcy'.[1] With a great sense of destiny, this autocratic, vain woman embarked on a life's mission to protect and defend her legacy, the kingdom of England, which was to become her substitute lover, husband and child, and to prove that she had indeed 'the heart and stomach of a king'.

Part of Elizabeth's legacy was Ireland, which remained, despite the best efforts of her wily father, a country without political cohesion or racial homogeneity; an island in close and dangerous proximity to England but which English cartographers had not as yet accurately mapped; a country which in its present state was the antithesis of everything that the sovereign Elizabeth and her renaissance age represented. Gaelic Ireland seemed barbarously medieval by the standards of England and continental Europe. More significantly, its outmoded political, social and religious structures, its dogged rebellious attitude to the 'civilising' attempts of the English Crown, its intertribal dissension and its consistent lack of common purpose, made it a potential attraction to England's foreign enemies. In 1558 Ireland, with her myriad of independent lords and chieftains, confronted Elizabeth with a similar problem faced by her grandfather Henry VII in England decades previously. Then the great English feudal lords had also strained at the royal bit before being short-reined into submission and acknowledgment that their royal overlord was invested with a God-given power over them. The Tudors demanded, and had received, the total loyalty and acquiescence of their feudal barons in England. Now it was the turn of the independent chieftains and lords of Ireland to proffer a similar obeisance. But the Irish lords were to prove reluctant to relinquish the powers and privileges they enjoyed by right of Gaelic custom and law. Elizabeth was not to have her way in Ireland without a protracted, expensive and bitter struggle.

Elizabeth's supposedly liege lords in Ireland were a mixed bunch. In Leinster the earls of Kildare, the Leinster Geraldines, had, during the reigns of Henry VII and Henry VIII, reached the pinnacle of their power. Henry VIII feared their power in Ireland and their inherited Geraldine tendencies towards independence. Their star finally fell when a hot-blooded young scion, Silken Thomas, son of the ninth earl, convulsed the House of Kildare into a hasty rebellion and provided Henry with the excuse he had long awaited. The rebellion led to the execution in 1537 at Tyburn of Silken Thomas and his five uncles, and the demise of the Kildares as a potential alternative to the English monarch in Ireland. Henry hurriedly had himself confirmed 'King of Ireland' before any Anglo-Norman lord or Gaelic chieftain could snatch the title from him.

In Ormond the Butlers, after years of eclipse by the Kildares, had re-emerged as the champions of the Crown. In Black Tom, with his Boleyn connections and his close personal relationship with the young queen, a new chapter of Ormond supremacy in Ireland was about to begin. Black Tom's loyalty to and friendship with Elizabeth lasted to the end of her long reign. She referred to him as her 'black husband', which gave rise to much speculation that, while not her husband in the legal sense, Black Tom had been awarded the pleasure of the royal bedchamber. He was twenty-seven years of age at the time of Elizabeth's accession to the throne. As his nickname suggests, and as is evident from his portrait, he was a black-haired, dark-skinned, tall, well-set, elegantly attired courtier, handsome and charming, but also cruel and ruthless when the necessity arose. He was the veritable renaissance man, modern and confident in outlook and action. Just as his loyal ancestry, Boleyn connections and personal ability had struck Elizabeth's sensibility, so his good looks and charm had touched a chord in her heart. Black Tom was and would continue to be her favourite Irish noble, a fact that she made no effort to hide but preferred to flaunt by means of the personal and political favouritism she showed towards him. In 1559 she appointed him Lord Treasurer of Ireland, and he became closely identified with the Sussex faction at the royal court.

In 1558, Black Tom's neighbour and adversary, Garrett (Gerald), son of James FitzJohn FitzGerald, became the fourteenth Earl of Desmond. In Elizabeth's eyes Garrett was the antithesis of Black Tom. His ancestry made him politically less acceptable, and, from a physical point of view, the delicate, pale, vain, melancholic, temperamental Geraldine aroused no passion in her Tudor heart. Henry VIII had desired that Garrett, like Black Tom, should have an English upbringing and education at Court. But in the wake of the execution of his kinsmen, the Geraldine Kildares, Garrett's father saw little reason to entrust his son to the care and attention of the Tudor king. Consequently Garrett was reared and educated in the hard school of Gaelic custom. He was fostered with the O'Moriartys in Kerry and was subjected to the rigorous physical training required of a potential Gaelic warrior, leader and ruler. But he also aspired to more learned ways and was given to the composition of verse.

Lest his literary and general melancholic disposition arouse doubts as to his physical ability to succeed his father to the earldom, and in accordance with the Gaelic custom which ordained that 'every heir or young chieftain of a tribe was obliged in honour to give a public specimen of his valour before he was owned or declared governor or leader of his people', Garrett led his followers 'to make a desperate incursion upon some neighbour or other that they were in feud with; and they were obliged to bring by open force the cattle they found in the lands they attacked or die in the attempt.'[2] The MacCarthy clans of Carbery and Muskerry were singled out by the young Geraldine lord to demonstrate his prowess. Not only did the MacCarthys pay the price of Garrett's initiation in the customary penalties of cattle and booty but, to further emphasise his abilities, he captured and imprisoned Lord Muskerry's son for good measure. Such was the tough school of warrior initiation with its origins in the legendary Celtic world, in which the son and heir of the Earl of Desmond was reared.

But Garrett's succession to the earldom was fraught with controversy. It had originated when Maurice, the son of the twelfth Earl of Desmond, married his own first cousin, by whom he had a son called James. A nephew of the twelfth earl, James FitzJohn, Garrett's father, disputed the right of James to succeed his father on the grounds of consanguinity. The matter was settled, not by law but by the sword, when James was murdered by James FitzJohn's brother. But James FitzJohn then found his way to the earldom disputed on the grounds of his equally prohibited marriage to his own grandniece, the daughter of Maurice Roche, Lord Fermoy, by whom he had a son known as Sir Thomas Roe FitzGerald. Yielding to pressure from his subchiefs, who feared another bloody succession dispute, James FitzJohn divorced his first wife and married Mór O'Carroll, the daughter of the chieftain of Ely O'Carroll, by whom he had Garrett, his recognised heir, born in 1532, John, later known as Sir John of Desmond, and five daughters. By a later marriage to Ellen, daughter of Donal MacCarthy More, he had another son called James 'Sussex' FitzGerald. Upon Garrett's succession to the earldom in November 1558, Thomas Roe, the disinherited son, unsuccessfully appealed his claim to the earldom of Desmond to the English court.

Garrett's father was a vigorous supporter of the ill-fated House of Kildare and one of the principal activists in the league formed to protect and reinstate the only surviving member of the Kildare dynasty. After the disbandment of the league he had, however, submitted to the Crown and was subsequently created Lord Treasurer and governor of Munster. By his fourth and final marriage to Katherine Butler, the second daughter of the eighth Earl of Ormond, and by various marriage alliances between other members of the Butler and Desmond families, he had mitigated somewhat the endemic rivalry and rancour that existed between the two families and thereby brought a period of peace to Munster. Well might the annalists, with a sense of impending doom, mourn his death in 1558. 'The loss of this good man', they recorded, 'was woeful to his country, for there was no need to watch cattle or close doors from Dúnchaoin

[Dunquin] to the green-bordered meeting of the three waters [i.e. the rivers Suir, Barrow and Nore].'[3] The scene was set for the enactment of a drama that had all the ingredients of a tragedy of Shakespearean proportions. With the fate and fortune of the two great aristocratic dynasties lying in the hands of two young and untried heirs, Ireland waited with bated breath for the storm to break.

But the young Desmond heir had already aroused his rival's enmity by his sensational marriage in 1550 to Black Tom's mother, Joan, the Dowager Countess of Ormond. Scarcely twenty years old, Garrett had thus become Black Tom's step-father. Twenty years Garrett's senior, Joan was the daughter of James FitzGerald, the eleventh Earl of Desmond, and was thus Garrett's own second cousin. On the death of Black Tom's father, Joan had subsequently briefly married, at the Crown's insistence, the Lord Justice, Sir Francis Bryan. But it was alleged that she had already fallen for the pale melancholic heir to the Desmond dynasty even before her marriage to Bryan. And Garrett was obviously attracted to his older cousin. The prospect of such a marriage gave rise to considerable speculation and anxiety in various quarters. It was recorded, for example, that great 'displeasure' had arisen 'between Lady Ormond and Lady Desmond re the Countess of Ormond's practice to marry with the heir of Desmond'.[4] The English administration was appalled at the potential consequences of the union. Black Tom was still a minor, and the government feared that the gaelicised Desmond heir would bring 'the uncyville and Yrishe'[5] customs of his house to bear on the loyal House of Ormond. Consequently the Crown intervened, and Joan was summarily 'sent for into Inglande and bestowed as wife to Sir Francis Bryan'.[6] Bryan died in February 1550, and even at his funeral, which was attended by Garrett, 'the Countess of Ormond's practice to marry with the heir of Desmond'[7] was common knowledge. The Lord Chancellor urged the countess to show some restraint, and reluctantly Joan promised him 'upon hir honor that she wolde lyve sole for one yeore'.[8] But in affairs of the heart promises are made to be broken, and by May 1550 Joan and Garrett were married.

The marriage was the sensation of the day, and at Kiltinan Eleanor's family too heard of the unlikely union which had become the butt of many crude jokes and was the principal topic of conversation from the courtyard fire to the great hall. But initially the marriage had a stabilising effect on the young heir of Desmond. Under Joan's quiet influence, her husband, on the death of his father in November 1558, despite the claim of his dispossessed half-brother, assumed the earldom. Her concern that Garrett should be confirmed in his doubtful title by the Crown bore fruit when he agreed to go to London, where 'with a willing mind and intention',[9] the new earl made his submission in style before the new queen, 'he being well attended on by one hundred prime gentlemen, waytering and attending upon him'.[10] This impressive show, however, cut little ice with Elizabeth who, with her calculating Tudor eyes, coldly surveyed the proud Geraldine peacock who flaunted his power before her, and mentally made a note to clip the wings of so overbearing a subject. Elizabeth knew the controversy that surrounded his title, but, as her own title to the throne was held equally in doubt, for the moment she smiled frostily at the swaggering Irish lord and graciously confirmed him in his title and immense estates.

Garrett's inheritance comprised over half a million acres of land. Rents forthcoming from the estate amounted to over £7,000 per annum, 'a prodigious revenue in these times and perhaps greater than any other subject in Her Majesty's dominion'.[11] Together with their feudal rents, successive earls, as they had gradually adopted Gaelic law, also claimed its privileges. Garrett was entitled to the traditional tributes and payments known as 'cuttings and spendings' from the many Gaelic chieftains who held under him. These tributes varied widely both in content and extent. When, for example, the earl travelled through the territory of an underlord, the expenses he incurred for food, drink and lodging were borne by his underlord. He received specific dues in kind from the territories under his control, varying from wood and candles to drink and cattle. He 'cessed' or quartered his armed followers, horses and hunting hounds on the country. The earl and his family were entitled to 'cuddy' (*cuid oíche*) or entertainment for the night in the houses of the gentry within his lordship. If he did not avail in person of the cuddy, the equivalent cost in meat, flour, whiskey, honey, or a money payment was forwarded to his castle in lieu. If the payments and tributes due to the earl were not readily forthcoming they were likely to be extracted by force and, to judge from the many complaints made against him by his dependent lords, at times Garrett was wont to exact more than his due.

Foremost among the privileges pertaining to the Desmond earldom under Gaelic law was the highly prized right of the 'rising out' whereby, whenever his standard was raised, whether in rebellion or against a neighbour, the earl was entitled to receive the armed support of every member of his house and every dweller upon his lands. It was claimed that 'no less than fifty lords and barons paid them [the Earls of Desmond] tribute and were ever ready to march under their banner'.[12] Such power, if vested in a lord hostile to the Crown, posed a grave threat, and as her reign progressed Elizabeth had every reason to fear and try to extinguish it. The Earl of Desmond claimed jurisdiction over some of the most powerful chieftains and lords in Munster. His power was centred in counties Limerick and Kerry and parts of Cork, but his influence extended over a much wider area. He claimed a disputed overlordship of the three MacCarthy clans: MacCarthy More, MacCarthy Muskerry and MacCarthy Reagh. In northern Kerry the FitzMaurices, kinsmen and hereditary marshals to the earls, often resisted his claim of jurisdiction over them. The Barry septs of County Cork, the Knight of Kerry, the Knight of Glin and the White Knight, together with the FitzGeralds of Imokilly in County Cork, the earls' hereditary seneschals, all were allied to the House of Desmond.

Together with his vast acres, Garrett had also inherited many castles and manors, the principal being Askeaton, Newcastle, Kilmallock and Shanid in County Limerick, Tarbert, Castleisland, Castlemaine and Dingle in County Kerry. His principal residence was Askeaton castle, built in 1199, situated on an island on the River Deel. A sixteenth-century account described it as:

> the one great castle built of square plan, a chief house of the Earl of Desmond, having at each angle of the same a round tower, with various places and chambers in each tower. And there is at the south corner, on the western side at the south part, a high square tower or peel, built for defence, within the walls, and also there were within the walls of the said castle many buildings, namely a large hall, a large room, and an excellent chamber, one garden and, in the same, two fishponds. And outside the walls, and near them, are divers orchards and gardens.[13]

Perched on its rocky plateau, the castle commanded a fine view east and south to where the dark forest of Kylemore stretched for miles into the distance towards the Galtee and Ballyhoura mountains.

The Earl of Desmond claimed overlordship of the port town of Youghal from which he had an annual chief rent of £71 6s 8d, together with administrative privileges within the town, and was also in receipt of the 'custom and cocket of Kinsale'.[14] His extensive household comprised a secretary, lawyers, versed in both Gaelic and English law, a personal physician who held in payment 'a ploughland free for his service and a tenement in Youghall',[15] constables who guarded the earl's other residences, a seneschal, a marshal, a standing army of galloglass, a large company of bards and rhymers, countless retainers, servants, tradesmen, labourers and hangers-on. The entire earldom was divided into 'highly localised units, each unit with its own castle or town house'.[16] To conquer the lordship presented major difficulties because 'victory was not symbolised by the capture of any one town or castle but was the result of encroachment and penetration until every castle had been destroyed or yielded up'.[17] The earls tended to rule their palatinate by an amalgam of Gaelic and English laws, and brehons or Gaelic judges were employed to arbitrate in disputes. Gaelic customs of dress, language and law flourished. The earls jealously guarded the palatine rights conferred on them by the Crown, while they just as assiduously sought to preserve the wide-ranging privileges granted them by Gaelic custom. In effect they sought and acquired the best of both worlds.

The first years of Garrett's marriage passed without major incident as Joan exerted her influence on her son and young husband and kept them out of each other's reach. Garrett busied himself within his lordship, establishing his authority over his liege lords and chieftains, exacting the customary dues and tributes, and punishing recalcitrant client lords. His aversion to any interference in his lordship extended also to the Crown. English officials and administrators who arrived in Munster gaped in disbelief at the existence of this relic of feudalism, operated by an autocratic, gaelicised earl who refused to acknowledge not only their presence but the authority of their sovereign mistress. When a confrontation over succession arose among the O'Briens of Thomond, Garrett backed the Gaelic contender for office, demonstrating his preference for the Gaelic system and leaving Elizabeth in no doubt where his loyalties lay.

In 1560 Joan's restraining hand seemed to weaken when a disagreement arose between Garrett and Black Tom over payment of her marriage settlement. Garrett claimed the rent from the manors of

Clonmel, Kilsheelin and Kilfeakle as Joan's dowry. Black Tom refused to pay. Garrett attempted to extract the rents by force. Black Tom responded by invading Garrett's lands. Garrett retaliated by denying Black Tom passage through his territories to collect his right of prisage at Youghal and Kinsale. Recourse to law would have been the practical way to resolve the dispute, but where the Ormond–Desmond feud was concerned, legal niceties did not enter into the equation. The galloglass were mustered, the liegemen summoned to arms, and the place of battle, Bohermore, County Tipperary, selected. But, the annals record, as the 'two great hosts had come front to front and face to face, the great God sent an angel of peace to them, so that concord was established between the hosts'.[18] The 'angel of peace' referred to was Joan who, for fourteen days, as her son and husband faced each other in open hostility, traversed the drawn battle-lines and eventually succeeded in effecting a reconciliation.

In the event Elizabeth ordered both lords to her presence. Black Tom obeyed the summons immediately, but Garrett made vague excuses and declined to appear at the English court. A personal letter from the Queen demanding his presence in London went unanswered for a month. Joan cajoled and counselled and reluctantly Garrett acquiesced. In 1562, accompanied by an even more impressive retinue than previously, he presented himself before Elizabeth and her Privy Council. 'Being charged before the Council with openly defying the law in Ireland, he answered contumaciously, and when called to order, refused to apologise.'[19] Elizabeth swore in her harsh voice and spat with anger, as was her wont, at the impudence of her subordinate vassal and committed him into custody. She afterwards wrote to soothe an anxious Joan and in a friendly tone explained that 'a little gentle imprisonment'[20] would do her vain young husband the world of good. But evil tongues and court gossip whispered in Garrett's ear that it was Joan who was responsible for his detention so that her son might be further favoured by the Queen. Garrett listened and wrote impulsively to reprimand his wife. Joan implored the Queen's secretary to inform her husband as to her innocence, declaring with a certain pathos, that she had continually sought for 'them both to be perfect friends, as two whom I love as myself'.[21]

But Garrett's confinement had the desired effect. Denied his freedom and hard-pressed for money, he swallowed his pride and in 1563 signed a treaty with Elizabeth. He promised to pay his dues to the

Crown, to maintain English law and order within Desmond, to abolish Gaelic law and practice and to prohibit the unrestricted movement of bards and rhymers within his lordship. In 1564, after a further stay in custody in Dublin, he was finally reunited with his lordship and his wife.

Joan, however, did not long survive her husband's return. On 2 January 1565, worn out, perhaps by the constant pressure of keeping her husband and her son from each other's throats, Joan died and was buried in Askeaton abbey. That Joan loved Garrett, and loved him deeply, cannot be disputed. Joan Butler FitzGerald was not a silly middle-aged matron who sought to prolong her youth by an amorous dalliance with the pale, poetic, warrior earl. 'By birth she was among the noblest women of the realm, by inheritance one of the richest . . . admired for her maturity and intellect',[22] a confidante of Queen Elizabeth, a healer of old wounds. With the death of Garrett's first countess, died also the last prospect of peace in Munster.

Chapter 3
The Lady of Desmond

How hight that Amazon (says Artegall)?
And where, and how far hence does she abide?
Her name (quoth he) they Radigund doe call,
A princess of great power and greater pride.

SPENSER, *THE FAERIE QUEENE*, III

I t is perhaps a quirk of fate that, despite the ongoing feud, it was from the House of Butler that the Earl of Desmond should choose his new countess. On the surface it appeared that the earl sought to heal old wounds and re-establish connections with the House of Ormond which had been severed by Joan's death. But the reverse was in fact more likely, as both the manner and choice of Garrett's future bride could serve only to further antagonise his rival. For Joan Butler was no sooner laid to rest than her husband began a frantic courtship of Black Tom's kinswoman, Eleanor Butler, the daughter of his out-of-favour liegeman, the Baron of Dunboyne.

At nineteen years of age, Eleanor was within marriageable age and had received her share of proposals. Either the suitors had proved unsuitable or the marriage settlements unsatisfactory, for in 1565, despite her good looks and connections, Eleanor was still available. Her father's dispute with his brother still raged, with Black Tom Earl of Ormond ranged firmly on the side of her uncle. Relations between the Baron of Dunboyne and his powerful overlord remained strained. Consequently the Earl of Desmond's choice of Eleanor as his future bride seemed deliberately motivated to exploit the differences between Black Tom and the baron. From the evidence of their subsequent relationship, however, it is more likely that the impulsive earl fell head over heels in love with the baron's daughter.

They had had many opportunities to meet through the connections that already existed between their families. Eleanor's half-brother, Donal-na-Píopaí MacCarthy Reagh, the nephew of the chieftain of Carbery, was married to the daughter of the earl's half-brother. Garrett's sister was married to Edmund Butler, Black Tom's brother. Their most recent meeting might well have been at Askeaton, for the funeral of Garrett's late countess. There Eleanor had perhaps fallen for the aristocratic earl, his pale, sensitive face starkly contrasted by the black velvet of his mourning apparel. Like everybody else throughout Munster, she had heard the gossip about his unlikely union with the middle-aged Dowager Countess of Ormond. While contemporary accounts, generally written by his adversaries, accuse Garrett of being weak, coarse, vain, hypersensitive and void of judgement, there is no doubt that he was attractive to women, particularly strong-willed women, to whom he appeared handsome, pensive and totally misunderstood; someone to be protected both from himself and his adversaries. 'Behind him Desmond left no cool-eyed observers; he moved through his age enveloped in rumours and turmoil, and if his actions repelled some, the riddle of his personality irresistibly drew others.'[1] Joan Butler had been a mature and intelligent woman. Eleanor Butler was also of a similar intelligent stamp, and both were irresistibly drawn to Garrett.

The entire Dunboyne household was thrown into disarray as the impatient earl conducted his ill-timed courtship at the same hectic pace as he was wont to gallop his horses. There is little doubt that Eleanor returned his advances. Her knight had arrived, albeit from an unexpected quarter. Eleanor's intelligence and beauty had a powerful impact upon the complex personality of her suitor, that strange mixture of poet and warrior. His love for Eleanor and his penchant for verse perhaps inspired his only composition to have survived, aptly entitled 'Against Blame of Women':

> *Speak not ill of womankind,*
> *'Tis no wisdom if you do.*
> *You that fault in women find,*
> *I would not be praised of you.*

Sweetly speaking, witty, clear,
  Tribe most lovely to my mind,
Blame of such I hate to hear.
  Speak not ill of womankind.

Bloody treason, murderous act,
  Not by women were designed,
Bells o'erthrown nor churches sacked.
  Speak not ill of womankind.

Bishop, king upon his throne,
  Primate skilled to loose and bind,
Spring of women every one!
  Speak not ill of womankind.

For a brave young fellow long
  Hearts of women oft have pined.
Who would dare their love to wrong?
  Speak not ill of womankind.

Paunchy greybeards never more
  Hope to please a woman's mind.
Poor young chieftains they adore!
  Speak not ill of womankind.[2]

Eleanor and Garrett were married at Kiltinan in late January 1565. The storm-clouds on the horizon would prevent the sun from shining for long on their union. For Eleanor was destined to become involved in a grim episode of history which would culminate in the most appalling personal tragedy and loss imaginable.

The earl and his new countess began their married life at Askeaton castle. Eleanor had a substantial dowry from her father, and Garrett endowed her with the castle and town of Bridgesford, County Tipperary, as part of her jointure. To judge by their later correspondence, despite their traumatic life together, Eleanor was devoted to Garrett, who in turn proved a respectful and caring husband. Her marriage introduced her to an environment markedly different from what she had been used to at Kiltinan and, in the more gaelicised and robust Desmond household, she strove to walk a diplomatic tight-rope with the Desmond clans and followers who despised the very name of Butler.

She accompanied Garrett on a tour of his lordship. His client lords received her with the hospitality and deference due their overlord's countess. She viewed the great Desmond castles of Askeaton, Newcastle, Castlemaine, Shanid and the rest with a bride's eye to future adjustments and refurbishment. For the moment she was content to accompany her lord and his retinue on a tour of inspection of his estates as he received the rents, services, homage and entertainment due his station, and enjoyed the festivities and pleasures of her brief honeymoon.

But political developments in Ireland waited for no such pleasant dalliances, not even for the great Earl of Desmond, whose impulsive spirit in any case was easily provoked especially where his feud with the rival House of Ormond was concerned. Eleanor was about to witness the intensity with which the two rivals were determined to pursue their differences. This time the row was sparked by Garrett's claim to rents from Sir Maurice FitzGerald, Lord of Decies, in Waterford. The Decies was originally part of the Desmond estate, but Sir Maurice now claimed to hold it by feudal tenure from the Crown. Garrett, however, insisted on his right to the overlordship of Decies, which, he proclaimed, 'is and always hathe beene a member of the house of Desmonde and in the rule and governance of the saide Earle and his ancestors'.[3] Sir Maurice appealed to the Earl of Ormond for protection. Black Tom readily agreed. Garrett thereupon summoned a hosting. His dependent lords and clansmen flocked to his standard, anxious for any chance to avenge themselves on their Butler enemies.

The intensity of their hatred doubtless surprised and dismayed Eleanor as she watched the Desmond forces mass before Askeaton. The mail-coated MacSheehy galloglass, battle-axes slung over their shoulders, formed the vanguard, as they would in battle when their ferocious strength and inborn hunger for slaughter was unleashed on their opposing counterparts, the MacSweeneys. The lightly-armed kern with their short Irish bows, targets and swords milled impatiently around the gateway. Inside the courtyard the horses attended by horseboys awaited their masters, who emerged from the castle clad in protective helmets, mail-shirts and jackets of quilted leather. Each carried a sword and dagger in his belt and a long spear. Garrett himself took command of this hot-blooded and impatient force. As he swung into the saddle, his standard was raised and the ancient war-cry of the Desmond Geraldines erupted in a roar. Amid shouts of 'Shanid abú!' Garrett, fourteenth Earl of Desmond, led his army to war against the hereditary enemy.

Eleanor watched her husband and his soldiers disappear from view, enveloped in the long woollen cloaks which would serve both as shelter and bed for the duration of the campaign. This was her first parting from Garrett, and she experienced a sense of loneliness and an even greater sense of fear for his safety. She was also uneasily conscious of her own vulnerability and isolation in an alien lordship. But the loneliness and fear would of necessity pass. Her training and personal experience had conditioned her to accept her husband's involvement in the unending litany of feuds, disputes, raids and rebellions, the hallmarks of the volatile society to which they all belonged. She busied herself in the administration of her husband's estate. Her inexperience and her Butler origins might well have made her task more difficult, but Eleanor Butler FitzGerald proved to be no pushover when it came to asserting her rights. From the moment of her husband's departure she determinedly set about establishing her position and authority in Desmond.

The years of skirmishing and verbal warfare between Garrett and Black Tom finally ended on 1 February 1565 at the ford of Affane near Lismore. This time no 'angel of peace' appeared to separate them. The rents of Decies were forgotten as, faced by the Ormond forces, Garrett put spurs to his horse and personally led the charge against his enemy. A brief but fierce battle ensued until Garrett, in a sharp encounter with Sir Edmund Butler, was 'stryken doune by shott of hagbut throughe his leg and woundid dangerously in III severall places of his body, besides divers bruses'.[4] Some three hundred of his men fell in battle, while others, who tried to swim to safety, were hacked to pieces by the Ormond galloglass along the banks of the Blackwater. Garrett was taken prisoner by an exultant Black Tom. As he was being carried shoulder-high on a litter from the battlefield by his enemies, they taunted him by asking: 'Where now the great Earl of Desmond?', to which Garrett haughtily replied: 'Where he belongs, on the backs of the Butlers.'[5] Brave words indeed. But for Garrett and Eleanor, Affane was to result in humiliation, imprisonment, loss of prestige, physical and mental deprivation, and the start of the slippery slope to rebellion and ruin.

The Queen was incensed at the entire episode and angrily ordered both earls to her presence. From Elizabeth's point of view, the Affane incident was an insult to her dignity and sovereignty, two attributes jealously guarded by the Tudors. Affane was the last battle fought between two private armies in these islands and, as such, it accomplished little but provoke the Queen's anger. 'It was impossible for a reforming government to ignore this assumption by nominal loyalists of a right to settle a family dispute by an appeal to arms.'[6] The two offending dynasts were to be put straight on the matter by an irate sovereign. Meanwhile, Black Tom exacted his personal revenge on his vanquished enemy. For six weeks he had Garrett incarcerated in his jail at Clonmel until the Lord Justice ordered both himself and his prisoner to Waterford. Fearing that he might be adjudged of equal guilt by the Crown, Black Tom was determined that the Earl of Desmond should be seen in public as the defeated and discredited villain of the piece, and himself the aggrieved but victorious party. He consequently had Garrett bound in chains and paraded through Waterford 'with sounding of trumpett and gunne shott, in suche tryumphant sort as though he were an open enemye or traytours rebell . . . the whole inhabitants of the cyttie staring and wondering and diversly speking thereon to his shame and dishonour'.[7] The jeers and catcalls of the citizens rang in Garrett's ears as he was led, sick, stumbling and dishevelled, through the streets. It was a bitter humiliation for the proud Geraldine earl.

News of the defeat of Affane and of Garrett's capture by the Butlers was brought to Askeaton by the defeated Desmond clansmen. Eleanor immediately set out for Waterford. She found Garrett in great agony from the wound in his thigh, a wound which was never to fully heal. Together they discussed the likely outcome of his capture and Eleanor soothed his feverish ramblings and bitter outbursts against the Butlers. Garrett entrusted the administration of his estates to her before being conducted to England to answer, with Black Tom, in person to the Queen for their presumptuous and precipitate action. To add to his discomfort, Garrett suffered greatly from sea-sickness on the trip. Consequently it was a haggard and ragged shadow of the vain, swaggering noble of their former meeting who was carried on a litter into the royal presence to answer for his crime. Garrett expected little mercy and even less justice from the angry Queen, well versed in his enemy's version of events.

At Court the Ormond–Desmond feud became entangled in a wider political intrigue between the Sussex and Leicester factions. Robert Dudley, the Earl of Leicester, had emerged as the Queen's favourite and there was some trepidation in the Sussex camp, that her admiration ran to such lengths as to encourage speculation that she had found herself a prospective husband. Sussex defended Ormond and lauded his loyalty. He berated the Earl of Desmond, accused him of treason and of being an oppressor of his neighbours. Leicester, with the backing of Sir Henry Sidney, favoured Desmond, and they cautiously indicated that his claim over the Decies was no more than an assertion of a right enjoyed for generations by successive earls of Desmond. While Elizabeth was critical of the conduct of both adversaries, she reserved the sharper edge of her tongue for Garrett. Both earls were forced to enter into recognisances for £20,000 and to agree to abide henceforth by the Queen's law. In an attempt to bridle Garrett's influence in Munster, MacCarthy More, over whom he claimed supremacy, was created the Earl of Clancar. Temporarily chastened, but undoubtedly relieved, towards the end of 1565 Garrett was permitted to depart for Ireland, while Black Tom chose to remain at court.

Garrett returned to Eleanor not yet fully recovered from the wounds he received at Affane and bearing also the mental scars of his further alienation from the Crown. Eleanor listened as he bitterly complained about the humiliation he had endured in the English court and the favouritism displayed by Elizabeth. He had been cold-shouldered and snubbed, while his rival, Black Tom, equally culpable, had been favoured by the Queen and her officials. Even the Leicester–Sidney faction had merely used him as a pawn in their political schemes and court intrigues. Eleanor soothed the ruffled pride of her aggrieved husband. She urged him to maintain his relationship, however tentative, with Leicester and Sidney as a means to counter-balance Black Tom's influence, as well as the antagonistic, ambitious petty officials in the Crown administration in Dublin. Initially Garrett seemed to take her advice and pursue a more loyal course. He refused to be drawn into a confederacy with the restless chieftain, Shane O'Neill of Tyrone, and even journeyed to Drogheda to meet Sidney, recently reappointed chief governor of Ireland, to offer him his services in the campaign against the Ulster chieftain.

Beneath the surface, however, the Geraldine–Butler feud simmered on. Factions from both sides raided and counter-raided the territory of the other. Both lordships were in a constant state of disorder. In the continued absence of Black Tom, his brothers contributed to the chaos in Ormond by their intemperate treatment of his dependent lords, tenants and town citizens, while the feud between Eleanor's father and uncle continued unabated.

After his ineffectual foray into Ulster against Shane O'Neill, Sidney turned south to attempt to cool the seething cauldron of lawlessness and malpractice which, by now, seemed on the point of boiling over and plunging all Munster into ruin. He first took in hand the feud between the Baron of Dunboyne and his brother and promptly had them, together with their quarrelsome wives and Eleanor's eldest brother James, committed to Dublin Castle. He next moved against Black Tom's brothers and sent them for trial at Clonmel. Sidney then turned his attention to the vast, sprawling territory of the Earl of Desmond. Reports and rumours of the unbridled lawlessness of Garrett's estates, the excesses of his rule, and the intolerable exactions he demanded from those over whom he claimed suzerainty, had reached Sidney. But neither he nor the Queen comprehended the determination and intensity with which the earl guarded the hereditary powers and privileges of his position, nor the fervour with which his adherents accepted his overlordship, which bound him to them as much as it did they to him.

For just as the Tudors claimed divine right to receive loyalty and exert total authority, so the Earl of Desmond claimed, by ancient Gaelic and feudal law, the loyalty and dues of his tributary lords. Garrett's estate exceeded that of any other lord either in Ireland or England. His income, both in money and in kind, was immense, yet he paid not a penny to the Crown, either in tax or cess. He used the revenue to subsidise his private army to enforce his will. He brooked no interference in the administration of his estates and meted out a harsh and summary justice based on the Gaelic principle that the strong must naturally overcome the weak. He was proud, even vainglorious, but in this he was a typical product of a society that expected such traits in a leader. He was an autocratic dictator, reared to expect homage, power and wealth. The Crown administrators and officials sent to dislodge him from his lofty perch he considered mere lackeys and underlings to be contemptuously dismissed. He was an absolute ruler by right, and this he intended to remain.

Eleanor presided over her husband's household and received the constant flow of chieftains, emissaries and spies who brought news of happenings in Ulster, Ormond, Dublin, London and the continent. Friars and priests came ashore at Youghal and Kinsale and beat a path to Askeaton to give tidings of the great religious crusade being contemplated on the continent against the 'heretic queen'. The wider political developments, with their religious undertones, did not concern the Earl of Desmond. The real news related to his lordship and its immediate enemies. Smarting at his treatment by Elizabeth and needled into action by his ambitious brother John and his military captains, like a Celtic warrior the Earl led his raiding parties at will. What Eleanor thought of his reckless behaviour is open to conjecture. The wild excesses of her husband and his followers, she realised, however, were bound to invite the attention of the Crown. Eleanor attempted to restrain her husband's more outrageous undertakings, more apt than he to see through the ill-advised plots of his brother. But for Garrett there was little choice but to play the Gaelic chieftain, keep his competitors for power within his own family at bay and still the wagging tongues that, on any sign of weakness on his part, might reopen the controversy surrounding his right to the earldom in the first place.

The number of his followers was legion and legendary. All the footloose and landless swordsmen of Munster flocked to his table and followed in his wake. The contrast between the earldoms of Ormond and Desmond was, in some aspects, remarkable. Black Tom assiduously flaunted his loyalty to Elizabeth while secretly retaining within his lordship many of the practices for which the Queen berated the Earl of Desmond. He had, however, made noticeable efforts to administer his estates by the English system, yet without foregoing any of the traditional dues and privileges he received under the Gaelic system. By his show of allegiance and a more circumspect and pragmatic administration of his lordship, Black Tom, in contrast to Garrett, presented to Elizabeth the commendable image of a loyal and anglicised Irish lord. Garrett, by his very nature and inability to adapt and play the politician, appeared the antithesis.

Incensed at the situation in Desmond, Elizabeth ordered Sidney to bestir himself and find out

why such rebells and offenders as be under the rule of the Earle of
Desmond and his brother John . . . have not ben apprehendid by them
or why the said Earle or his brother . . . have not ben charged and
made answerable thereto being to be committed to prisons as they
ought to be.[8]

The Queen could not forget that Sidney had favoured the Earl of
Desmond at court, and she was suspicious that he might deal leniently
with him at the expense of her protégé Black Tom. 'Of which two
persons,' she reminded Sidney, 'without any private respect of either of
them, it is . . . most easiest to judge which of them aught to recyve favor
and countenance.'[9]

With the royal accusation of favouritism ringing in his ear, Sidney
hurried to Youghal to confront the object of the Queen's anger. But
Sidney well realised that any reform of the feudal lordships of
Ireland must bring him into conflict, not only with the Earl of
Desmond, but with the Earl of Ormond as well. Sidney planned to
establish a militarily backed presidency in Munster with the aim to
'undermine the power of the feudal lords by depriving them of their
palatinate jurisdiction, by prohibiting the maintenance of private
armies and by truncating their power'.[10] The loyal Earl of Ormond
would be affected as much as the disloyal Earl of Desmond. But Black
Tom was at the seat of power in London and had access to the Queen
who, in any event, had been less than enthusiastic for Sidney's
proposal which, she deemed, would necessitate further Crown
expense.

When Sidney suggested Sir Warham St Leger for the post of council
president, the Queen, prompted by Black Tom, gave full vent to her
disapproval. 'Wee did mislyke in deede to see you so addicted to the
favour of the earle of Desmond', she fumed, 'as to the place St Leger
the president of that Counsell, whose inward preferrid friendship
towards the Earle of Desmond was notorious.' 'And', she added,
perhaps echoing Black Tom's sentiments, 'the old inimitye that St
Leger's father bore to the Earle of Ormond's father, whome he brought
to his end heere in England by prosequuting of him so as we assure
you nether needid We the information of the Earle of Ormond to
disallow St Leger to be president.'[11] While astounded at such overt
prejudice, Sidney had little alternative but to let the presidency issue
rest for the moment. Ormond's objection to St Leger merely masked

his opposition to an English presidency in Munster *per se* and its likely effects on his own power.

Eleanor and Garrett were at Youghal, where Eleanor was delivered of their first child, Margaret. Garrett's spies brought news of Sidney's progress through his territory. As Sidney drew closer to Youghal Garrett's sense of grievance at the intrusion increased. He called for a 'rising out' of his tributary client lords and armed followers to show Sidney just who was master in Munster. As he rode through the Munster countryside, Sidney reported the waste and untended state of Garrett's domain to the Queen:

Like as I never was in a more pleasant country in all my life, so never saw I a more waste and desolate land . . . and there heard I such lamentable cries and doleful complaints made by that small remain of poor people which yet are left, who (hardly escaping the fury of the sword and fire of their outrageous neighbours, or the famine which the same, or their extortious lords, hath driven them unto, either by taking their goods from them or by sending the same, by their extort, taking of coyne and livery) make demonstration of the miserable estate of that country. Besides this, such horrible and lamentable spectacles there are to behold as the burning of villages, the ruin of churches, the wasting of such as have been good towns and castles, yea, the view of the bones and skulls of your dead subjects, who, partly by murder, partly by famine, have died in the fields, as in troth hardly any Christian with dry eyes could behold.[12]

Early in 1567 Sidney confronted Garrett at Youghal, where the earl made little attempt to hide his displeasure at the Lord Deputy's presence. Sidney ordered an investigation into Garrett's long-standing dispute with Black Tom over possession of Kilsheelin castle. The investigation duly found in favour of the Earl of Ormond. The decision provoked Garrett into a passionate tirade, in Sidney's presence, against the Crown. He swore that no English sovereign should ever have jurisdiction within his territory and 'that he would never disperse with the old state of his family, but would have five gallowglasses where he had formerly had one'.[13] Sidney brushed aside the earl's intemperate outburst and, with some sympathy, attempted to excuse it to the Queen on the grounds of her preference for the Earl of Ormond which, as he had warned her, made Garrett 'grow desperate for that he cannot have his causes ended between the Earl of Ormond and him, in which matters I suppose each doth the other wrong'.[14] But mindful of his duty as a loyal servant of the Crown, Sidney also pointed out that if Garrett did rebel and was defeated, his lands could be confiscated and 'thereby the Queen to be made mistress of a great part of the realm'.[15] For the first time the idea of confiscation of the Desmond estates was, albeit hypothetically, propounded, and the attention of land-hungry speculators in England became fixed on the vast acres ruled by such an irresponsible and disloyal subject.

As Garrett sought to put his threat into action, Sidney attempted to clip his wings by inviting the earl's dependent lords to make submission to him personally, independently of their overlord. Garrett acted to counter Sidney's move, and soon messengers were bringing him word that the traditional Desmond allies had answered his call to arms and a thousand armed men were mustered to await his orders. Sidney's force in Munster numbered only two hundred. With the odds in his favour, Garrett attempted to leave Youghal to assume control of his army. Sidney forestalled him and in March 1567 committed the irate earl under guard in Youghal.

Eleanor was recuperating after the birth of her child. Her husband's rash behaviour made her greatly fear the consequences. She had tried to curb his intemperate conduct towards Sidney, the only potential English ally he had. But he would not be restrained and became even more incensed as he watched his tributary lords troop in, one by one, and submit to the Lord Deputy. Sidney listened as they recited long lists of complaints against Garrett, whose overbearing treatment 'so injured and exacted upon by him as in effect they are or were become his thrals or slaves'.[16] Sidney ordered Garrett to accompany him to Limerick, while Eleanor remained at Youghal. Moving towards Limerick with his small force, with Garrett in tow, Sidney received reports that the earl's army intended to attack. He pre-empted the danger by placing the earl under arrest, and with this insurance was able to pass without hindrance through the Desmond heartland to Limerick. From there the proud Earl of Desmond was brought captive through Limerick, Galway, Athlone and back to Dublin, where he was confined to prison in Dublin Castle, branded by Sidney as 'a man void of judgement to govern and will to be ruled'.[17]

News of her husband's imprisonment was relayed to Eleanor, who greatly feared the effects of this new humiliation on his mental and physical well-being. His brother, Sir John, to whom Sidney had conveyed the administration of the Desmond estates in the earl's absence, went to Dublin to seek terms for his brother's release. But shortly after his arrival he found himself sharing the same cell as Garrett. Shades of the fate meted out by Henry viii to the House of Kildare were revived. Was Henry's daughter about to order a similar brutal chastisement on the House of Desmond? All Ireland awaited the fate of the earl and wondered in awe at the seizure of such a powerful lord. Even Elizabeth appeared somewhat aghast at the temerity of her Lord Deputy in seizing Desmond on his own ground with such a small army. In Munster there was little reaction to the imprisonment of the earl except from his kinsman the Knight of Glin who took the field with his son Thomas. They were eventually captured and condemned to death. By a legal loophole the Knight escaped his fate, but his son was hanged, drawn and quartered in Limerick. 'There is a tradition that his mother was present at his execution, seized his head when he was beheaded and drank his blood and collected for burial at Lislaughtin abbey the parts of his dismembered body in a linen sheet.'[18]

Meanwhile Garrett languished with his brother in Dublin Castle, complaining bitterly to Sidney about the treachery of his capture. Sidney sought the Queen's pleasure as to the fate of his troublesome prisoner. But Ormond had the Queen's ear in England, and in September 1567 Elizabeth ordered that the earl and his brother should be transferred to the Tower of London. Eleanor's worst fears were realised. She hurried to Dublin and received permission to visit her husband. There was no indication of what lay in store in London. But they both realised that his absence from Desmond was bound to be exploited by his enemies from both within and without. The old Gaelic dictum 'a lordship without a lord is a dead lordship'[19] was very much a reality in gaelicised Desmond. Few could be trusted. Officials and officers in the Crown's pay now cast envious eyes on the Desmond estates, reckoning up their potential as a means of revenue both for themselves and their royal mistress. Garrett's step-brother, Thomas Roe FitzGerald, the disinherited contender for the earldom, waited in the wings to reassert his claim by whatever means offered him the best opportunity of reinstatement. Garrett's cousin, James FitzMaurice FitzGerald, was the most able and likely contender to take his place in his absence. But he too would have to be watched lest his unexpected promotion made him unduly ambitious.

Eleanor alone could be trusted, and once again Garrett entrusted her with the administration of his estates. He urged her to write regularly with details of her stewardship and to be vigilant in collecting his rents and dues. For in the grand Geraldine manner Garrett insisted on being escorted to his London prison by a princely retinue of followers. He intended to hold court in the traditional style, even though Elizabeth intended his palace to be a dungeon. But there were no multitudes of willing peasants in London to provide the earl with the means for this vain display. The rents and dues from his estates must pay for his self-indulgent and expensive outlay. Eleanor returned to Munster to begin the unenviable and daunting task of holding the fort in her husband's absence.

Garrett and Sir John, accompanied by a hundred followers, were sent to London in December. Sir John fell ill during the voyage, and there was 'much ado to get him to Lichfield', where their escort reported they were 'thus constrained to tarry there to see what he will do tomorrow, when if there be any health in him they will travel towardes London'.[20] They eventually reached the capital where the brothers were lodged under confinement in the Tower. The terms of their custody permitted them access to their followers who daily flocked to the prison. From his cell Garrett, while the money lasted, kept 'open house' and a hospitable table for his dependants, generally holding court as if he were at home in the great hall of Askeaton.

While Garrett kept up the brave show in England, Eleanor was left with the responsibility of both funding her husband's extravagances and safeguarding his interests in Munster. As she had anticipated, the vacant earldom unleashed the unquiet ambitions of Garrett's relatives. In order to foment unrest within Desmond, rumours of the earl's death were circulated, and there was little Eleanor could immediately do to counteract them; the borders of her husband's territory were far-flung and communications primitive. The rumours provided the opportunity for the main contenders to throw their hats into the ring and revive their claims to the earldom. Garrett's step-brother, Thomas Roe, 'taking advantage of his brother's misfortunes . . . took upon him to command in chiefe the Earledome of Desmond'.[21] It was rumoured that Thomas Roe was supported in his bid for power by the Earl of Ormond. Thomas Roe was stopped in his tracks, however, as James FitzMaurice FitzGerald, proclaiming that his own interest in the vacancy was merely to preserve his cousin's rights, 'leaps into the lists, challenging any man that durst presume to question the Earle's right'.[22]

Eleanor viewed the motives of both contenders with suspicion. Their bid to usurp her husband's position seemed likely to split the lordship apart as both prepared to implement their claims by force. She acted swiftly to pre-empt their plans and summoned a hosting of Garrett's retainers and galloglass. Like an avenging eagle she swooped on the two claimants and took them into custody until she could establish Garrett's will in the matter. After some time she received his instructions from the Tower to appoint James FitzMaurice FitzGerald as 'captain' in Desmond during his absence. He further urged his dependent lords 'to aid the countess and James FitzMaurice in collecting rents and in keeping the peace'.[23]

Eleanor's suspicions about FitzMaurice's motives were unappeased. Garrett had been absent for almost six months, and his volatile sub-lords and chieftains needed an overlord to both protect and direct them. As the situation stood, any contender with even the vaguest claim to the lordship, but with sufficient strength to enforce it, could usurp Garrett's position. Her husband was far removed from the real situation and, she felt, placed too much trust in his cousin. Eleanor could not be sure that FitzMaurice's motives were as unselfish as he publicly proclaimed. Until her suspicions could be allayed Eleanor decided to keep FitzMaurice and Thomas Roe under lock and key.

She had also to contend with the Crown Commissioners in Munster, who also sought to take advantage of her husband's absence to extend their authority into his lordship. In addition, she was under pressure from the Commissioners to deliver her two prisoners into their custody. But Eleanor well realised that such action on her part would achieve little but to incur the wrath of their respective followers and lead to even greater disorder within the lordship under her care. She knew she had to play for time.

The Commissioners summoned her to Waterford, but she fobbed them off, pleading the unsettled and poor state of her husband's country and her own deprivation. 'I can scant abyde in one house past two dayes and two nights,' she told them, 'though it be wynter, but trudging and travaylinge by day and ptly. by night from place to place meaninge to appease the fury of their lewd attempts the best I can.'[24]

She had set out in January 1568, in the depths of a severe winter, to quell the rumours of her husband's death, to appease the anxiety of his dependent lords, and to determine their views on the proposed appointment of James FitzMaurice FitzGerald as the earl's temporary replacement. On her journey she tried to collect the rents due to her husband, but, as she informed the Commissioners (no doubt in order to dispel any hopes they might have of securing a share for the Crown) the state of the country was so poor that she 'could not find in my harte to take up myne owne dutys of the inhabitants there'.[25] But the Commissioners insisted on a meeting to discuss the situation in Desmond and urged her by return messenger 'to lett us understand yor determinate answear whether yo will come to us or we to yo in any convenient place'.[26] They further ordered her to deliver her two prisoners to the Crown and to ensure that all the tributary lords of Desmond submit to the Commissioners. But following the abduction and imprisonment of the earl, Desmond's sub-lords refused to meet the Commissioners, unless under Eleanor's protection, whom they acknowledged as the earl's true representative.

Despite her suspicions of the ulterior motives of FitzMaurice and Thomas Roe, Eleanor was loath to hand her prisoners over to the Crown. Desmond needed a strong lord at the helm, especially at this decisive time. She subsequently extracted pledges and securities for Thomas Roe's release from the Munster lords, Roche and Power, and endorsed Garrett's choice of James FitzMaurice to act in a caretaker capacity until his return. She then released them, pretending to the irate Commissioners that it had been perpetrated 'by the rude people the erle's captens of galloglasses, constables and other of the countrey'.[27] With her husband's lordship for the moment under control and in relative peace, Eleanor set out, escorted by Hugh Lacy the Bishop of Limerick, to keep her long-postponed appointment with the Crown Commissioners at Cork. To keep them at bay she promised not to impede the extension of English law into Desmond, though qualifying her promise by stressing that it applied only 'as far as my good will may thereunto extend'.[28]

During 1568 Eleanor maintained a steady flow of correspondence with her imprisoned husband. From the Tower Garrett continued to urge her to be vigilant in his interests in Munster and to endeavour to collect his rents, of which he was in dire need. The Queen had reduced her allowance for his upkeep, considering it altogether contrary to her parsimonious nature that such an unfaithful subject, together with his overbearing retinue, should be maintained at her expense. Garrett's health began to deteriorate in the damp, unhealthy confines of the prison. He became withdrawn and silent as he brooded over the humiliation and injustice of his detention. His thoughts were constantly on Munster and in one letter uncharacteristically rebuked Eleanor for her apparent tardiness in sending him news from home. Otherwise the tenor of his letters to her was warm and loving; they were generally addressed to 'the Right honourable and my veray lovinge wife dame Elinor Countesse of Desmond in Ireland',[29] according her all the respect and affection pertaining to her position as his countess and wife. In his letters he frequently sent his commendations to Eleanor's mother, the Baroness of Dunboyne who, on the death of her husband in 1567 and after their release from Dublin Castle, had continued to be harassed at Kiltinan by Peter Butler and his Ormond supporters. The heir of Dunboyne, Eleanor's brother James, a minor, had been sent to England to further his education at Cambridge. In a letter to his step-brother, whom he addressed as 'Mr Thomas of Desmond', Garrett instructed him in his behaviour towards Eleanor:

> *This shalbe to desire you not to fayle as my trust is no less in you, to be vearie kindlie towardes my Ladie my wif, and that she maie not slacke nor perceive the contrarie but your good will and yt you and everie of yours, as you tender my good will and advoid my displeasure.*[30]

His seneschal, John FitzEdmund of Imokilly, he instructed to aid and protect Eleanor.

Conditions in the Tower continued to worsen. Elizabeth's stop to the carnival atmosphere found Garrett now lodged 'without furniture and left to suffer from the cold'.[31] His vexation was exacerbated when he was compelled to appear before endless inquisitions to answer for his conduct within his own lordship. There were plenty of paid spies and informers ready to talk. He was accused of providing meat and drink to proclaimed traitors in Munster. Disdainfully he explained the Gaelic custom of liberal hospitality, but denied that he had aided any treasonable offenders. Reasserting the inherited powers conferred on him by right of the palatine status of his lordship, he loudly proclaimed to his inquisitors that he had sole authority to rule and to administer justice without regard to the Queen's sheriffs, judges or administrators. His judges could scarcely comprehend such seemingly outlandish claims which harkened back to the bygone age of the independent barons of feudal England, long since moulded into obedient subjects by successive Tudor monarchs. That such a political dinosaur as the Earl of Desmond could still exist, even in Ireland, was beyond the comprehension of their Elizabethan minds.

Evidence of raids on his neighbours, of the disorder in his lordship and of intrigue with O'Neill against the Crown was produced against him. The whisper of treason began to circulate. Visions of the executioner's block, at Tyburn, and the jeering mob flashed before his mind. The pale ghosts of his Kildare kinsmen came to haunt him. Not willing to place his head entirely in the lion's mouth, in July 1568 he made a submission to the Privy Council at Howard House:

> *I, Garrett, Earl of Desmond, knowing myself to have offended the Queen's laws and to stand in great peril of life and forfeiture of all my lands and goods; and besides knowing myself to be in danger of forfeiting £20,000 wherein I stand bound to Her Majesty by recognisance: therefore, to obtain her favour, I submit myself to her mercy and clemency, and do offer to Her Majesty all my possessions, thereof to take into her hands so much as she thinks convenient and to dispose of the same for benefit of the realm of Ireland, at her pleasure and I grant and promise that within days after her pleasure shall be signified to me, what castles, lands or liberties she shall think good to take, I will make assurance thereof to Her Majesty, her heirs and successors.*[32]

With the imperious Geraldine where she wanted him, on his knees, and 'so far as the law went, Elizabeth now had Munster at her mercy, but she kept fast hold on her prisoners until time should declare how far the law coincided with the facts'.[33] Garrett had saved his neck from the block, but at a terrible cost to both his pride and his pocket. His fate still hung on a thread, for, despite his submission, he was still in prison, destitute, ill and friendless. His sole hope depended on his wife's ability to counter the intrigue, greed and double-dealing directed against him from every quarter. The outlook in the summer of 1568 looked as grim as the cold, grey stones of his prison cell.

Suddenly a new threat to the stability of Munster emerged and, for a time, seemed likely to spawn the unlikeliest of alliances between the rival houses of Desmond and Ormond. While his plan to establish a presidency in Munster had been forestalled by the machinations of the Earl of Ormond, Sidney now raised the idea of colonisation as a means to extend the Crown's authority in the province. His proposal was examined by the English government. Sidney envisaged the establishment of English settlements 'as oases of civility in a desert of barbarians'.[34] Lands confiscated by the rebellion of their Irish owners, or land held by tenure that could be proved faulty or uncertain, would provide the means to subvent the proposed settlements. The Queen looked favourably on the proposal as a less expensive method of conquest and in keeping with the mood of discovery and colonisation in vogue among English financial entrepreneurs and intrepid, land-hungry adventurers. The settling of the disorderly areas of Ireland with English farmers, yeomen, artisans and soldiers, and the establishment of English shire practices therein, seemed practical and augured well for a more stable and less expensive administration.

Elizabeth's domestic and foreign problems had intensified. Scotland, in complicity with the ever-scheming Mary Stuart and her French Catholic allies, threatened revolt. 'The life-and-death wrestle between the Reformation and the unreformed Church had already settled into a permanent struggle between England and Spain.'[35] While the struggle was, as yet, fought 'unofficially' by Elizabeth's privateers who plundered Spanish treasure ships as they returned from the Americas, Munster, with its unstable political situation, unreformed religion and strategically situated harbours like Youghal, Kinsale and Dingle, could yet provide Spain with the backdoor access to England.

The colonisation of Munster was greeted with enthusiasm in England. First into the fray, with a dubious claim originating from the Norman conquest, came Sir Peter Carew of Devon, an enterprising Elizabethan soldier and adventurer. Carew claimed lands in Cork, Kerry, Waterford, Meath, but also the barony of Idrone, the property of the Earl of Ormond's brother, Sir Edmund Butler. The ire of the loyal Butlers was unleashed when Sidney had the claim confirmed by the Irish Privy Council. On the strength of Carew's initial success, scores of enthusiastic English adventurers, including Sir Richard Grenville, Sir Humphrey Gilbert and Sir Warham St Leger, set their sights on the rich land of Munster in a mission of plunder on a grand scale. To the majority of these pirate-adventurers, Ireland was as remote and unknown as the far-off Americas, peopled by a race as alien as the Red Indians, governed by savage chiefs and mysterious brehons, an ideal terrain for the ambitions and energies of restless young men in search of wealth and adventure.

To add to the growing anxiety of both Gaelic and gaelicised landowners Sidney, on his return to Ireland, had failed to bring back the Earl of Desmond. Fear spread among the Irish chieftains and lords including the normally loyal House of Ormond. Ormond's brother declared 'that no man of Irish descent could be safe'[36] from the seizure of either his land or his person. Sidney convened a parliament in 1569 which was primarily 'used to promote the policy of conquest'[37] and which caused further unrest. In Ulster Shane O'Neill, recently murdered, was deemed 'attainted, the name of O'Neill extinguished and the Queen entitled to Tyrone';[38] thereby sounding a clear warning to every lord and chieftain 'that there could be but one sovereignty in Ireland'[39] and that possession of their lordships was no longer guarantee of legality of tenure by English law.

The first wave of adventurers landed in Munster and laid claim to lands and castles in the vicinity of Cork, possessions of the Earl of Desmond and MacCarthy More. James FitzMaurice FitzGerald seized his chance to exploit these developments and convened a conference of Geraldine leaders, informing them that 'their chief and his brother were condemned to death or at least to perpetual imprisonment'.[40] Garrett's continued confinement, the uncertainty over land titles, the threatened colonisation, combined with the unlikelihood of Elizabeth being reconciled with the papacy, gave James FitzMaurice the opportunity he sought—to broaden the basis of the local struggle over land and lordship into the wider international religious and political crusade against Elizabeth. To seek international recognition and material assistance for his new-found cause, FitzMaurice sent Maurice FitzGibbon, papal appointee to the See of Cashel, to King Philip of Spain. FitzMaurice next sought to make common cause with the brothers of the Earl of Ormond, still smarting under Sidney's chastisement and Carew's threat to their lands. The brothers agreed to become involved, though, they maintained, not against the Crown but 'against those that banish Ireland and mean conquest'.[41] The prospect of an alliance between the usually loyal House of Ormond and the rebel House of Desmond, aided by foreign enemy intervention, sent shivers of apprehension down Elizabeth's spine. She ordered Black Tom back to Ireland to resume his responsibilities in Ormond, but gave no such commission to the still captive Earl of Desmond.

Eleanor observed the unfolding events and wondered at the unnatural alliance being forged between FitzMaurice and the Ormond Butlers. They were no friends of her own family, and even less of the Desmonds. They had lately terrorised her mother and plundered her father's estates. She was suspicious of FitzMaurice's real intention, as he promoted his religious crusade. The question of religion mattered little in Munster, and FitzMaurice's use of it she saw as merely a means to subvert her husband's authority and position. She also feared the leadership abilities of FitzMaurice. In the continued absence of their overlord, and under the constant threat of colonisation and encroachment by the Crown, the loyalty of her husband's followers might waver. Caught in a dilemma between the Queen's refusal to release her husband and the unfolding ambitions and designs of FitzMaurice, she could do little but await developments and keep alive the fast-receding memory of her husband among his people.

Chapter 4
Exile

We have been here much molested with the erle of Desmond's wief . . . pretending that she hath not brought with her wherewith to mayntayne her owne charge nor the charge of her husbande . . .

QUEEN ELIZABETH TO SIR HENRY SIDNEY, 17 APRIL 1570

In July 1569 James FitzMaurice FitzGerald raised his crusading banner over Munster and with fire and sword swept through the province with the avenging fury of a convert hell-bent on doing the Lord's work. In Ormond his confederates, the Butler brothers, plundered and raided the countryside on the less lofty but nonetheless bloody mission of defence of their land. Confronted by the 4,500 men of this diversely motivated force, the newly-settled English planters and their families fled for their lives and cowered for safety behind the high protective walls of Cork, Kinsale and Youghal. Leaving a trail of corpses, looted and burnt-out houses and hovels, bare fields and thousands of cattle stampeded into the wilderness, FitzMaurice arrived before the gates of Cork on 15 July 1569 and ordered the mayor to 'destroy out of the town all the Huguenots with the first wind'.[1]

Sidney proclaimed the Butler brothers and FitzMaurice traitors, and Carew commenced a campaign of retaliatory but indiscriminate slaughter in Ormond. News of the atrocities spread. In Connaught the earls of Clanrickard and Thomond bestirred themselves into action and united with their Geraldine and Butler counterparts to defend their land. In Leinster the Earl of Kildare wavered in the direction of his Geraldine kinsmen. Black Tom prepared to return to Ormond and made no secret that 'anti-Geraldine though he was, if the lands of the ancient owners were to be seized by strangers, then he would make common cause with his countrymen'.[2]

The situation was getting rapidly out of hand. The Queen made Sidney her scapegoat. She berated him for tarring Black Tom's brothers with the same brush as FitzMaurice, blithely ignoring their participation with him in besieging Kilkenny. Upon the arrival of their brother at Rosslare in August, however, they deserted FitzMaurice and, spurning Sidney, submitted instead to Black Tom. Shortly afterwards Carew's colonisation schemes in Ormond were abandoned. Sidney was ordered by the Queen to leave the Butlers to their own devices and to concentrate his efforts against FitzMaurice.

At Sidney's approach FitzMaurice fell back from Cork and sought shelter deep inside the Kerry mountains. For a second time in a matter of months Munster was subjected to a baptism of slaughter and rapine as Sidney retaliated with the same ferocity as FitzMaurice had shown to the planters. The earls of Clanrickard and Thomond promptly submitted, together with many of the confederates. Deserted by his erstwhile allies, FitzMaurice established his camp within the inaccessible fastness of the Glen of Aherlow. His first attempt to promote a religious confederacy, linked to international developments, had failed. But he had sufficient political awareness to realise that the question of religion had not, as yet, penetrated as a political issue in Ireland, which was 'merely a pawn in the great game of European diplomacy'.[3] He could afford to lie low for a while, consolidate his position and formulate his plans to raise his banner another day.

But FitzMaurice's hasty action and Sidney's reprisal focused the attention of the Crown once more on the lordship of the Earl of Desmond. Eleanor soundly cursed the ill-advised revolt which had presented the Crown with the opportunity to establish garrisons in the abandoned castles of Garrett's tributary chieftains who had followed FitzMaurice. The countryside bore the scars of the revolt and, as Eleanor testified, 'was utterly distroid and wasted by the unhappie rebellion of James Fitzmorrish'.[4] She found it impossible to collect the rents and dues owed to her husband, and whatever meagre sums were forthcoming were summarily expropriated by the Crown to redeem the expenses incurred in suppressing the revolt. Oblivious to the state of affairs within his lordship, Garrett begged her to come personally to him with as much money as she could obtain for the relief of himself and Sir John, both of whom, he told her, 'greatly lack apparel and other necessities and especially money'.[5] Their situation in prison had deteriorated to the level of common felons. But there was little that Eleanor could do to relieve their condition. She wrote to Garrett of the desperate conditions prevailing in Desmond which had prevented her from collecting 'no pte of yor rents or other duties that maye enable me to repaire toward you'.[6] She held FitzMaurice responsible for the destruction and voiced her suspicions about his true motives, which she saw as being 'to bring you yf he could in further displeasor but also usurpe all yor enheritance to himself'.[7] The ostensible religious overtones of FitzMaurice's revolt cut little ice with Eleanor. The misery and depression she suffered at this time is evident in a letter to Garrett in which she confided: 'I pray God send us joyfull meeting or me shorte departure out of this world.—Yor loving miserable wief Ellynor Desmond.'[8]

She sought permission from Sidney to go to her husband and moved to Kinsale in anticipation of his reply. Whether out of a sense of genuine sympathy for her plight, or with the intention of using her as a means to secure the release of the earl (a better alternative from the Lord Deputy's point of view than have to contend with the more dangerous aspirations of the earl's deputy, FitzMaurice), Sidney secured Eleanor a pass into England. Accompanied by her husband's lawyer and friend, Morris Sheehan, who throughout the traumatic years that were to follow was seldom from her side, and a small company of servants, Eleanor arrived in Bristol in the early weeks of 1570. From there she journeyed down the long, bleak road to London.

It was Eleanor's first visit to the great metropolis but, as she made her way through the maze of narrow, bustling streets, flanked by the wooden-fronted houses, taverns and shops, there was little time to wonder or admire. Hers was a mission fraught with danger and uncertainty. Her means were meagre, and the awesome task that confronted her, to effect her husband's release, would take every ounce of her energy, ability and resources. She had to move the mind of a resolute, autocratic queen whose known antipathy towards her husband seemed as unyielding as the hard, grey stone of his tower prison. She was conducted through the grim, dark corridors of the infamous Tower, and as the heavy iron-bound door closed with a shuddering bang behind her, she was reunited with a husband whom she scarcely recognised.

They had been apart for eighteen months. The once handsome, proud, richly-attired noble was no more. In his place stood a trembling, gaunt and shabby figure who with red-rimmed eyes cried out his welcome and his fear. The reality of their awful dilemma was perhaps temporarily banished as for a moment a beam of happiness shone on their reunion and briefly lighted their gloomy surroundings. Through the prison bars they looked down on the slow-moving, muddied waters of the Thames, flanked by a jumble of dingy, riverside buildings, and thought perhaps of Askeaton and the rushing Deel and the green pasturelands of Limerick. Eleanor related the tidings from Munster and the changes that had occurred in Desmond during Garrett's absence. It was of the utmost urgency that he should find a way out of the Tower and back to Ireland to salvage what remained of his lordship and his authority. But with Munster subdued, there seemed even less likelihood that the Queen would see any reason to restore him. If, however, Munster was to relapse into disorder, then the heavy cost of restoring peace and the Queen's known aversion to paying the piper, allied to Sidney's advice, that the vacant Desmond lordship was the source of internal discord and a temptation to England's enemies, might well have the effect of making Garrett's restoration seem the lesser of two evils. Consequently FitzMaurice had to be encouraged in his religious rebellion and foreign intrigues. But before Garrett's return to Ireland could be contemplated, Eleanor first set about securing his release from the Tower.

From both financial necessity and a desire to be with her husband, Eleanor took up residence in the Tower. The ancient stronghold, situated in the south-east corner of the old city of London, on the north bank of the Thames, built by William the Conqueror, was initially constructed as a secure enclosure within the surviving Roman city walls. Within this enclosure the imposing White Tower was erected. Over succeeding centuries the site developed with the addition of a series of smaller towers, connected by high curtain walls and surrounded by a moat. Eventually by the sixteenth century the Tower complex was to encompass some twenty-three individual towers, a chapel, and various lodgings, gardens and walks. Henry VIII was the last monarch to occupy it as a residence, and it gradually came to be used as a prison to lodge important political prisoners.

One of its towers, the Beauchamp Tower, had a tragic association with the FitzGeralds. It was in the apartments of this tower, following in the tradition of former inmates, that Silken Thomas, to pass away the days leading to his execution, started to carve his name on the brick wall. The inscription, still visible today, was abruptly cut short, however, at 'THOMAS FITG' as the executioner of Tyburn interrupted the doomed engraver. Like his kinsman, the Earl of Desmond had also been allotted an apartment in one of the towers. The degree of comfort in the cold, cheerless rooms depended on one's own means or the generosity and influence of friends outside. Garrett's distinct lack of both meant that there were for him few comforts to ease the agony of his imprisonment.

From the Tower Eleanor daily sallied forth to Whitehall, Westminster and further afield to Greenwich and Richmond, wherever Elizabeth and her court happened to be in residence, to seek her husband's release. From the fringes of the court circles and cliques she importuned, bribed and cajoled the influential and corrupt in her endeavour to obtain access to the Queen. She endured humiliation and defeat as backs were turned and doors slammed in her face. Her lack of means was reflected in her meagre and threadbare wardrobe. The powdered, coifed and bejewelled court ladies and their elegantly attired male counterparts, would have little truck with the down-at-heel countess from Ireland. The powerful Ormond faction spied on her every move as she picked her way through the spider-like web of intrigue and double-dealing on the long and perilous road to the Queen. A cash handout here, a promise of land there, it was a costly mission which soon absorbed her slim resources. In desperation Garrett wrote directly to Elizabeth's chief secretary, Sir William Cecil, explaining that as 'verie extreme necessitie' had prohibited Eleanor from continuing 'her sute for my delyverance into the cyttie of Londone', he was appealing to Cecil 'to have rememberance the futherance of her sute'.[9] On foot of her husband's message, Eleanor redoubled her efforts, and eventually her persistence was rewarded. In May 1570 she was informed that Elizabeth had, albeit reluctantly, agreed to grant her an audience.

The audience was held at Hampton Court. The ill-feeling that the Queen bore her husband was extended to Eleanor. She realised that her petition to the unfriendly, short-tempered Queen must be couched in humble and repentant tones. With cold, calculating eyes the older Queen looked down on the younger countess who knelt before her and listened to her plea for sustenance for herself and her husband and for his release from the Tower. Eleanor promised in return to steer her husband on a path of loyalty and obedience.

Elizabeth appeared unmoved by her request, and her attitude was reflected in the atmosphere of her court, which evinced little friendship or support to the Irish countess. It was dangerous to appear sympathetic to the wife of a rebel, personally out of favour with the Queen and currently awaiting his fate in the most dreaded prison in the land. A friendly look, a quick word of consolation or encouragement to his wife could be misinterpreted. Elizabeth's impenetrable face gave little indication of the likely outcome of their meeting, and Eleanor withdrew from the royal presence to her prison home to await the outcome.

She had not long to wait. In a letter that bristled with indignation and impatience at Eleanor's dogged persistence and her alleged penury, Elizabeth informed Sidney that

> We have been here much molested with the erle of Desmond's wief who pretending that she hath not brought with her wherewith to mayntayne her owne charge nor the charge of her husbande and on the other parte we have been at no smale charges with him and his synce his comying over.[10]

As ever, the cost factor involved in the maintenance, however frugally, of the Desmonds was Elizabeth's preoccupation. To rid herself of the burden, she acceded to Eleanor's request and ordered their removal from the Tower to the custody of Sidney's protégé, Sir Warham St Leger, on whom she also dumped the cost of their maintenance. Eleanor, Garrett, Sir John and fourteen servants were subsequently transferred from the Tower and lodged at Leeds castle, the country estate of St Leger in Kent.

Garrett and Eleanor were well acquainted with their jailer. St Leger held a fee farm from the Earl in Desmond at a rent of 53s 4d per annum. He had obtained additional land west of Cork city, in recompense for financial assistance to Garrett during his period of captivity. St Leger's known antagonism to the Earl of Ormond and his friendship with the Sidney faction at court had initially drawn Garrett to him. Anxious to expand his estate in Munster, St Leger had provided his destitute landlord with money, but at a price. In any event, Eleanor had accomplished the first step towards achieving her husband's repatriation. And after the long months of captivity in the Tower, the relative freedom of Leeds castle and the fresh summer air of the Kentish countryside must have acted as a tonic to the physical and mental well-being of Eleanor and her husband.

For a few short months of the summer of 1570 they enjoyed partial liberty in unfamiliar but pleasant surroundings. But soon St Leger's resources began to feel the strain of their upkeep. In October 1570 he complained of the dire straits of both himself and his prisoners. He begged the Privy Council for 'a warrant for receipt of money for their diet; otherwise', he threatened, 'I shall be constrayned to bring them to court, being not able, by my greate losses sustayned in Ireland, to beare the chardges thereof any longer'.[11] The earl and his family, St Leger complained, had not 'any thing of their owne to relieve them selfes withal, having your honnrs not so muche as to buy them a pair of shooes, nor have not had since their cominge in to my chardge and stand in despair to have any thing out of their owne country'.[12] No rents were being forwarded from the earl's estates in Ireland. He and his retinue were totally dependent for their food, clothing, shelter and necessities of life on their reluctant custodian. Garrett in captivity had cost Elizabeth more than when unrestrained in Desmond. Yet Elizabeth was not prepared to risk sending him back to Ireland. St Leger's protest of impoverishment fell on deaf ears, and the straitened conditions into which he and his aristocratic charges had fallen were allowed to continue.

In December 1570 the long-postponed decision to appoint a president in Munster was reached. The Queen nominated Sir John Perrot to the office with explicit instructions to seize 'the castle of the Earl of Desmond in Kerry [i.e. Castlemaine] ... for the use of the Lord President and Council and also to seize the Liberty of Kerry which Desmond claimed as a palatine'.[13] By the establishment of a presidency and the negation of the Earl of Desmond's hereditary palatine rights in Kerry, Elizabeth sought to undermine the power he exerted by right of Gaelic law over his tributary lords and to institute English law and administration in its stead. The choice of Perrot as President and the 'vigorous career of law enforcement and the discouragement of Gaelic institutions'[14] that he was about to pursue put him on a collision course with the House of Desmond. Sir John Perrot, the supposed illegitimate son of Henry VIII, a bluff, energetic, if somewhat imprudent, Elizabethan knight, had been educated with the Earl of Ormond at court, and initially showed little enthusiasm for his new appointment in Ireland.

News of the new regime in Munster, and of the Crown's intention to render him powerless, filtered through to the Earl of Desmond, adding to the torment that afflicted his mind. In his captivity in England it was to be expected that the distracted earl would champ at the bit that restrained him from his patrimony and power. By now St Leger had been forced to move himself and his destitute charges from Leeds castle to his town house at Southwark, across the river from the Tower, a grim reminder to the Desmonds of their vulnerable circumstances. The house was unfashionably located 'east of London Bridge beside a depot for municipal building materials. The house had once been a friary in the country, but grown up about it was Bankside, a rowdy neighbourhood of breweries, brothels, the Clink Prison and the Paris Garden bear pits.'[15] It was a dark, damp building, far too cramped for the two large households compelled to reside there in varying degrees of poverty and despair. The fog, damp and stench of the Thames seeped through every chink and hole in its timber-faced façade, while the cries, shouts and curses of the squalid tenement area that surrounded it permeated to further disturb and harass the inhabitants.

Eleanor bravely soldiered on. She was now pregnant, and the misery and unhealthiness of her surroundings added greatly to her discomfiture. Garrett's health, reprieved by the brief sojourn in the Kentish countryside, succumbed again to the unwholesome environment and inadequate nourishment. The bills for the attendance of physicians and for pills and potions mounted. In desperation St Leger again beseeched the Privy Council for some relief and even offered to go to prison to free himself from the financial responsibility of his imposed guests. Too ragged to be seen by her peers in public, and in dread of the low dockland society that surrounded her, Eleanor was forced to remain cooped up within St Leger's house and was very ill throughout the duration of her confinement. Eventually, through the good offices of Sir William Cecil, a sum of £130 was sent for their relief, which, according to St Leger, 'hath ben ymployed uppon necessary apparel and phisick, they having been all very sick, the lady his wife yet so, and his lordship and Sr John but lately recovered. Their health cannot be long,' he warned, 'being pent upp in so little a rome altogether.'[16] St Leger once again pleaded that he might 'be delivered of them, whereby I may bend myself towarde Ireland to seek to recover some pte of my losses'.[17] The rich pasturelands of his prisoner beckoned the jailer.

In the stifling, deprived environment of their Bankside abode Eleanor was delivered of a son in June 1571, whom they called James. The birth of a son, heir to the great Desmond dynasty, should have been an occasion of great jubilation and festivity but for the circumstances of the infant's birth and the dark shadow that hung over the fate of his father, his mother and his inheritance. In their drab surroundings Eleanor and Garrett briefly celebrated the joyful event. News of the birth was less joyfully communicated to the royal court, where the continuation of the 'cankered' rebellious Desmond line was hardly considered an event for celebration. Nor was the birth of a son and heir to the Desmond title and estate welcomed by all the Desmond party at Southwark. Over the months a rift had grown between Eleanor and Sir John. The Desmond historian Russell later concluded that after Eleanor 'had become the mother of that young son the Ld. James, Sr. John of Desmond was out of all hopes to enjoy or inherite the Earledome after his brother's death; whereas before the birth of that child he conceived otherwise'. [18] But the strain of their long captivity, destitute condition, frequent illness and close confinement had, even before this, driven a wedge between Garrett and his brother. Their frequent arguments merely intensified when Eleanor bore the earl a son. Sir John had anticipated that Garrett's frail health would succumb to the harsh conditions of his long imprisonment, and that he would then succeed to the earldom. He had not foreseen that Eleanor would choose to leave Ireland to be with Garrett, or that his brother would withstand the rigours of prison and father a son.

Eleanor, for her part, viewed Sir John with deep suspicion, and the rift that emerged between them in London was never to heal. She suspected him of evil intentions towards her new-born son, whom she guarded like a lioness. The safeguarding of the infant's life and his inheritance was to become her sole aim. Oblivious to the intrigue and danger that surrounded him, the young Desmond heir, sickly from birth, fought for life, which was to prove as unfortunate as the circumstances of his birth.

Shortly after the birth of his son it came to the earl's attention that his brother had offered, in return for his own freedom, to accept a commission from the Crown to suppress James FitzMaurice. And it appeared that he had also convinced Sir John Perrot, who in August 1571 advised the Privy Council that Sir John should be returned to rule in Munster instead of his brother. The earl protested to the Privy Council that if permission was thus granted to Sir John, it would only serve to undermine his own position in Munster and, as he phrased it, 'geve me occasion to thinke that your honnours do either suspect my trewe and loyall service towards my soveraigne Lady the Queene or els do judge me unhable to geve them the overthrowe'.[19] The rebels, the earl maintained, 'who besedes that they are traytours to her Matie so have they bene utter enemyes and spoylers of all my patrymony',[20] which to a degree was true. In the event, however, Sir John's proposal, even with the endorsement of Perrot, did not find favour with the new Lord Deputy, Sir William Fitzwilliam, who bluntly advised Lord Burghley: 'God keep both Sir John of Desmond and base money out of Ireland.'[21]

The birth of his son in captivity and destitution, his wife's protracted illness, uncertainty about the state of his inheritance in Ireland, and, above all, the Queen's negative response to his continued pleas for repatriation—all drove Garrett to acts of recklessness in his desperate desire for freedom. Throwing caution to the winds, he openly abused the semi-free status that had been allowed him. St Leger complained that he was no longer able to control the earl, who, he claimed, 'refused to go down to Kent with him and in his absence had rashly ranged into sundry parts of London'[22] outside the confines of his allotted parole. St Leger 'prayed to be delivered of him or to have command to keep him prisoner without liberty'.[23] Garrett had been granted the liberty of Southwark, Bankside and the marshes west of Lambeth Palace. Tormented by his obsession to return to Munster, he roamed the narrow streets and alleys and hung around the seedy riverside taverns, desperately seeking some scheme for his deliverance. He listened to the chimerical plans and projects offered by the waterfront confidence tricksters and rogues who filled his head with wild plans of escape but who, with the earl's deposit of gold in their grasping hands, simply slunk away and disappeared among the milling dockside crowds.

Whispers of the frantic attempts by the Earl of Desmond to effect his escape back to Ireland reached the court and reverberated abroad where it became entangled in the more complex web of international intrigue. The St Bartholomew's Day massacre of 4,000 Huguenots in Paris, masterminded by the Catholic Queen, Catherine de Medici, and her son Charles IX, coupled with the excommunication of Elizabeth by the Pope, had finally polarised the European power struggle of England, Spain and France into a religious conflict. In Ireland the initial attempt by FitzMaurice to 'use religion as a catalyst to make a common cause of local grievances'[24] appeared a more serious threat in light of international developments and attracted the attention of Elizabeth's enemies on the continent. Papal emissaries were despatched to Ireland. Sir John Perrot intercepted Edmund O'Donnell with letters to the Geraldine leader from Pope Gregory XIII. Agents from Rome had also infiltrated England to exhort the remnants of the Catholic aristocracy there.

In his daily prowls along the Thames dockside Garrett was watched lest he too should be contacted by papal or Spanish conspirators. Both Eleanor and Garrett had secretly written to encourage FitzMaurice in his revolt as a means to obtain their freedom and reinstatement in Desmond. Some of their letters had been intercepted by Perrot, who cautioned against allowing the Earl of Desmond return to Munster and recommended to Elizabeth that he should be restrained indefinitely in London. Garrett and Eleanor also wrote to the Earl of Leicester to inform him of their plight and of the condition of the Desmond estate in Munster. To further exploit the prevailing court factions, their trusted confidant, Morris Sheehan, was sent to Leicester armed with details of their version of the Desmond–Ormond dispute over the lordship of the Decies and the ownership of Kilfeakle and Kilsheelin, which, as Garrett informed Leicester, 'are wrongfully witholden from him by the saide Erie of Ormonde'.[25] Not to be outdone in the subterfuge the Earl of Ormond arrived in London and invited Garrett to dine with him. Black Tom made sympathetic noises about his rival's miserable plight. Lulled into a false sense of security Garrett readily accepted his rival's offer of help. But the Earl of Ormond and his cronies, as part of their vendetta against their opposite camp at court, and also in the hope of augmenting their fortunes out of Garrett's estates in Munster, had set a trap for the unsuspecting captive, who unwittingly found himself implicated in a more sinister political plot of international dimensions. Shortly after his meeting with Ormond, captain Martin Frobisher introduced himself to Garrett in a Bankside tavern. Frobisher offered to effect the earl's escape to Ireland for a suitable fee, together with the island of Valentia in lieu. Garrett eagerly agreed to the proposal and, elated at the prospect of freedom, and encouraged by Frobisher, talked wildly of treason, foreign schemes, intrigues and rebellion, all of which Frobisher reported back to Court.

But before Garrett could be apprehended, events in the international political arena intervened to have him unexpectedly restored to his lordship. Elizabeth's change of heart sprang from her fear—and Eleanor's hope—that the dangerous and unstable situation that was developing in Munster would get out of hand. Exhorted by promises from the papal and Spanish courts, James FitzMaurice FitzGerald had emerged from his retreat and raised the banner of crusade aloft once more in Munster. The English President, Sir John Perrot, despite his initial resolve to wipe out the rebels and to eradicate all semblance of Gaelic law and custom in the province, was by 1572 forced to admit that he was merely whistling into the wind. Despite the severity of his rule, the rebellion still raged and Munster was more ruinous and desolate than when he had taken office. Well might Perrot wonder, as he wearily led his surviving hungry, underpaid soldiers through the wastelands of Munster in search of FitzMaurice, what it took to conquer such a wild land and such headstrong lords. There were no words of encouragement from the Queen, only impatience at his lack of success against FitzMaurice and incredulity that the bogs and marshes of Munster could so relentlessly soak up her precious revenue. Gradually Perrot was forced to adopt some of the Gaelic customs which he sought to destroy. He learned the advantage of ambushes by small numbers of lightly-armed soldiers, and how Gaelic rather than English military dress was better suited to the climate and terrain of Ireland.

Perrot's war with FitzMaurice had developed into a personal vendetta. This was turned to his advantage by FitzMaurice when, with characteristic rashness, Perrot allowed himself to be drawn into a well-planned trap, from which he barely escaped with his life. His pride had been dented and his energy sapped by the unceasing, unrewarding campaign against an elusive enemy. He resolved to resort to the ancient Celtic method of single combat in an attempt to bring the inconclusive war with FitzMaurice to an end. FitzMaurice accepted his challenge, but insisted on the use of Gaelic weapons, the sword and dart, and stipulated that both combatants should wear Gaelic attire. At the appointed time and place the English President duly arrived, sporting his short, pleated tunic, tight worsted Gaelic trews and leather quilted jerkin. Thus arrayed for battle, the former champion of the Queen's tiltyard waited for his Gaelic adversary. The hours passed, but FitzMaurice failed to appear. Finally FitzMaurice's bard approached and spoke his master's message to the waiting Perrot:

> *If I should kill Sir John Perrot, the Queen of England can send another President unto this province; but if he do kill me, there is none other to succeed me or to command as I do, therefore I will not willingly fight with him, and so tell him from me.*[26]

All Munster soon knew about Perrot's humiliation, and when the news reached the Queen only the restraining hand of Burghley prevented Perrot's recall. Perrot redoubled his efforts against FitzMaurice and vowed 'to hunt the fox out of his hole'.[27] Driving him back into the Kerry mountains, he took the strategic Desmond fortress of Castlemaine, but the elusive FitzMaurice still evaded him. Then, in February 1573, FitzMaurice unexpectedly submitted to the President who pardoned him, maintaining that like 'a second St Paul'[28] FitzMaurice had seen the error of his ways. But FitzMaurice was merely playing for time, waiting for developments to unfold on the continent that would enable him to resume his crusade in Ireland with even greater vigour.

From Eleanor and Garrett's point of view, FitzMaurice's rebellion had accomplished the objective for which they had hoped and plotted. The rebellion made it impossible for the colonisation process started by Carew to make headway in Garrett's lordship during his absence. It had demonstrated to the Crown that the earl's removal had not produced the results anticipated, namely the extension of English law and custom throughout Desmond. His removal merely exchanged one Gaelic leader for a far more dangerous and able one. Elizabeth had seen no improvement in her finances resulting from the long imprisonment of the Earl of Desmond. On the contrary, she had to dig even deeper into her pocket to support her prisoner and his retinue in England, while at the same time endeavouring to suppress an expensive rebellion within his territory in Ireland.

In the hope that the wayward earl had learned his lesson and that he might conform, if only to ensure his son's succession to his estates and title, Elizabeth signified her intention to rid herself of her tiresome prisoner. After much discussion, terms for his release were agreed. Garrett undertook to be

> *answerable to the laws, ordinances and statutes of the realm, as the Earles of Kildare and Ormond are, and shall assist the Queen's ministers in Munster to serve and execute and process writs and the levying of her rents, customs, subsidies, services and duties.*[29]

He also promised to apprehend all known malefactors within his territory, to renounce all foreign jurisdictions, and to put down the remaining vestiges of FitzMaurice's rebellion. He agreed to the suspension of his palatine liberties in Kerry, pending an investigation as to their legality, and to the forfeiture of such castles in his lordship, recently seized by Perrot, for as long as the Crown deemed it necessary for the public good. In theory, Garrett effectively signed away the hereditary powers and privileges of his earldom enjoyed by the House of Desmond for centuries; in practice, however, the Crown had yet to prove its ability to hold that which had been forfeited. But in the spring of 1573, after an exile and imprisonment lasting six years, freedom meant everything to the Earl of Desmond: freedom from humiliation, squalor, fear and poverty. For Eleanor, cooped up with her child in St Leger's house, still weak from the ordeal of the birth, from undernourishment and the unhealthy atmosphere of her surroundings, the prospect of freedom and return to Munster was as heady as potent wine.

Shortly before their departure for Ireland the prisoners were ordered to appear before the Queen. Still unable to conceal her personal dislike of Garrett, Elizabeth instead concentrated her attention on Sir John, to whom 'she gave a privy nip, that as he hath a good wit, so he should hereafter use it wele'.[30] The Queen seemed better disposed to Eleanor than at their previous meeting and, knowing Eleanor's ability to control her husband's rash nature, urged her to direct him on a more loyal and law-abiding course. The Queen perceived the ragged condition of the Desmonds and, in a rare display of generosity, ordered presents 'of some silks for apparel and some money in reward.'[31] Garrett boldly asked that the Earl of Ormond should also be returned to his lordship—as a means, he maintained, to deter rebels driven out of Desmond from seeking refuge in

Ormond. For Garrett could not let the opportunity pass to remind Elizabeth that there were others in Ireland who had, despite their proclaimed loyalty, harboured rebellious subjects, not to mention relations, within their lordships but whom she had not thought fit to punish as he had been. Moreover, he would prefer to have his enemy in sight in Munster than at court in London, where Black Tom could more effectively intrigue against him. The cold eyes of the Tudor Queen flashed dangerously at his suggestion.

Before they set out on their journey Eleanor had to endure one final heartbreak. It was decided that her infant son, scarcely two years old, should be left in care in England. There is no evidence to suggest that the child was demanded by the Crown as a hostage for his father's future loyalty. On the contrary, the evidence points to the fact that he was presented to the Queen by his parents on their own initiative. He was taken into the care of their mentor, the Earl of Leicester, who stated in a later letter to Garrett and Eleanor that

> *Yor Ls request for the presentinge of yor sonne to Her Matie I have also accomplished. Her Highness accepteth of him and taketh yor offer of him in very good pte as I have signefied by lres to my Lady yor wife and by cause he is yet too younge to be brought hither, Her Matie hath taken ordre for his plasinge until he shal be fit to be removed.*[32]

The child had been sickly from birth, and Eleanor may well have considered that the long and arduous journey to Ireland might further compromise the infant's welfare. It was, however, more likely that the decision to leave their child in England sprang from fears for his safety from Garrett's own relatives and competitors in Munster. The rift between Eleanor and Sir John of Desmond had continued to widen. The unsettled state of her husband's lordship and the uncertainty of their future there were hardly conducive to the safety and health of the heir to the earldom of Desmond. Under the patronage and care of the powerful and friendly Earl of Leicester, her son's life and future might be better assured.

Despite despatches from the President of Munster, who unceasingly had advised the Queen against Garrett's restoration, the Desmonds were permitted to depart for Ireland. They were conducted there under the charge of the newly-appointed vice-treasurer, Sir Edward Fitton. Rumours of Perrot's opposition to their return reached them in

London; and, suspecting that Fitton and Perrot were in league, Garrett, Eleanor and Sir John made a dash across England and Wales for Beaumaris in search of a quick passage to Ireland. But Fitton caught up with his fugitive captives, and eventually the entire party set sail for Dublin. They landed at White Friars in Dublin on 25 March 1573 after an exile of almost six years.

Chapter 5
A Troubled Homecoming

There went he and the Countess towards
Loughgure, where a nombre of the freeholders of
the Countie of Lymerick met hym. He and his
wiefe put on Irishe rayment and made
proclamation that no deputie nor constable nor
sheriff should practise their office in his countrey.

JUSTICE NICHOLAS WALSHE TO LORD DEPUTY FITZWILLIAM,
24 NOVEMBER 1573

The joy of liberty was short-lived, and the nightmare of captivity looked set to continue. No sooner had Garrett, Eleanor and Sir John disembarked at the walls of Dublin than they were promptly taken to Dublin Castle where they were held in 'easy restraint'[1] at the behest of Sir John Perrot. Perrot had long resisted the Earl of Desmond's restoration and, as he doused the embers of rebellion in Munster, saw even less reason for the earl's return. Eleanor, while not personally held in custody, chose to remain with Garrett in Dublin. They were permitted daily access to the city and once again incurred much expense as they strove to maintain themselves in some state conducive to their rank and position. But Eleanor's main preoccupation was to pacify and control her husband. Garrett was incensed at his further detention. He accused the crown officials in Dublin and in London of a breach of faith. What right had they to restrain him, the Earl of Desmond, set at liberty by the Queen? His lack of political cunning was once more exposed as he made wild threats and treasonable outbursts against the Crown.

Eleanor realised that her husband was close to breaking-point. Despite her pleas for caution, he could not control his sense of anger and outrage before the sneering faces of the petty Castle officials, who reported his every word and goaded him into even more damning utterances. He could not be restrained even in the presence of Perrot, who contemptuously reported 'that Desmond was devoid of reason and that nothing could be done with him'.[2] Perrot urged the Queen to have him speedily returned to England, as he considered him 'more fit to keep Bedlam than to rule a newly reformed country'.[3]

Garrett's brother, Sir John, played his cards more cautiously and, promising to uphold English law in his territory, was allowed to depart for Munster. Eleanor became suspicious at the ease with which her brother-in-law obtained his release from Perrot, who had previously indicated to the Queen his readiness to accept Sir John in preference to Garrett as leader of the Geraldines in Munster. To thwart Sir John's ambitions, Eleanor decided to accompany him back to Munster. Lack of money and the collection of the overdue rents of his estates were used as the excuse to explain Eleanor's sudden departure. 'Such rentes and duties as were owing in my country', Garrett complained to the Irish Privy Council, 'were taken up by suche as tooke little cause to heere in what beggered estate I lyde there in Dublin.'[4]

Eleanor found Munster in relative peace, slowly recovering from the ravages wrought by the rebellion and Perrot's subsequent reprisal. As Askeaton loomed into view, despite her undoubted fatigue, she felt a warming sense of homecoming after her long and bitter exile. Her daughters awaited to be reunited with her. As news of her arrival spread, Garrett's tributary lords and dependent clansmen came to seek news of their overlord and to give an account of themselves during his absence. She listened to their complaints about the encroachment of Perrot's administration into their domain. The return of their overlord they hoped might restore their traditional rights.

In July the news of Perrot's sudden departure from Ireland, due, it was said, to ill-health, spurred the Munster lords into action to bring about Garrett's release. Glin castle was seized and the surrounding countryside plundered. James FitzMaurice intensified negotiations with Spain and Rome to revitalise interest in his religious crusade. At the same time he divorced his wife on the grounds that she had conducted an amorous correspondence with his erstwhile ally, Edward Butler. He promptly remarried O'Connor Kerry's widow and thereby gained access to the strategic O'Connor castle of Carraigafoyle on the Shannon. Munster was in a restless state once more.

In Dublin the Council began an investigation into the legality of Garrett's privilege of palatine rights in Kerry and adjudged it to be void. There was henceforth to be but one legal palatinate in Ireland— that of the Earl of Ormond in Tipperary. The Crown's preference for one earl over the other was once more blatantly exposed. While Garrett fumed in captivity in Dublin Eleanor kept him in touch with developments in Munster and redoubled her efforts to secure his release. But Garrett also received intelligence from England to the effect that the dreaded nightmare, his return to captivity to the Tower, was being actively propounded by Perrot at Court. As the Crown had failed to honour the terms of his release, Garrett considered himself free from whatever promises he had made to the Queen. He waited while Eleanor co-ordinated plans to effect his escape from Dublin.

On a chilly morning in early November 1573 the Earl of Desmond informed the Mayor of Dublin, in whose custody he had been placed, of his intention to join a stag hunting party to the city environs. This was customary, according to the terms of Garrett's detention, which stipulated that he must return to the mayor's custody each evening. But at Grangegorman Garrett gave the hunting party the slip and, accompanied by the faithful Morris Sheehan, rode south through the territory of his kinsman the Earl of Kildare without hindrance. There they were met by Rory Oge O'More and Piers Grace, two prominent rebel leaders, who, with a guard of 'some hundred kerne and shot of the Moores',[5] escorted the earl safely through the midlands to Béal an Droichid where Eleanor waited. Together they hurried on towards Limerick.

News of the Earl of Desmond's dramatic escape spread rapidly. As if awaiting the return of a messiah, his followers flocked to see him at the Geraldine lake fortress of Lough Gur. The crowds had already assembled as the earl and countess rode down towards the lake shore. With a great cheer of welcome, which reverberated over the still waters, they surged forward to greet their overlord. For many of the wildly cheering clansmen the reappearance of their almost forgotten lord was like a resurrection from the dead. As he climbed stiffly down from his horse, the misery of his long years of imprisonment was etched on his haggard features and on his threadbare hose and worn shoes. It was an emotive and highly-charged meeting between the earl and his loyal Desmond retainers and clansmen. Later, as was subsequently reported to the Lord Deputy, the earl 'and his wiefe put on Irishe rayment and made proclamation that no deputie nor constable nor sheriff should practise their office in his countrey'.[6]

Symbolically donning the clothes and speaking the words expected of a Gaelic warrior chieftain, the proud Geraldine thus appeared triumphant before his people. All the pent-up anger, frustration and humiliation which he had endured at the hands of the Crown spilled forth. This was his hour of glory, the destiny of which he had dreamed and from which he had drawn solace and comfort in the long, dark nights in his Tower cell and in his destitute lodgings in Southwark. The traditional retainers, dependants, galloglass and kern of his house pressed excitedly around him, their roars of welcome acting as a stimulus to his long-suppressed ego. Vain and dangerous threats against the Crown and rash promises of a return to Gaelic ways gushed forth incautiously as he basked in the adulation of his supporters, 'knowing no God, no prince but the earl, no law but his behests'.[7] With exultant cheers, the Earl of Desmond and his countess were escorted home to Askeaton.

Eleanor listened, with some misgivings, to the indiscreet outbursts of her husband and perhaps wished that he had spoken with more restraint. It was an emotional reunion for him and it was natural that he should vent his spleen on the Crown which had broken faith with him so often. His health had suffered considerably from his enforced detention, and the doubts of his Gaelic followers as to his fitness to receive and command their allegiance had to be assuaged. There were many competitors waiting in the wings should he appear incapable. On the other hand, as Eleanor realised, partly as a result of the events that had occurred in Munster during his exile, and partly because of the recent developments on the international front and their possible effects on Ireland, a return to the old ways would be strongly resisted by the Crown, which had established a foothold in Garrett's lordship which it intended to retain.

To survive, Eleanor knew, they must adapt to the changing political parameters. She had personally experienced English power, its commitment, philosophy to progress and change, its unity of purpose, its lust for exploration and exploitation. The Earl of Desmond, as leader and protector of the cause of Gaelic Ireland, was doomed; but if he adapted to the changing circumstances relentlessly being promoted by the Tudor political machine in Ireland, he would not only survive but, perhaps, retain his power like his neighbour

Ormond. Perhaps it was Eleanor who influenced Garrett to write to the irate Queen regarding his flight from custody in Dublin. It may have been Eleanor's idea too that she should take the blame for her husband's unlawful escape, to mask the real reason. For Garrett excused his unauthorised departure to Munster as having resulted from his concern for Eleanor, 'in whose care in myne absence, having no thing els to lyve upon . . . did pricke so deeply that I camme away without your lycence with intent faithfully to serve her matie as becommeth a true subject'.[8] With tongue in cheek, Garrett assured the Queen, 'if I thought my staye there [in Dublin] had ben ane way a further cause to your highness service, I would [be] well contented to end my lyfe there in captyvitie'.[9] For the moment there was little Elizabeth could do but grit her teeth at the insolence and audacity of the Irish earl.

Garrett's fiery speeches to his supporters brought immediate and predictable results. Castlemaine and Castlemartyr, which had taken Sir John Perrot so long to capture, were seized. Garrett ordered the English strongholds in Glin and Castletown to be razed to the ground, and he granted Glin, Carraigafoyle and Tarbert to his cousin James FitzMaurice. Rumours of foreign-based conspiracies circulated, and a servant in the Earl of Desmond's livery was reported to have been sighted at the Spanish court. The earl revelled in his freedom and power. His dramatic escape from Dublin had enhanced his prestige among the Gaelic and gaelicised grandees. O'Neill and Clanrickard sought an alliance. To those on friendly terms Garrett loudly declared that 'he would rather have an old mantle in Munster than a torn silk gown in England'.[10] With less likely allies, such as the redoubtable Butler brothers, he was more circumspect: he stoutly professed his loyalty to Elizabeth but his independence of her administration in Dublin—for fear, he claimed, of being subjected again to the extremities he had suffered in the past. To emphasise his argument, 'he exhibited the patched and pieced hose and shoes which he had been forced to wear continually in England'.[11] The Butlers were unimpressed and refused to be drawn into another Geraldine-led conspiracy. Defence of their lands was one thing, but intrigue with alien powers against the Crown was another matter entirely. Like bees to a honey-pot, however, the idle swordsmen of Munster swarmed to Garrett's gates. Soon his army numbered over a thousand, all of whom had to be fed and maintained at his people's expense.

The Lord Deputy, Sir William Fitzwilliam, could do little to curb the earl's increasing power in Munster. Lack of money and poor coordination of resources and manpower in his administration resulted in turmoil in every province. In Connaught the restless sons of the Earl of Clanrickard, Elizabeth's 'impudent imps', plundered unchecked throughout Galway. Turlough Luineach, chief of the O'Neills in Ulster, was known to be plotting with the Scots and the Spanish. In Leinster the O'Mores raided at will through King's County and Queen's County, and even the Pale was subjected to attack. In Ormond the palatinate of Black Tom was said to be as disturbed and wasted as Desmond. The Lord Deputy and his vice-treasurer, Sir Edward Fitton, were at each other's throats and could not agree on tactics to quell the maelstrom. Finally, at the end of his tether, Fitzwilliam begged the Queen to relieve him of his post in Ireland. With her administration and military commitments in Ireland stretched beyond their limits, Elizabeth was compelled to pursue a policy of reconciliation towards the Earl of Desmond. She despatched warrants to Dublin which formally, if belatedly, granted the self-liberated earl his freedom. She urged him to make peace with her Lord Deputy and to disperse his private army, which she realised well outnumbered her own in Munster. But the earl reckoned that he negotiated from a position of strength and, flushed by his reception and success in Munster, boldly replied that if the Queen would remove her garrison from nearby Kilmallock, he would find little need to maintain so large an army.

In an attempt to breach the dangerous gulf developing between the Earl of Desmond and her administration in Ireland, Elizabeth consented that Edward FitzGerald, the brother of the Earl of Kildare, should negotiate with his imperious kinsman. But Garrett proved reluctant to negotiate with anybody. Fearful that the ever-widening gap between the Queen and her husband should become an unbridgeable chasm, Eleanor urged him to at least hear what FitzGerald had to offer. While he awaited Garrett's decision FitzGerald stayed at Eleanor's old home, Kiltinan castle. As floods on the Shannon prevented Garrett from a planned rendezvous with the Earl of Clanrickard, reluctantly he acceded to Eleanor's advice to meet the Queen's emissary instead.

Eleanor was pregnant again and unable to accompany her husband to the meeting. The earl set out with Sir John of Desmond,

James FitzMaurice and Andrew Skiddy, the judge of the palatinate of Kerry, to meet FitzGerald at Clonmel. FitzGerald assured the earl that the Queen did not seek to dispossess him but merely wished to be assured of his loyalty and his compliance with the promises he had made in England. Garrett flatly refused to go to Dublin, but indicated his willingness to meet with the Lord Deputy on the borders of his own territory instead. He refused to hand over Castlemaine and Castlemartyr to captain Bouchier, the English constable at Kilmallock, but offered them to FitzGerald, who, he knew, had no commission to accept them and no means of holding them. Beyond this, as FitzGerald reported to the Queen, Desmond would not be moved. Elizabeth had little option but to pardon the earl, which she did reluctantly in the hope that 'he would restore such castles as either we were possessed of before the time of his escape or any other that we should like to be delivered into our hands'.[12] Once back in the safety of Askeaton, however, Garrett flatly refused to forfeit any of his fortresses. Elizabeth thundered against her luckless Lord Deputy as Garrett claimed a moral victory over the Crown, a thing abhorrent to Elizabeth's Tudor sense of sovereignty. 'We think ourselves touched in honour', she raged, 'that the earl may have cause to think that we should now seek upon him a thing very unfitting for the place and quality we hold.'[13]

Garrett's moral victory over the Crown further enhanced his standing among his peers. With rumours of alliances and intrigues, domestic and foreign, Eleanor realised that her husband was now becoming the lynch pin for a wider conspiracy of opposition to English rule in Ireland. She knew her husband's unsuitability to adopt the mantle of leadership of a Gaelic alliance against England. Garrett was not endowed with the strength, charisma or commitment necessary to mould the highly individualistic tendencies of the Gaelic and gaelicised lords into an effective, organised and patriotic alliance, where personal ambition must become secondary to a common cause. But Gaelic society was, as ever, divided and unable to either spawn or succour such a national alliance. Every lord sought independence of his neighbour as much as of the Crown. It would require the services of a ruthless, powerful leader, driven by a vision of nationhood, to lead and unite such an assortment of independently-minded egotists. Garrett FitzGerald, 14th Earl Desmond, was no such visionary.

Eleanor's objective was to make her husband secure in his title and estates. But to attain that seemingly realistic and understandable ambition, she realised Garret must first come to terms with the changing political scene. Elizabeth was adamant that Ireland's autocratic lords, whose independent tendencies she viewed just as much an affront to her sovereignty as a threat to England's security, must be brought into line. They must either accept the new political parameters, affirm their loyalty to the Crown, and thus retain the power and privilege allowed them by law, or rebel and risk losing everything. Garrett's temperament and character would, in any event, make a painful transition inevitable. But there were other forces, more sinister in their motivation and more clandestine in their operation, from within the Desmond family itself, that sought to make that transition even more difficult. To Eleanor these powerful interests were as devious and dangerous as the most ruthless agents of the Crown. Both groups cast envious eyes on her husband's estates and plotted his alienation from the Crown. For Garrett to make the transition from a sovereign lord in his own right to a loyal earl of the realm she knew would take time.

Eleanor sought to gain that time. She wrote to the Lord Deputy to reassure him of her husband's loyalty. Initially her letter would seem to have had the desired effect, and Fitzwilliam and his army remained in Dublin. As Garrett ruminated over his position in Munster his liegemen ran riot throughout the province. James FitzMaurice captured captain Bouchier and kept him prisoner, while Garrett's galloglass, the MacSheehys, seized the Mayor of Limerick. Hundreds of kern and clansmen flocked to Askeaton and looked to their indecisive overlord to provide them with work for their weapons and food for their bellies. Reports reached Dublin and London that Desmond had now at his disposal an army of 3,000 men-at-arms, that he had captured Kilmallock and Cork, and that he intended to deliver Valentia Island to the King of Spain, with whom he was said to be in constant communication. It was also said that he intended 'to purge the country of the name of England'[14] and that he would listen to no counsel but that of the rebel leader James FitzMaurice.

Under pressure from all sides, Garrett brooded over his position. In the great oak-beamed hall of Askeaton the earl listened as the Desmond bard O'Daly solemnly intoned the valorous deeds of his ancestors. The bard recited a litany of treachery and deceit perpetrated against the House of Desmond by successive English monarchs. Words of exhortation flowed from his lips as he listed the heroic tales of Nesta's sons and the first Irish Geraldines. Low, deep-throated growls erupted from the bearded chieftains, seated at the trestle tables, as O'Daly bewailed the cruel fate meted out to the earl's kinsmen, the Geraldine Kildares, at Tyburn. The assembly was brought to its feet as the bardic recitation reached its climax denouncing the late treacherous imprisonment of the earl and the subsequent attempts of the English to usurp his power and patrimony. 'Shanid abú!' cried the bard.

In the emotionally charged atmosphere the wooden drinking-cups, overflowing with the heady wine of Spain, were raised, as lord, chieftain, constable and captain saluted their pale, brooding overlord seated impassively at the top of the hall. 'Shanid abú!'—their answering roar of allegiance seemed to lift the great beams from their stone corbels and fly south over the dark mass of Kylemore to strike terror into the heart of any faint-hearted or doubting inhabitant of Munster. Beside her husband, Eleanor looked on in fear at the upraised faces and frantic eyes of his supporters, who in their wild homage to her husband also demanded their age-old right to his leadership in the defence of their antique Gaelic world.

As reports of the lawlessness in Munster continued to reach her, Elizabeth angrily berated Fitzwilliam for his apparent unwillingness to move against the Earl of Desmond. Fitzwilliam attributed his inaction to Eleanor's stalling intercession on her husband's behalf. 'The Countess with her contynuall impertinancie', Fitzwilliam complained, 'and constant assercions of his conformitie made me to hope he wolde in tyme prove so conformiable as she reported him.'[15] Eleanor's action had been successful in staying Fitzwilliam's hand but, in any event, Fitzwilliam was about to be pushed aside in favour of Elizabeth's new favourite, the dashing, extrovert, Walter Devereux, Earl of Essex.

Essex came to Ireland in August 1573 in the vain hope of conquering Ulster for his royal mistress. But the Ulster chieftains, as Essex found to his cost, did not part easily with their territories. Their resistance, together with the insubordinate conduct of his demoralised soldiery, whose fear and hatred of Irish warfare and irregular pay made them desert in hundreds, had tarnished the gilded image of Gloriana's shining knight. Essex now sought to make amends. The seemingly impossible task of reconciling the Earl of Desmond to the Crown seemed an appropriate challenge. Essex wrote to Garrett, seeking a meeting and urging him to free himself from 'ill counsellors who hiss you on to that which is evil'. [16] Echoing Eleanor's fears, Essex advised Garrett:

> My lord, consider well of this and look into the case deeply and give care unto the sound and faithful counsel of your friends and stop the ears from hearkening unto them which seek by their wicked counsel to destroy yourself and to overthrow your house. [17]

Essex wrote in similar vein to Eleanor and urged her to use her influence to persuade her husband to meet him. Eleanor's counsel prevailed, and Garrett finally agreed to hold discussions with Essex at Waterford. He was accompanied by Eleanor, James FitzMaurice and sixty horsemen. On 1 July 1574 they halted at a bridge some three miles outside the city, where they were met by the Earl of Kildare. The Desmond party refused to enter Waterford without a safe protection, which they promptly received—for twenty days' duration. Garrett, with Eleanor by his side, accompanied by the Earl of Kildare, rode into Waterford and were received by Essex at his rooms in the city. After a series of meetings, on the advice and under the personal protection of both earls, Garrett and Eleanor agreed to go to Dublin, where Garrett's case was again to be examined before the Council.

Despite Essex's friendship and protection, the journey to Dublin must have been a difficult and fearful one for the Desmonds. Eleanor might well have wondered whether the faith she had in Essex would be vindicated. Her husband's dread of further imprisonment had become an obsession. The nightmare of Dublin Castle, the Tower and Southwark was still a vivid, raw reality. Could a sense of honour and good faith exist in their present circumstances? Would Essex keep his word? Eleanor had placed her trust and her husband's life and liberty in his hands. But unknown to her, or to Essex, the Council in Dublin had received a stinging missive from the Queen, who demanded immediate action against the Earl of Desmond. In her anger she ordered Fitzwilliam 'to proclaim him traitor and to proceed against him with all celerity'. [18] And now the object of the Queen's anger rode unsuspectingly into their presence.

The Desmonds were met with an icy reception in Dublin. Stung into action by the Queen, the members of the Council made little attempt to hide their antipathy towards Garrett and their distrust of Essex. The latter was not permitted to accompany Garrett into the council chamber or to plead in favour of his case. Outside Eleanor waited anxiously for the outcome and hoped that her headstrong husband would restrain his temper and not play into the hands of his antagonists. But the councillors were not in a placatory mood and summarily demanded that the earl abide by the articles he had concluded with the Queen in England. Garrett contended that they had been signed under duress, but that he would agree to be bound by them as part of a more general settlement; otherwise the terms of the articles would, in effect, render him the only undefended lord in the country and thus easy prey to his many enemies. Goaded by the overbearing attitude of his inquisitors, he refused to hold his estates at the Crown's pleasure or to forfeit those of his castles which it had seized before his restoration. He would accept the Queen's pardon, but would not on any account 'repair into England to be a spectacle of poverty to all the world'[19] in order to receive it. Asked to submit pledges for his future conduct, Garrett pointed out that both his son and his youngest brother, James, still a minor, were in the keeping of the Crown. 'If neither my son, being my only son, nor my brother, whom I love, nor the possession of mine inheritance, as before granted can suffice,' he bitterly told his tormentors, 'then to the justice of God and the Queen I appeal upon you all.'[20] But his appeal fell on deaf ears.

In the Council's opinion, the Earl of Desmond was not in any position to make demands, but should be prepared to accept whatever decision regarding his future they deemed appropriate. Temporarily in the Council's power but also under Essex's protection, Garrett reacted quickly when rumours of his impending imprisonment and removal to London reached his ears. Flight from Dublin was now imperative, and he called on Essex and Kildare to honour their pledges of protection. Essex was disgusted at the nature of the Council's proceedings against the Earl of Desmond. 'The manner of Desmond's answer might with honour have suffered a toleration,' he protested. 'The mischief is without remedy, for I am bound with the Earl of Kildare, by our words and honours, to safe-conduct Desmond to the confines of Munster.'[21] Essex was as good as his word, and, despite some resistance, he and the Earl of Kildare conducted Garrett and Eleanor safely away from Dublin and out of the clutches of the Council.

Throughout the long journey towards Munster Garrett's companions continued to exhort him to comply with the Queen's demands. At Kilkenny they were joined by the Earl of Ormond, who, carefully making sure that Essex was within earshot, loudly harangued Garrett, urging him to mend his ways and become a loyal subject. Antagonised by the presence of his enemy, and as the safety of his lordship drew near, Garrett grew more reckless and sneered contemptuously at Ormond's advice. Let the loyal Earl of Ormond dispose of his private army, and he, Desmond, would do likewise, but not before. At the borders of Desmond Eleanor and Garrett parted with their escort and, surrounded by their own clansmen, returned to Askeaton. From Eleanor's point of view the mission had been an abject failure. The Crown continued to make impossible demands on her husband, demands which not only would leave him undefended but would also be opposed by his dependent lords and clansmen in Munster whose own security was dependent on the strength of their overlord. The Queen persisted in her personal dislike and distrust of him. There were elements in Desmond too who welcomed Garrett's further alienation from the Crown for their own designs. Eleanor had sought to attain the middle ground for her husband but, so far, without success.

With the Queen's threat of being proclaimed a rebel hanging over his head, Garrett summoned a meeting of his kinsmen and tributary lords at Askeaton. It was as a result of this conference that the famous 'combination' or deed of association was compiled—though the date of this document was to be hotly disputed in later years. According to one version of events, the deed was signed on 18 July 1574, while another version places it exactly four years later, in 1578. Even if (as seems likely) the latter date is correct, the language of the document graphically reflects the unsettled conditions in Munster and the truculent mood of its principal leaders at the time of Garrett's return from Dublin. The signatories to the deed stated bluntly that they 'with one accorde doe counsell and advise the Earle not to consent nor yield to any more than in his answer [to the Council in Dublin]'. They further advised him 'to defend himself from the violens of the Lord Deputy' and forewarned the Crown that they intended 'aiding, helping and assisting the Earl to maintain and defend this our advice against the Lord Deputy or any other that will covet the Earl's inheritance'. [22]

The document unequivocally states the reasons which compelled Garrett and his adherents to undertake such a course of action. They did not stem from any great desire to remove or replace the English presence in Ireland, nor from any intention to join in an international conspiracy against Elizabeth. They arose from a basic and distinct desire to preserve their hereditary lands, powers and privileges. The deed of association was signed by Sir John of Desmond and by nineteen of Garrett's liege lords and kinsmen. Noticeably absent was the name of James FitzMaurice FitzGerald. However, the problems of dating the document make it difficult to determine the reason for FitzMaurice's non-participation; it may have resulted from a decision to distance himself from any movement which did not further his own designs in 1574 or, as is more likely, to his absence on the continent, if the deed was dated in 1578.The intentions of Garrett and his adherents were soon brought to the attention of the irate Queen. The aspirations of the Munster lords and chieftains, however legitimate, were deemed by the Queen a deliberate affront to her sovereignty. She was furious to learn of Garrett's permitted departure from Dublin Castle and again vented her anger on the unfortunate Fitzwilliam. 'We gave you no such authority', she wrote, 'to give a protection to him to come and go but to come safe and receive his pardon.'[23] The earl it seems might be given safe conduct to the Castle but not out of it. The intolerable situation drove the angry sovereign to try to bribe Sir John with a promise of some part of his brother's lands, even extending her offer to James FitzMaurice 'or any other of the leaders of his confederates, alluring them from him by such offers as seem reasonable'.[24]

Eleanor's distrust of Sir John and FitzMaurice, and her suspicions concerning their designs on her husband's patrimony, were further heightened by the Queen's offer. This, combined with the fear of her husband being proclaimed a rebel, prompted Eleanor and her husband to take the unusual and later controversial step of enfeoffing Garrett's estates to Eleanor's brother, Lord Dunboyne, Lord Power and John FitzEdmund FitzGerald of Cloyne, in trust for them during their joint lives 'with provision for his daughters and final remainder to his son'.[25] They intended to make Garrett's property legally secure from both the Crown and family rivals, so that it could eventually be passed on to their son, who, should his father die proclaimed a rebel, would otherwise forfeit his right to inherit. The document was later to be no more than a paper defence, however, against the steely intent of the Crown to gain possession of the vast Desmond estates.

Meanwhile the Earl of Ormond was seeking an explanation for the seizure by Desmond partisans of his castle of Derrinlaur on the Suir. Garrett refused to answer. In August Black Tom, with the backing of Lord Deputy Fitzwilliam, took matters into his own hands. They surrounded the castle and ran a mine beneath the walls. Before they could spring it the garrison attempted to escape but were intercepted, put to the sword and the castle captured. Fearful that similar tactics might be used against his own castles, Garrett surrendered the disputed Castlemaine to the Queen. Eleanor followed her husband's action with a personal letter to Elizabeth. She assured the Queen that her 'husband's departure from Dublin procedid not (God I take to witness) through any evill intencion towards yor Matie or dignitie but rather incencid by ungodly disturbers of the comon tranquillitie to conceave otherwise of your worthy honor than he had cause'.[26] She excused her long delay in answering previous letters from the Queen on the grounds that 'I durst not untyll nowe, that he hath both hastely repentid and duetifully performid suche things as was required by yr Matie Deputie and Councell of him, ones oppen my lyppes nor put penn to paper to intreat for your highnes mercifull clemency for him.'[27] In view of her husband's submission, Eleanor asked the Queen 'to restore him unto favour'.[28]

Eleanor's appeal and Garrett's submission had the desired effect. Weary of the entire episode, the Queen agreed that the Earl of Desmond 'was in theory to reign supreme as a feudal prince and be a loyal subject'.[29] But independent feudal princes were an anachronism to the Tudor mind and to their concept of royal absolutism. The Earl of Desmond, on the other hand, would not—and indeed could not—abandon the role in Munster which was his fateful inheritance. There could, however, be only one winner in the struggle, and from the beginning the odds appeared to be decidedly in favour of the Tudor queen. Garrett's fate and fortune depended on how quickly and astutely he could make the transition while retaining as much of his hereditary power as the changed political circumstances allowed.

Eleanor at last breathed a little easier. The threat of proclamation and attainder had receded. Elizabeth had not pushed Garrett beyond his limits. Her relief was further heightened in March 1575 when James FitzMaurice, together with his family and some other members of the Munster Geraldines, sailed from Glin for Saint-Malo in France. FitzMaurice departed ostensibly 'for the recovery of his health and to make friendship to come to the Queen's favour'.[30] In fact it was common knowledge that he sought international assistance to continue his religious campaign in Ireland. Whether he had Garrett's consent and blessing for this undertaking is uncertain, but it does not seem likely. For Garrett, at Eleanor's insistence, had refused to give FitzMaurice additional land in Munster as a reward for his services. Thomas Russell, the Desmond historian and an ardent supporter of FitzMaurice, writing later in 1638, blamed Eleanor for FitzMaurice's exile:

> *For Dame Elleynor Butler, Countess of Desmond, and then the mother of one only sonne, opposed herselfe against this James FitzMaurice and with reasons, persuasions, teares and imploreings, persuaded the Earle, her husband, not to dismember his patrimony, but rather for to leave it whole and entire to his only son James FitzGarrett, who was then a young child.*[31]

Russell propounded the belief that Garrett was either, as he states, 'conjured by his wife or rather not well established in his witts'[32] to deny FitzMaurice an estate.

Eleanor saw little reason to deprive her son of any part of his inheritance, particularly for FitzMaurice. She wanted her son returned to her care, and her husband's future conduct must not jeopardise that possibility. Consequently when Garrett's kinsman and ally, the Earl of Kildare, was suspected of intrigue against the Crown and imprisoned, and when it was expected that 'Desmond will make extraordinary broils to revenge him',[33] Garrett, with Eleanor's restraining hand on his sword and on his lips, did and said nothing. Their son James was now four years old, and her longing to be reunited with him was intense. But still more intense was Eleanor's determination to protect his inheritance from the grasping ambitions of her husband's family. With Garrett reinstated in his lordship and with James FitzMaurice in exile, Askeaton seemed at last a safe haven for the young heir of Desmond. Garrett and Eleanor opened negotiations with the English government for the child's return. Initially it seemed that their request was to be granted, as James was brought from London to Bristol, where he was placed in the care of a Thomas Chester. With some impatience, Garrett asked the Earl of Leicester to intervene and to obtain a licence 'to have the child brought hither, where', he assured him, 'he will not put Her Majesty or me to any charge until he be able to go to school, at which time I will return him thither'.[34] But the English Privy Council, pending further 'trial and proof of his [Garrett's] obedience and good conformity',[35] ordered that the child continue to be detained in Bristol.

Despite the temporary setback concerning her son's return, Eleanor's hopes for a more balanced treatment of her husband by the English administration in Ireland and at the English court were further heightened in the late summer of 1575 by the news of the reappointment of Sir Henry Sidney as Lord Deputy of Ireland. Sidney generally tended to take Garrett's side at Court and in the Council in Dublin in an attempt to balance the inordinate influence and power of the Earl of Ormond. In Sidney's opinion, Black Tom had become, by virtue of the Queen's preference of him at Desmond's expense, too powerful a subject and a threat to the balance of power in Munster. At last it appeared that Eleanor could look forward in hope of better prospects.

Chapter 6
Diplomacy and Intrigue

I vow to God . . . I know her to bee as wicked a woman as ever was bred in Ireland and one that hath ben the chief instrument of her husband's rebellion. And if she bee licensed to go out, your lordship shall doo as good an act as ever you did in your life to this realme to cause hir hed to be stroken of or else to be kept in perpetuall ymprisonment.

SIR WARHAM ST LEGER TO LORD BURGHLEY, 15 MAY 1581

Atimorous peace descended on Munster. The acrimonious struggle for power had temporarily exhausted both sides. Desmond retreated to Askeaton to lick his wounds and consolidate his position. The Dublin administration, under the leadership of Fitzwilliam, appeared as exhausted as the country it had attempted to subdue. Harassed by an unending series of disorders, wearied by a constant stream of abuse from an uncomprehending sovereign, and hampered by a continuous shortage of money and supplies, Fitzwilliam gladly resigned, and in September 1575 Sir Henry Sidney reluctantly resumed the reins of office.

Although overtly the Crown had accomplished little in the lordships of either Desmond or Ormond since the incident at Affane, English policy towards Ireland had, nonetheless, undergone radical change. Until Affane Elizabeth had been content to tolerate the independent tendencies of her Irish earls. As late as 1565 her chief secretary, Sir William Cecil, had cautioned the then Lord Justice of Ireland 'to stir no sleeping dogs in Ireland untill a staff be provided to chastin them if they will byte. Many things in common weales are suffered that are not liked.'[1] But the sleeping dogs had been roused and strained at the reforming leash of the Crown, which searched frantically for a suitable stick with which to control them. It could be the olive branch of submission and loyalty or the sharp, prickly thorn of confrontation. Ormond had chosen the first option, and, while Desmond had initially inclined towards the latter, he had been given a chance to choose again.

The English government had changed its earlier wait-and-see policy towards Ireland and had embarked on the difficult road of reconquest. The change of policy stemmed from various reasons. Over the decade Ireland had become a major drain on Crown revenue. Official expenditure had soared from £18,975 in the 1560s to £31,847 in the 1570s, which, even taking the inflation of the day into account, was more than the state coffers could afford or the parsimonious Elizabeth would tolerate. Furthermore developments in international politics also demanded more positive action. The threat of foreign intervention in Ireland by England's continental enemies and its menacing potential as a backdoor to England, haunted English minds. The revolt by James FitzMaurice and his flirtations with a wider international conspiracy which sought 'to use religion as a catalyst to make a common cause of local grievances',[2] had frightened the English government. FitzMaurice's continued contacts with the French, Spanish and papal courts did little to allay the fear that Ireland might well become a base for the Counter-Reformation.

There was further alarm at the prospect of a confederacy between the powerful, independent Irish lords such as Desmond, O'Neill and the Earl of Kildare. If such a confederacy received foreign support, it could well extend throughout the country and attract the Catholic lords of the Pale, already embroiled in a bitter dispute with the Crown over the payment of cess. And there were other interests which would welcome a more vigorous assertion of English rule in Ireland. While Elizabeth might chastise her officials for the disorderly state of the country and the enormous expense of reconquest, English financial investors in the various colonisation ventures felt positively defrauded. Furthermore, royal administrators, like Sidney, Fitzwilliam and Perrot, who had sacrificed their careers and their health, as they trudged through bogs and over mountains in a thankless attempt to subdue, inch by inch, the rebellious land, felt understandably frustrated. The time for reassessment had come, and in the present lull the Crown took stock.

Despite the continued detention of her son, the next few years were to prove a welcome period of relative tranquillity and normality for Eleanor. Imprisonment, exile, deprivation and loneliness had been her lot as Countess of Desmond. Her moments of happiness with Garrett had been fleeting. They were constantly torn apart by the political maelstrom that raged around them. Yet their union had become strengthened and revitalised. Throughout the years of her life with Garrett, Eleanor's primary concern and *raison d'être* for her every action was to protect her husband's political and physical well-being and to safeguard the Desmond inheritance for their son. With an iron will and fierce physical energy, she braved every threat to those objectives. Time after time, both by virtue of her letters and personal mediation, she demonstrated her undoubted intelligence and political acumen as she interceded for her husband when he spoke treason too loudly or was suspected of some ill-advised conspiracy. Almost every letter from Garrett to the Queen or to the Privy Council was accompanied by a letter from Eleanor, moderating the more arrogant tones of her husband or seeking to dissuade the Crown from forcing him into an impossible position. She was his adviser during negotiations with government officials, and her restraining hand held him in check while, with the other hand, she strove to keep the English administration at bay.

Eleanor understood better than anyone and was witness to the tremendous pressures exerted on her husband from all directions— pressure from the Gaelic lords of Munster, who expected him to observe and protect their customs and privileges; the self-inflicted pressure imposed by his inordinate sense of position and lineage; and pressure from the English Crown, the most potent threat that had emerged to undermine his prized inherited powers, assiduously guarded by his ancestors for generations. Garrett looked to his wife to share the burden that seemed at times likely to overwhelm him. In the whirlpool of intrigue and subterfuge that swirled around him, hers was the voice of calm and reason, the one voice he could trust. Imprisonment he held in fearful dread, a nightmare to which he would never again submit as long as he lived. Eleanor well realised that if the Crown, for any reason, attempted to deprive him of his liberty, the effect would be to make a rebel of her husband. This she sought desperately to avoid. Lords who rebelled against the Tudors seldom emerged victorious, and, as witnessed by Shane O'Neill's fate in Ulster, upon their demise their inheritance was forfeited. Eleanor endeavoured her utmost to prevent a similar occurrence happening to her husband.

Respite from the turmoil and trauma of the preceding decade also afforded her time to enjoy the more personal pleasures pertaining to her position as Countess of Desmond. In the shady, tree-lined walks among the gardens and orchards that surrounded Askeaton castle, she resumed some semblance of a normal lifestyle. During the preceding unquiet years her daughters, fostered among close relatives and friends, were now reunited with their parents. Their number was increased by the birth of another daughter, Ellen. Askeaton reverberated with the happy sound of its Geraldine family in residence again after many years of absence and exile. In the splendid fifteenth-century hall, on the west side of the castle, lighted by the famous traceried windows, the Earl and Countess of Desmond presided over more joyful festivities than Askeaton had known for some time. The great hall vibrated to the warm, noisy clangour of Gaelic hospitality. The earl welcomed his many followers to his table, not merely out of hospitality, but also because in Gaelic Ireland, where 'every Irish overlord held sway over people rather than territory',[3] a lord's prestige and power was measured by the number of his liegemen. While the English Crown might rant and rave over the existence and extent of the Earl of Desmond's personal army, the reality in Gaelic Munster decreed that without it the earl's power and ability to rule was compromised.

Without his army, the earl, in effect, forfeited his ability to protect himself and his dependants, the primary function of his role as Gaelic overlord. But the actual upkeep of his army was the duty of his overburdened and overtaxed peasantry whose plight, both in the Gaelic and anglicised parts of the country, was deplorable. Overlords were demanding and harsh masters. They showed little mercy, and little was expected from them. The peasantry bore the brunt of their master's excesses, both in war and in peace, with a blind obedience. If hatred towards Garrett and his house surfaced in their hearts, it was quickly subdued. As their earl and countess, dressed in silken finery, rode past their cabins, they briefly left the plough or the reaping-hook to raise the loyal shout of 'Shanid abú!' with a mixture of pride and fear instilled in them for generations.

The long summer days were spent hunting, following the swift red deer over the plains of Limerick and Cork and into the dark forests

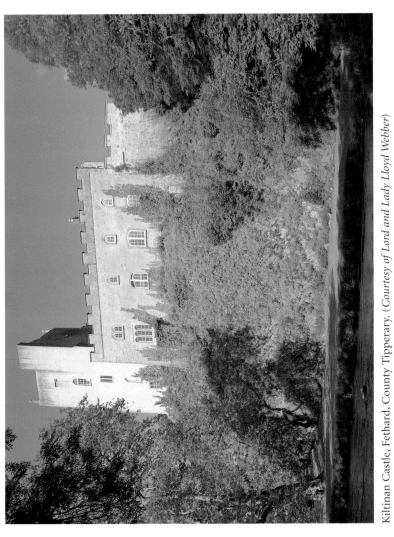

Kiltinan Castle, Fethard, County Tipperary. (*Courtesy of Lord and Lady Lloyd Webber*)

Thomas Butler (Black Tom),
tenth Earl of Desmond.
(*Private collection*)

Principal sixteenth-
century lordships.
(*Private collection*)

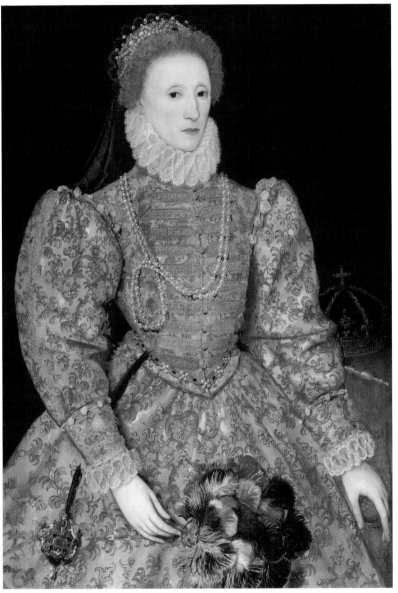
Queen Elizabeth I. (© *National Portrait Gallery, London*)

Askeaton Castle, County Limerick. (*Department of the Environment, Heritage and Local Government*)

Newcastle West, County Limerick. (*Department of the Environment, Heritage and Local Government*)

As the fame of your ma:ties singler mercy is spread throughout the
whole world whereof I your ma:ties lo:all subiect have emonges diuers
others most plesauntly tasted. So the remembranc therof
is the most ioye and Comffort vpon Earth I have: Moost
noble m:rs if I have not followid and performid accordinge my
Duetie your ma:ties directions and the promyses I made before
your highnes when I last departid your princely presenc
I renounc god, And do most humbly referr me to the
Report of your ma:ties gou:no:r and Coun:ell. Though my
husbands dealinge sinc his departur from dublin proceadid
not god I take to witnes throughe eny evill intencion
towards yo:r ma:tie or dignitie: but rather inconcid by ungodly
disturbers of the comon tranquillitie to conceave otherwise
of your worthy gou:no:r then he had Canse: yett I durst
not vntyll none that he hath both hartely repentid and
duetifully performid suche thinges as was requirid by yo:r
ma:tie Deputie and Coun:ell of him ones oppen my lypps
nor put penn to paper to intreat for your highnes merifull
Clemency for him. But sinc that he is reconcylid and
hath most humbly submittid himself to your ma:tie:
I with all humblenes in most humble wise do hartely
beseich yo:r ma:tie to vouchsauff of your accustomd mercy
to restore him vnto your ma:ties favo:r: And so with the
remembrance of my most bounden duetie: I beseche
god to preserue your ma:tie longe to Reigne ou:r vs,
from yo:r ma:tie Cyttie of lymrick the xij of septembre
1574

your ma:tie most humble and
loyall subiect

Eleanor, Countess of Desmond to Queen Elizabeth, 12 September 1574. (*The National Archives*, UK)

Sir Henry Sidney leaving Dublin Castle (note heads of executed Irish chieftains). (*Derricke, 1581*)

Tower of London. (© *Jack Sullivan / Alamy*)

Leeds Castle, Kent. (© LOOK Die Bildagentur der Fotografen GmbH / Alamy)

Hampton Court Palace. (© *David Levenson / Alamy*)

King Philip ii of Spain.
(© *National Portrait Gallery,
London*)

234

68

68

By the Queene

to the countesse of Desmond

Right deere and right welbeloved cousine we greet you well. Understanding by sundry lres and messages
deliuery knight our viceroy in Mounster, of the good affection you do beare vnto vs and to our Crowne, to addresse him
to conteynue in his dutifull obedience towardes his Iointreasure, we will let no longer tyme passe, but signifyinge
vnto yow our owne good lykinge of your care and good mynde in that behalf, And ymie now have herely praise
for it. And as yow haue this testimonie, &c. We doo doubt not but yow will contynue still to the good example
& ghyvin yow [...] all do the part of a Noble woman, [...] we never [...] &c, &c, [...] yow [...] towardes your
Lustiness, [...] to be of good contentment. And to yow selfe and our people [...] about you great good & praise
to the pleasing of thalmyghtie God, whose [...] thriftes to be regarded. And [...] your vertuous actions and praysefull
[...] proiectes. [...] we shall require to your comfort. And towardes Almyghtie God, to regard [...] sundrey [...]

Geven vnder our Signet at our Mannor of Greenwych the xvjth of July 1577 [...]

Geven :: B

Eleanor, Countess of Desmond to Queen Elizabeth, 30 September 1578. (*The National Archives, UK*)

[Manuscript letter in Elizabethan secretary hand, largely illegible]

... 1578

Eleanor, Countess of Desmond to Queen Elizabeth, 30 September 1578. (*The National Archives, UK*)

24 ~~51~~ 61 585

Right honorable I have received yo[u]r comfortable l[ett]re: And as I am most bound to praye for the preservacion of my soveraign Lady the Quenes ma[jes]tie for that her highnes would vouchsafe to remember me her humble and obedient subiect not onely with that yo[u]r l[ett]re but also with her ma[jes]ties most gracious and comfortable l[ett]res of the first of march last which I have received the second of maye to my greatest comfort and ioye. So have I alwaies had according my bounden duetie a respect to the s[er]vice of her ma[jes]tie in all my actions: And will so contynewe duringe liefe: And for eny thing touching the breache of my lord my husband his duetie: Surely I am well assured that he standeth as fast and sure a subiect to her ma[jes]tie, And willbe as ready to venture himself and all he hath in her ma[jes]ties quarrell as eny within this Realme, And hath taken as great payne and care for the quiett of this province as becometh one of his calling, the report whereof I leave to the declaracion of those in aucthoritie here that therewith are acquainted: Desiring yo[u]r honour not onely to take in good p[ar]te this my first l[ett]re of so little acquayntance, but also that you will knowe and then visite me with a favour kynde of yo[u]rs for the which I willbe thankfull, And here sending sent unto you by this bearer as a token of my good will [illegible] which I praye yo[u]r honour to take in good worth. I hartely take leave from Dongill the last of Septemb[e]r 1578

yo[u]r honors assured frend

E. Desmond

PUBLIC RECORD OFFICE

61

Eleanor, Countess of Desmond to Queen Elizabeth, 30 September 1578. (*The National Archives*, UK)

Sir Walter Raleigh. (*The Bridgeman Art Library*)

William Cecil, Lord Burghley. (© *National Portrait Gallery, London*)

Author at memorial to the Earl of Desmond at Glanageenty, County Kerry. (*Private collection*)

Earl of Ormond's castle, Carrick-on-Suir. (*Department of the Environment, Heritage and Local Government*)

King James i. (© *National Portrait Gallery, London*)

Eleanor's tomb, Sligo Abbey. (*Department of the Environment, Heritage and Local Government*)

Katherine FitzGerald, the 'old' Countess of Desmond. (© *National Portrait Gallery, London*)

of oak and ash. The evening silence was punctuated by the tolling of the prayer-bell from across the Deel, as the monks from the Franciscan abbey intoned their Te Deums over the bones of dead generations of Geraldines. And in his travels, just as the sovereign Elizabeth in England was wont to quarter herself on her subject lords, so the Earl of Desmond exercised similar but more ancient rights within his lordship. When he went to Tralee to collect his dues and rents, a fair was held to honour his presence. It was attended by travelling merchants and traders who sold their wares and paid taxes to the earl for the privilege. The mayors of Cork, Youghal and Limerick, over whom he claimed suzerainty, put on a brave show, opened their gates, displayed banners of welcome, entertained their lord lavishly, and breathed a sigh of relief and counted the cost when his official visit terminated. The earl presided over the palatine courts of Tralee and Any, appointed court officers, and was the ultimate arbiter in all judicial proceedings within the palatinate, dispensing justice by Gaelic law intermixed with elements of feudal law. Ships from Spain and France kept him in touch with developments abroad and also kept him provided with fine furnishings, wines for his table, and silk, taffeta and velvet for his and his countess's wardrobe. Whispers of more serious transactions reached Desmond from time to time. Spies in the earl's pay brought reports of FitzMaurice's travels to the French, Spanish and papal courts in search of assistance to raise the banner of crusade once again over Munster. But the threat which sought to shatter the tranquillity, that like a soothing salve had almost healed the painful sores of the previous years was, as yet, far removed.

As if to augur a continuation of the peaceful respite, Lord Deputy Sidney embarked on 'a mission of inquiry, conciliation, and administrative settlement'.[4] In response, the Earl and Countess of Desmond greeted him at Dungarvan and offered to conduct him through Munster. Despite their differences at their last meeting, which had resulted in Garrett's long imprisonment in England, Eleanor knew that Sidney's antagonism towards the Earl of Ormond could be made work in her husband's favour. She was also determined that Sidney should recognise that Garrett was the premier lord in Munster, with as much authority, and as capable to rule his palatinate, as the supposedly loyal Earl of Ormond. Sidney was suitably impressed. In a spirit of friendship and cordiality the earl and countess escorted him into Cork city, where they were received by the citizens, as Sidney duly reported, 'with all joyfulness, tokens and shows, the best they could express'.[5] Eleanor's brother, Lord Dunboyne, joined their party at Cork, together with Garrett's brothers, Sir John and Sir James, who had lately been freed from captivity in England.

Following the Earl of Desmond's lead, the Munster nobility assembled to attend the Lord Deputy. Thither came, as Sidney related, the chieftains of the three branches of the great MacCarthy clan: 'The Earl of Clancar, by the Irish styled MacCarthy More, was accompanied by his countess, the sister of the Earl of Desmond, and his infant children, the Baron of Valentia and the Lady Ellen. . . . The Lord of Muskerry, the wealthiest chieftain of the sept . . . and the Lord of the fertile lands of Carbery, Sir Donagh MacCarthy Reagh . . . accompanied by his two sons, Florence and Dermod Moyle.'[6] They were joined by the Earl of Thomond, the Archbishop of Cashel, the Bishop of Cork, the viscounts Barry and Roche and the Baron of Lixnaw. To this glittering array of Munster aristocracy were added Gaelic chieftains, O'Sullivan, O'Callaghan, O'Donoghue and O'Driscoll. As a further manifestation of Gaelic custom, Sidney received the five MacSheehy captains of the Desmond galloglass, bound in hereditary allegiance to their Geraldine overlord, though, as Sidney astutely observed, their status was hardly that of subordinates, 'the greatest being both in fear of them and glad of their friendship'.[7] And there too, as he gallantly reported to the English Privy Council, 'the better to furnish the beauty and filling of the city, all the principal lords had with them their wives during all the Christmas who truly kept very honourable, at least plentiful, houses'.[8] Sidney concluded his account by pointing out, perhaps as an incentive to widowers and bachelors in England; 'to be brief many widow ladies were there also, who erst had been wives to earls and others of good note and account.'[9]

It was a great social event, and, as such, a rarity in the troubled times, a bright and joyful occasion, on the surface at least, as the interrelated Munster aristocracy mingled under the watchful but, for the moment, benign gaze of the English Lord Deputy. For Eleanor it was an opportunity to meet and exchange news with her sister, brother, half-brother, nieces and nephews and her many other relatives among the assembled nobility. It was Christmas time, and the festive season was lavishly celebrated. As principal lady of the province, Eleanor entertained Sidney, his entourage and the Gaelic nobility and hosted banquets in their honour. The wine flowed freely, and the music was loud and merry as English and Gael celebrated the festive season of 1575.

Alongside the gaiety and pageantry, however, lay the hard political realities. Eleanor captured the Lord Deputy's ear to spell out the pressures to which her husband was being subjected. She entreated Sidney to show patience and forbearance and promised to encourage her husband along the path of loyalty. But she also reminded him that Garrett's encounters with the Crown had, so far, done little to inspire his trust and obedience. Surrounded as he was by the trappings of the Gaelic world of which she spoke, Sidney could not fail to appreciate her dilemma, and accordingly spoke with friendliness and encouragement to her husband.

But neither did Sidney allow the festivities to deter him from his duties. In the new year he set about the more serious business of his office. He presided over the court in Cork and heard civil cases tried by English law. He undertook an inspection tour of the city's defences and made provisions for their improvement and upkeep. On 1 February 1576, accompanied by Eleanor and Garrett, he departed for Limerick, where they received a reception equally as hospitable from the mayor and citizens. The only ominous note struck by the Lord Deputy during his tour of Munster was to recommend a speedy appointment to the vacant post of President of Munster. He prophesied the return of James FitzMaurice and warned the Privy Council 'that all the loose people of this province will flock unto him. Yea,' he continued, drawing on the knowledge he had gleaned from his talks with Eleanor, 'the lords, though they would do their best, shall not be able to keep them from him.'[10]

After Limerick, Eleanor and Garrett parted company with the Lord Deputy, as he continued on his journey into Connaught. They returned home to Askeaton, where life continued in relative peace. Garrett saw to his vast estates, collected his rents, and exercised his customary privileges as overlord. To reiterate his palatine privilege and to stem any doubt in the minds of his tributary lords in the wake of Sidney's visit, he summarily ordered the Baron of Lixnaw and the freeholders of Clanmorris to attend at his palatine court at Tralee. In his own country the Earl of Desmond's power must still be seen as absolute.

Despite Sidney's recommendation, the vacant presidency of Munster was not filled until the summer of 1576, when Sir William Drury was appointed second president of the province. A native of Suffolk Drury had previously been governor of Berwick. He had a distinguished military career, both by land and sea, in England and on the continent. From nearby Askeaton the Earl of Desmond anxiously watched the build-up of English military might as Drury established his headquarters at nearby Limerick and embarked on his presidency in a way that was bound to bring him into collision with the uneasy earl. Drury wrote enthusiastically to the Privy Council: 'I began the assizes in Cork,' he reported, 'where I hanged to the number of 42. Of which some were notable malefactors, one pressed [i.e. pressed to death] and two gentlemen of the chief of the MacSweeneys hanged drawn and quartered.'[11] Drury next turned his attention to the lordship of the Earl of Desmond. He was determined to curtail the influence and power of the earl, which he reckoned was a threat to his position as President. In order to compel the earl to reduce his army, which far outnumbered his own, he compiled a register of the earl's followers, for whose future conduct he held the earl personally responsible. He next attempted to extract cess, in money and in kind, from the earl's tenants in order to defray the expenses of his office. The earl bristled with anger at Drury's blatant attack on his customary rights. Contemptuously ignoring the Lord President, Garrett complained directly to the Privy Council but to little avail.

Drury next struck against the earl's most prized hereditary privilege, his palatine court of Kerry, which had previously been deemed void by the Irish Privy Council. Drury further contended that the palatinate had become the refuge of all the 'evil-doers' of Munster and proposed 'to make a passage for law and justice to be there exercised', as he considered 'that it would not be safe among a great flocke to leave a scabbed sheepe nor good for a commonwealth to have nurseries for sinne'.[12] Drury started out for Tralee with the intention to establish Crown courts to prosecute offenders by English instead of Desmond law. But the 'scabbed sheepe' of Drury's despatches called out his army and barred the Lord President's way. Drury reported to the government that Desmond had declared war on the Crown.

A direct confrontation, and one that was likely to have far more serious implications for Garrett than even Affane, seemed inevitable as the two forces formed battle-lines. If Garrett attacked or was drawn into battle he could expect to be proclaimed for treason, with dire consequences for himself, his lordship and his family. Eleanor swiftly interceded with Drury. A contemporary observer somewhat melodramatically reported:

> *Like a good Abigaell [she] went and met the lord president, fell upon hir knees, held up hir hands and with trilling teares praied his lordships patience and pardon, excusing as well she could hir husband's follie, saying that he had assembled all that companie onelie for a generall hunting.*[13]

While the lady's excuse was somewhat thin, considering the superiority of the earl's forces, Drury accepted the countess's version of events but nevertheless proceeded to Tralee. With great difficulty Eleanor restrained Garrett from attacking him.

Drury was merely one of the ever-increasing band of 'unattractive outsiders, arrogant and ruthless men whose system threatened a wide spectrum of the existing society, from the learned class, the jurists, poets, and musicians to the men of war'.[14] To the proud Earl of Desmond, the great, gaelicised lord of Munster, Drury was but a servant, a hireling, one of the contemptible 'English churls' of inferior degree. But Eleanor realised that Drury and his kind were merely a symptom and a symbol of the new English political attitude that had evolved towards Ireland. No matter how disdainfully the Earl of Desmond might regard him neither Drury, nor the policies he pursued in the name of the Crown, would go away. If Drury failed in his mission in Ireland, there were a hundred more to take up where he left off—and perhaps with even more ruthless intent.

In Connaught the Burkes strained against the severe rule of the new military governor, Sir Nicholas Malby. Drury received reports that Sir John of Desmond had incited the Burkes to rebel and promptly had him apprehended. When rumours reached Askeaton that Drury intended to arrest the earl as well, faced with the dreaded nightmare of detention, Garrett fled with Eleanor and their children into the furthermost part of Kerry. It was significant that rumours of Garrett's impending arrest had emanated from London, where Black Tom's influence at Court was as strong as ever. Garrett's flight and his point-blank refusal to obey the President of Munster or the Lord Deputy could only serve to alienate him further from the Crown. It was also to Black Tom's advantage that Garrett's reaction would serve to keep Drury fully-occupied in Desmond and leave him less time to pry into the state of affairs in his lordship of Ormond.

Professing his life to be in danger, the Earl of Desmond sounded the age-old call to arms. Soon over a thousand adherents flocked to his defence. Safe within the confines of his palatinate and protected by his hereditary men-at-arms, Garrett boldly announced that no rent or cess would henceforth be forthcoming to the Crown from his lordship. The question of cess had become a vexed issue, particularly in the Pale, where lords Baltinglass, Howth, Delvin and Trimleston had been committed to Dublin Castle when they too voiced their grievances on the subject. While the Queen acknowledged that the system required some measure of adjustment, she was indignant that such normally compliant lords should so boldly challenge her royal prerogative. By his pronouncement on the matter Garrett had, whether by design or by accident, linked his grievances with those of the lords of the Pale.

Eleanor spent the summer months of 1577 deep within the Kerry fastness, behind mountain, wood and marsh, hidden from Drury, who scoured the countryside in vain. But as summer gave way to autumn she became uneasy that Garrett's continued absence from the centre of his lordship might be usurped by others. She wrote to the Queen and Sidney to propose that it was fear of imprisonment that had caused herself and her husband to flee to safety. But there was no immediate reply to her letters. The Queen continued her policy of favouritism, instructing the Lord Deputy to ensure 'that the Earl of Ormond's landes should be exempt from all cess'.[15] In vain Sidney urged her to reconsider. Her decision would not only result in a decrease in much-needed revenue, but, in the present circumstances, would be seen by the Earl of Desmond as further proof of the Crown's discriminatory policy towards him. Mindful also of the situation in the Pale, Sidney further warned the Queen that it 'was a precedent to others to sue for like immunities'.[16] To placate the earl and to allay Eleanor's fears, Sidney sent messages urging them to repair to either Drury or himself. The English Privy Council further wrote to assure them that the rumours of Garrett's impending imprisonment were totally false. It was instigated, they intimated, 'no doubt by some of your private enemies, that practise and would be glad to draw you into any undutiful action that might purchase unto you Her Majesty's indignation to the overthrow of your state'.[17] Eleanor concurred with the sentiments expressed and cautioned Garrett against playing into the hands of his enemies and to make his peace with the Crown.

After much persuasion Garrett finally agreed to deal with Sidney, who forwarded the necessary letters of protection and arranged for the meeting to take place, significantly, at Kilkenny, the principal seat of the Ormond lordship. At a ceremony in St Canice's cathedral in February 1578 the Earl of Desmond formally submitted to the Lord Deputy. Garrett was in agony from the wound he had received at Affane, and Sidney was taken aback at the apparent deterioration in his physical condition. 'I suppose there is least danger in hym,' he assured the Queen, 'beinge such an impotent and weake boddye, as neither can he gett up on horseback, but that he is helpen and lift up, neither when he is on horsebacke can he hym selfe alight downe without healpe.'[18] Sidney reconciled Eleanor and a reluctant Garrett with Drury and, as he reported, 'made them ffriendes in as good sorte as I could'.[19]

Drury was every bit as reluctant to make peace with Garrett. He privately considered that the Lord Deputy had dealt too leniently with the troublesome earl, who, to Drury's mind, was the single greatest obstacle to peace and order in Munster. He was convinced that Sir John of Desmond, with the earl's consent, had conspired with the Burkes to incite the most recent rebellion in Connaught. His opinion was further strengthened when rumours circulated of a marriage between Lady Mary Burke, the daughter of the Earl of Clanrickard, and Sir John. He suspected that the Earl of Desmond and Sir John were also in collusion with James FitzMaurice in his endeavours to elicit help from England's enemies abroad. Sidney, on the other hand, sought to portray Garrett 'as the least dangerous man of iv or v of these that are next hym in right and succession (if he were gonne) and easieth to be dealt withall'.[20] Perhaps his critic and his erstwhile mentor both failed to consider the passionate tradition of birthright, obligation and privilege invested in the feeble body of the Earl of Desmond, a tradition which, if unleashed, could elevate the weak and indecisive earl into a noble and mighty warrior. But in February 1578, as Sidney watched Desmond, grimacing in pain, being lifted off his horse, he could not be blamed for dismissing such a possibility.

With another confrontation narrowly avoided, Eleanor felt a sense of relief at the outcome of their meeting with Sidney. She ministered to Garrett's physical ailments which, despite his relatively young age, had incapacitated him greatly. For as well as the discomfort and pain he suffered from the aggravated thigh wound, the earl was showing early signs of palsy, which was to develop over the succeeding years. But with incursions by the Lord President into his preserve momentarily halted, Garrett now had time to recuperate. All the signs augured well for a continuation of peace and the right environment for the earl to make a slow but steady adjustment to the changed political situation. The Queen too seemed affected by the air of reconciliation that had emerged. She wrote in friendly tones to Eleanor in appreciation of her

> good travail with your husband, to remove from him this vain fear of his apprehension and to leave off his number of followers. So have you declareth yourself no less wise and loving towards your husband for the preservation of his estate, which might easily have been utterly ruined if he had not by your good means been brought to the said submission. [21]

Sidney maintained a steady hand on the tiller of government in Ireland, and Garrett and Drury continued an outward show of harmony in Munster. As further proof of his loyal intent, Garrett delivered into the Lord President's custody certain malefactors who had recently committed crimes within his lordship. Among them was the 'most notorious woman in all the coasts of Ireland',[22] the female sea-captain and leader, Grace O'Malley (Granuaile) from Connaught. The earl's soldiers had captured this extraordinary woman as she led a raiding party from her ship in search of booty in Thomond. Drury communicated news of her capture and imprisonment to Sidney:

> Grany O'Mayle, a woman that hath impudently passed the part of womanhood and been a great spoiler and chief commander and director of thieves and murderers at sea to spoille this province, having been apprehended by the Earle of Desmond . . . his Lordship hath now sent her to Lymrick where she remains in safe keeping. [23]

Whatever part, if any, Eleanor played in yielding up the 'famous female sea-captain' to the Crown is not recorded, and her opinion and reaction to her husband's remarkable hostage is open to conjecture. She had doubtless heard tales of her exploits and extraordinary lifestyle as a sea-trader, pirate and mercenary. While pirates were numerous off the south and west coasts in sixteenth-century Ireland, a woman pirate of the calibre of Grace O'Malley was both a phenomenon and worthy hostage. Compassion for a woman's plight or a feeling of sisterhood did not concern Eleanor so long as the capture and handing over of Grace O'Malley served as a means to pacify the Crown and protect her husband and her family.

Despite the continued peaceful overtures, ominous storm-clouds began to gather on the horizon. In summer 1578 rumours came flying across the seas, propelled by emissaries from the papal and Spanish courts, that James FitzMaurice, suitably equipped, was homeward bound to raise the banner of crusade aloft over Munster. Messengers also brought despatches to Garrett and to the Munster lords to advise them that FitzMaurice not only requested but expected their support and readiness to lead their followers behind the 'banner of Christ'. James FitzMaurice was coming with enough gold and arms from Christ's vicar on earth to persuade any doubting Catholic mind. Eleanor's nightmare was fast becoming a reality. The cursory truce between Garrett and Drury also seemed destined to end with the recall in September of Lord Deputy Sidney, the sole buffer between Garrett and the more ruthless and grasping elements of the Crown. Drury was subsequently sworn in as Lord Justice in his place.

Eleanor and Garrett journeyed to Dublin to take their leave of Sir Henry Sidney. On 12 September 1578, as the tide lapped the city walls at Wood Quay, with much trepidation and some sadness, Eleanor watched Sidney's departure from Ireland for the last time. Sidney, perhaps better than most, had come to understand their great dilemma and whenever possible had made allowances in his dealings with her husband. Undoubtedly a loyal and often ruthless official, Sidney also possessed rare qualities often lacking in his contemporaries in the Irish service. Eleanor knew that many of her husband's treasonable outbursts and actions had never been reported by him to Court. He had shielded them from the arrogant petty Crown officials in Dublin. His personal and political antipathy towards the Ormond clique at court had, to a degree, worked to their advantage. There was a basic honesty and integrity about Sidney in his dealings with them. While ever the devoted servant of the Crown, and in no way prepared to tolerate the Earl of Desmond's inclination to rule as an independent magnate, he was nevertheless willing to allow him the space to adjust to the unpalatable but obligatory transition. As the ship slipped anchor and sailed away into the wide estuary of Dublin bay, Eleanor perhaps realised that with it went her hope for a peaceful resolution to their situation.

Rumours of an impending invasion intensified, and Eleanor wrote directly to the Queen to assure her of Garrett's continuing loyalty, declaring that he 'standeth as safe and sure a subject to her Matie and will be as ready to spend himself and all he hath in her Maties quarrell as any within the Realme'.[24] She also asked the Queen to have her son returned to her. Elizabeth promised to look into the matter. Eleanor sent the Queen 'as a token of my good will half duzen marten skins whereof I praye you some to take in good worth'.[25] To reciprocate the gesture, the Queen sent Eleanor a fashionable gown. Perhaps it was the self-same gown that Eleanor wore, to the admiration and envy of all, when she and Garrett presided at a banquet in Limerick held in honour of the newly-appointed Lord Justice. The atmosphere was cordial and the earl and Drury appeared on friendly terms. Drury reported of their meeting: 'We won the Earl and Countess of Desmond to agree to and subscribe to a compositon for the alteration of their wonted manner of coyne and livery and the converting thereof into a yearly rent of £2,000.'[26] Eleanor had persuaded her husband to relinquish the coyne and livery exactions, a privilege which was also a hallmark of his power and thus had brought him more than half way to meet the demands of the Crown. She now looked for some reciprocal sign. In relinquishing his ancient rights Garrett must not be seen to lose face and risk losing authority in Munster.

The Queen seemed eager to maintain and encourage the Earl of Desmond in his new-found loyalty. She wrote to both Garrett and Eleanor to assure them that 'it was never our meaninge (as by some hathe been most unjustlie and maliciouslie given out) to dispossesse our subjects of our saide realme of their livinges.'[27] On the contrary, her intention, she maintained, was to see them live in peace and justice 'whiche, if it hathe not been in our ministers there, whom we wilbe as ready to punishe with all severity, if they may be justlie convicted of that faulte'.[28] In a personal message to Eleanor, Elizabeth again thanked her for her good advice to her husband and promised that she would 'find Us your good and gratyous lady when said occasion shall faule out wherein We may shewe you the proofe of our good meaning towards you'.[29] As a token of her appreciation the Queen despatched to Lord Chancellor Gerrard of the Irish Privy Council 'a gowne of clothe of gold'[30] for Eleanor. The Chancellor, however, postponed the delivery of the gown until his meeting with the Earl of Desmond, when he personally placed it in Eleanor's hands with the express purpose, as he wrote, 'by her help to have gotten the better end for the worth'.[31] There were no free gifts forthcoming from the Crown.

Elizabeth, however, kept her promise and, early in 1579, Eleanor was reunited with her son. Almost six years had elapsed since she had seen James. Weak from birth, the years in custodial care in England had not improved his health. His English apparel, accent and outlook made him seem strange and different to his sisters who clustered around in wonderment at their strange, timid, brother. The restoration of the Desmond heir caused a stir among the Desmond tributary lords and chieftains, not least the earl's brothers, who saw in the child the demise of their own ambitions to the earldom. Like a stormy petrel, Eleanor's young son appeared as the harbinger of the great tempest that was about to break.

For on 18 July 1579 the peace of Munster was shattered by a holy thunderclap that reverberated off the high mountain peaks of Kerry and sent shock-waves careering across the country to frighten the Council in Dublin and stir Elizabeth and her government into action. James FitzMaurice FitzGerald, with a fleet of small ships, an army of 600 soldiers of Italian, Spanish, French, Portuguese, English and Irish origin, a quantity of arms and ammunition, a papal legate, a Spanish friar and a banner blessed by the Pope, landed at Smerwick harbour, and made their headquarters at the old fort of Dún an Óir. The banner was a significant feature of the enterprise. It bore the personal arms of FitzMaurice, with the motto 'In omni tribulatione et angustia spes Jesu et Maria'.[32] The small force was the net result of years of solicitation and exaggeration by FitzMaurice at the royal courts of Europe. But the royal heads of Europe, while they applauded the crusading zeal of the Irish chieftain, were less enthusiastic to back him financially. In Rome FitzMaurice met the English Jesuit Dr Nicholas Sanders, who not only helped him elicit the meagre support from the Pope which had made landfall at Dún an Óir, but offered to accompany the expedition to Ireland.

Sanders had a reputation as 'a cold humourless unbending zealot'.[33] A former professor of theology at the Catholic university of Louvain, he was the author of an abrasively bitter but highly erudite and influential anti-Reformation tract. In the years before his appointment as papal legate to Ireland he had travelled widely and had access to and the respect of the Catholic princes of Europe. He was a tireless worker with a burning religious faith and an equally burning hatred for all the Reformation represented. He saw in FitzMaurice and his mission in Ireland the means to put his counter-Reformation energy and enthusiasm into action. With a fierce determination and an absolute dedication to his principles, he turned his back on the serenity and security of Rome and willingly accepted the hardship of his Irish mission. Under his influence FitzMaurice declared his cause to be 'a war for the Catholic religion and against a tyrant who refuses to hear Christ speaking by his Vicar'.[34]

But FitzMaurice had tended to overemphasise the commitment of the Gaelic and gaelicised lords in Ireland to the aims of the Counter-Reformation, and had certainly overestimated the unifying ability of religion in Ireland. The discontent of Irish leaders sprang not from a sense of religious persecution by the English Crown, but from the Crown's endeavours to make Gaelic Ireland conform to English ways and with it a dilution of their power. Real religious persecution was, as yet, some way off and a revolt based on religious grounds alone was thereby unlikely to succeed. To mould their crusade in Ireland into an effective arm of the Counter-Reformation movement, Sanders and FitzMaurice needed 'to make positive revolt out of negative discontent'[35] and thus draw the lords and chieftains of Munster, especially the Earl of Desmond, into their religious net.

Under the influence of Dr Sanders, FitzMaurice despatched a letter to Garrett urging his support for the banner of Christ and for the restoration of the Catholic faith in Ireland. His exhortation was couched in ominous terms:

> God forbid that any Geraldine should stand in the field against the cross of Christ. I cannot tell what worldly thing would grieve me more than to hear not only that your honour would not assist Christ's banner but also that any other nobleman should prevent you in this glorious attempt. All that I write is spoken also to me good lady, your bedfellow, and to me good uncle, your brothers to all of whom I commend myself and also me bedfellow most heartily doth the like; trusting in Almighty God that as his holiness has made me Captain General of this holy war so your honour being head of my house will be the chief Protector and Patron of them, no less than me quarrel.[36]

The Pope, FitzMaurice further reminded Garrett and Eleanor, had promised that all who chose to fight under his banner should receive indulgences similar to those granted to those who had fought in the recent war against the Turks.

The arrival of FitzMaurice and his attempt to involve her husband in a religious crusade had finally turned Eleanor's nightmare into a grim reality. Her years of haggling and bargaining with the Crown to win sufficient time for her husband to adapt to the changing political circumstances seemed destined to be brought to nothing by the religious declamations of the returned exile. On a personal basis, there was little love lost between them, and she suspected that the religious overtones of FitzMaurice's mission to Ireland hid a deeper and more devious intent. She had heard that FitzMaurice had openly declared his aspirations towards the earldom of Desmond during his sojourn on the continent. His crusading banner displayed his personal coat of arms. Her husband was in poor health and daily seemed to grow more incapacitated. Gaelic society, she well realised, had little tolerance for physical weakness in its leaders. Her son was a child of eight years and a long way from his majority and inheritance. The sprawling Desmond lordship needed strong, steady guidance to safeguard it against the pressures being exerted on it by divergent interests.

The question of religion seemed to Eleanor a cloak to mask more basic motivations. Religion had never been a strong issue in the politics of the day in Ireland. Church property was often the target of attack and seizure by warring Gaelic chiefs, just as it had been, in recent years, by the Crown. Church laws had generally fallen into decline, particularly in relation to social issues such as marriage, where the old Celtic ethos prevailed. FitzMaurice himself was divorced, and numerous other examples among Eleanor's own family and peers bore out the assessment of a modern historian that 'Celtic secular marriage remained the norm in Ireland and Christian matrimony was no more than the rare exception grafted on to this system.'[37] The clergy were as lax in the practice and observance of their faith as the laity. The sacraments were performed haphazardly and many of the monasteries were in a ruinous and decayed condition. The real dilemma posed for Garrett and Eleanor by FitzMaurice's arrival was that, to preserve his status, Garrett, out of necessity more than by desire, might be prevailed upon to join the rebellion. If defeated he would then be proclaimed a traitor and his estates confiscated. If, on the other hand, the country were to rise in defence of the Catholic religion, and if the rising was successful, then Garrett could not afford to be left out in the cold. The only option was to play for time to determine which way the wind was likely to blow.

Garrett and Eleanor despatched innocuous letters to Lord Justice Drury to inform him of what he already knew, that James FitzMaurice had landed at Dingle. 'If need shall require,' Garrett assured Drury, 'I am ready with all mine to venture both my life and theirs in Her Majesty's quarrel.'[38] Drury was unimpressed. To test the earl's intent he ordered him to accompany an English detachment which was to set up camp some distance from the invasion force. Reluctantly Garrett agreed and with the English reconnoitred FitzMaurice's fortifications at Smerwick. Meanwhile his brothers, Sir John and Sir James, met secretly with FitzMaurice and Dr Sanders. The Geraldine historian Russell, writing in 1631, stated that Sir John actually agreed to join with FitzMaurice at this time, with the sole intention, as Eleanor had long since suspected, of deposing his brother. Russell further maintained that Sir John was motivated by 'a private grudge and hatred to ye Countesse of Desmond'.[39] Whether impelled by personal ambition or hatred of Eleanor, or inspired by the religious zeal of Dr Sanders, Sir John decided 'to performe some piece of service whereby hee might give them assurance of his faithfull meaning to doe them service and not to leave any after meanes to recant or shirke back'.[40] The 'piece of service' with which he chose to demonstrate his commitment to the crusade astounded everyone and was destined to have catastrophic repercussions for his brother.

Despite the protestation of loyalty of the Earl of Desmond, Drury sent Henry Davells, a Devonshire man long resident in Ireland and on friendly terms with the Desmonds, to copperfasten the earl's allegiance. Davells was particularly friendly with Sir John, who, it was said, was his godson. Davells inspected the camp at Smerwick, concluded that with a few score soldiers it could easily be captured, and requested the Earl of Desmond to provide him with the necessary troops. Unwilling to commit himself to either side, Garrett lamely excused himself on the basis 'that his musketeers were more fitted to shoot at fowls than at a strong place and that his gallowglasses were good against gallowglasses but no match for old soldiers'.[41] Davells, together with his associate Arthur Carter, the provost-marshal of Munster, set out from Smerwick to report back to Drury. They lodged overnight at an inn in Tralee. In the middle of the night, accompanied by his brother James and some supporters, Sir John burst into the room and murdered both Davells and Carter in their beds.

News of the murders was received with disbelief in most quarters. One opinion was that the crime was committed with the full knowledge and consent of James FitzMaurice, while others stated that he condemned the treachery of the act but not the act itself. Dr Sanders was said to have called the murder 'a sweet sacrifice before God'[42] and to have absolved Sir John and Sir James of the crime. For the Earl of Desmond the murder of Davells and Carter had even more far-reaching consequences. He publicly expressed his shock and revulsion and hurried back from Dingle to Askeaton. Garrett believed that the crime was intended to deliberately force his hand and alienate him further from the Crown. The Crown reacted predictably and Drury promised 'liberall rewarde to anie that should bring me the head of James FitzMaurice or of Sir John or his brother James of Desmond'.[43] Thus Garrett's brothers were formally proclaimed rebels by the Crown and placed in the same camp as James FitzMaurice.

But the murder of Davells and Carter had other implications. When FitzMaurice landed in Dingle Bay, Garrett had an army of over a thousand men under his direct leadership. Scarcely one month later, as he hastened back to Askeaton, less than sixty of his followers chose to follow him. The remainder, whether with or without his consent, now formed part of the new army under James FitzMaurice and Sir John of Desmond. It was rumoured in Dublin and London that the Earl of Desmond had, in fact, covertly allowed his army to aid FitzMaurice so that the earl himself could appear loyal until further aid arrived from Spain and until Irish lords, such as Clanrickard, O'Neill and Kildare, joined the crusade. However, it seems clear that ever since 1576, though the transition was undoubtedly painful, Garrett, with Eleanor's encouragement, had been making an attempt to conform to the demands of the Crown. But it could be argued that old habits die hard and especially in the case of the Geraldine earl, reluctant to accept any diminution of his traditional power which thereby could lead him to conspire in secret with FitzMaurice. It could be further argued that Garrett had little choice in the matter, and that his obligation to the Gaelic world that sustained him, and to his tributary lords and clansmen over whom he claimed jurisdiction, in turn demanded that, in the present circumstances, he should favour rebellion.

It was clear, however, that elements on both sides, for more devious reasons, sought to provoke the earl to throw off his loyalty to the Crown. He was in ill-health; if he died, it must not be as an attainted rebel. There was no advantage to be gained, either for Garrett or his son, from rebellion unless it could be assured of success. For this, more foreign assistance had to be forthcoming. Despite the promise of FitzMaurice and Sanders of further aid from the Pope and from Spain, none, as yet, had materialised, nor had FitzMaurice been successful in his attempts to extend the confederacy throughout the country. To Eleanor it appeared that Sir John had usurped her husband's control of his armed followers, who, exhorted by the preaching of Dr Sanders, had a new cause on which to expend their martial skills and energies, with the added bonus of booty and papal gold. Life under Garrett in recent times had tended to provide little scope or reward for their military abilities. A leader who could not mount his horse unassisted was scarcely fit to command, especially when a more able leader, such as James FitzMaurice, was prepared to lead them in his place.

While Garrett pondered his unenviable dilemma, Drury fell ill in Dublin. The newly-appointed President of Connaught, Sir Nicholas Malby, who with great severity had subdued rebellion in Connaught, began to harass the rebel army in Munster. FitzMaurice and Sir John struck camp at Smerwick and moved towards Limerick. They parted company, however, over a difference of opinion regarding the leadership of the enterprise. FitzMaurice, with a small group of supporters, hurried through Tipperary and Limerick in an attempt to outflank Malby and enter Connaught. Passing through the country of the Burkes of Castleconnell, FitzMaurice's followers removed two horses from under a plough and took some booty. Theobald Burke, the chief's son, pursued them, and in an ensuing fracas on 18 August 1579 FitzMaurice was shot dead. So ended the career of the man who, whatever his personal motivations, introduced religion as a political cause in Ireland, and as a means to consolidate resistance to the English Crown. Despite developments on the continent, however, the religious question in Ireland was yet an unsteady peg on which to hang the banner of revolution. The Gaelic annalists were fulsome in their praise of FitzMaurice. 'His death', they recorded, 'was the beginning of the decay of the honourable house of Desmond, out of which never issued so brave a man in all perfection.'[44] His former adversary, Sir John Perrot, acknowledged him as a 'man very valiant politicke and learned as any Rebyll hath byn of that Nation for any yers'.[45] But to Eleanor, FitzMaurice had been the monster of her nightmares, the one who sought, deliberately or otherwise, to dispossess her husband and her family and embroil them in a cataclysm that, once started, could end only in victory or abject defeat.

Sir John of Desmond assumed the vacant command of the insurgent forces in Munster. Meanwhile Sir Nicholas Malby proceeded to snap at the Earl of Desmond's heels, bombarding Lord Justice Drury and the Council in Dublin with accusations of his disloyalty. Drury determined to investigate the allegations against the earl. Accompanied by the Earl of Kildare, Eleanor's brother, the Baron of Dunboyne, and the Baron of Upper Ossory, Drury marched south, established camp near Kilmallock, and prepared to dislodge the rebel garrison at Smerwick, thereby raising the old contentious issue—the invasion of Desmond's palatinate. The pressures on the earl were now immense. Eleanor's brother counselled him to repair to the Lord Justice. At the same time Dr Sanders, Sir John and his clansmen pressed him to obstruct Drury's passage through his palatinate. His own pride cried out that he, the great Earl of Desmond, should not be ordered hither and thither by subordinates and Crown servants. The cloud of melancholy and despondency returned as the earl shut himself up in his fortress at Askeaton and brooded over the insidious trap in which he found himself.

Drury sent a delegation, led by the Baron of Upper Ossory, to negotiate. At first Garrett refused to meet them, but Eleanor prevailed on him to at least hear the baron out. The delegation was eventually ushered into the presence of the earl, who sat at a table with Eleanor by his side. The baron duly delivered Drury's orders to the earl to attend his camp at Kilmallock. At this intended slight Garrett's frail composure snapped, and with a sudden violent movement he upended the table and

*fell into an extreme rage protesting that he wolde never come to
William Drury nor where Malby was a counsellor, and that he wolde
presently be master of the fielde, that if the Justice came to Kerry he
should have nothinge there and rather than Englishmen should come
to Dingle he woulde rase the towne.*[46]

All the pressures that beset him seemed to erupt in a verbal outburst.
The palatine rights of his Kerry kingdom were the only vestiges of
prestige and self-respect that remained. If his sovereignty there was
violated by Drury, he would be left with nothing. It was unfortunate
that FitzMaurice and his army had chosen it as the launching-pad for
their crusade against Elizabeth. He alone, not the Lord Justice, would
see to the demolition of the fortifications at Smerwick and to the
dispersal and expulsion of the rebel army. His fury beyond all control,
Eleanor shivered as she listened to her husband rage on against the
Queen—

*the red calioghe [hag] let hir doe what she like, affirminge that she and
hir frendes had undone him and turning to a marchant of Lymericke
there present he said he wold leave Lymericke and Corke as naked as
his nayle.*[47]

The English emissaries present were hurriedly told by the earl's
retainers that the hag in question was the earl's wife, and this version
was duly reported to the Privy Council in London. But the Irish lords
present knew well the derisive nickname applied in Ireland to the red-
haired Queen of England.

The Baron of Upper Ossory and his fellow-delegates departed to
convey Desmond's reply to Drury as Eleanor and her brother tried to
placate the overwrought earl. Eleanor sent his secretary, Morris Sheehan,
to excuse his conduct. Drury agreed to temporise with the earl and
promised him safe conduct to his camp near Kilmallock. Garrett
eventually agreed to meet the Lord Justice, who received him
courteously and asked his opinion on how best the rebels might be
resisted. Garrett suggested that pledges should be first given by his
tributary lords, the Earl of Clancar and lords Barry and Roche, and
other lords in Munster over whom he claimed jurisdiction. By this
means, Garrett hoped the lords would be less likely to join with the
rebels and thereby undermine his position. But they protested

vigorously to the Lord Justice that, in order to prohibit the earl from joining forces with his brother, he should also be required to 'put in his onely sonne pledge for maintayning the warre against his bretherne'.[48] Smarting at this further insult from his dependent lords, Garrett went 'into a newe passion and started from the boarde'.[49] Drury, however, agreed with the lords' proposal and refused the earl permission to depart until his son should be delivered to him as hostage.

In trepidation Eleanor awaited Garrett's return at Askeaton. A party of his followers rode up to the castle and demanded that she deliver her son to be taken as a hostage to the Lord Justice. Eleanor refused. She could trust no one, least of all Garrett's supposedly loyal followers, most of whom had, in any case, defected to his brother Sir John. She decided to put her case to the Lord Justice in person. With a small guard she set out for the English camp, having first hidden her son in the lake fortress of Lough Gur. Drury received her graciously and sympathised with her anxiety over her son. He agreed to her proposal that in her own time she would place the child in the custody of the Mayor of Limerick. Thus having gained some precious time, Eleanor returned to the safety of Lough Gur.

Under the leadership of Sir John the crusade had meanwhile lost much of its original appeal and impetus. Sir John lacked the prestige and authority to extend the rebellion throughout the province or draw support from the local lords and chieftains. Dr Sanders knew there was only one person who could effectively revitalise interest in the crusade and to whose leadership the chieftains and clansmen would respond. But the Earl of Desmond still held aloof, reluctant to be drawn. He had little of FitzMaurice's crusading zeal. His own intransigence and the arrogant antics of the Crown officials in Munster were far more likely reasons for him to join the crusade. If the religious crusade could be used to stimulate 'the rankling sense of injustice dating from the Carew episode earlier . . . and the consequent sense of insecurity of tenure on the part of the great landholders',[50] then Garrett's present grievances against the Crown could be easily exploited for the cause of the Counter-Reformation. As the English administration seemed determined to humiliate and strip him of every remaining vestige of his traditional power so they, either intentionally or accidentally, pushed the earl towards Sanders.

The Jesuit besieged Garrett with letters and messengers to assure him that his secular status could be guaranteed if he assumed leadership of the spiritual crusade. Messengers arrived from Ulster and Connaught where the Mayo clans, under the leadership of Richard-in-Iron Bourke, the husband of his former captive, Grace O'Malley, awaited his call to arms. Spies brought news that Drury, who had again fallen ill in Dublin, had been unable to secure much-needed supplies and forces from the Crown. Sanders renewed his promise of additional aid from the Pope and the King of Spain and tempted Garrett with promises of the glory and prestige the Crown sought to deny him. Eventually Garrett made a secret rendezvous with Sanders and Sir John. Gradually he became more withdrawn from Eleanor, who saw her influence over him steadily eroded by the zealous exhortations of Sanders. She tried in vain to reason with him but, against the machinations of Dr Sanders, she was no match and, as was reported to the government, 'the corruption of the Erles disposition is such as manie tymes he nether regardeth frend nor wive'.[51] But for the present he maintained his show of loyalty and accompanied Drury on an expedition against the rebels, now led by his two brothers.

As her influence over Garrett lessened, Eleanor's fears for the safety of her son increased. She had established a good relationship with Drury; like Sidney, he was one of the few English administrators who had come to recognise her dilemma. For different reasons they both worked for the same objective, to maintain Garrett in some degree of loyalty to the Queen. Both had begun to falter under the pressure of their respective missions. Drury was in poor health and had been consistently denied adequate provisions to perform his duties in Ireland. And now news of Drury's imminent departure for England reached Eleanor—her last contact with the more reasonable elements in the English administration was about to be severed. The safety of her son weighed heavily on her mind. She feared that Sir John or Dr Sanders might kidnap James to ensure her husband's support. Garrett also feared for the safety of his son at the hands of his brothers, whom he later accused of attempting 'to imbrue their cruel hands with the blood of my wief and sonne, whom Sir John mortalie hated'.[52] Perhaps also with an instinctive sense of the turmoil that was about to engulf them, Eleanor decided that her child could only evade the taint of rebellion, if in the custody of the Crown.

Drury was the one person she could trust to ensure the boy's safety. She first journeyed with her son to Limerick city, where it was reported that

The Countesse of Desmond (with the Erles consent as shee saith) brought hir only son the Lord Garrett [sic, for James] to Limerick and delivered him as hir assurance (for so shee termed it) to the Attorney and Recorder, from whome he was sent for to the campe within two daies after, because it was doubted that the Erles faction in Limericke should convey him awaie and that the Lord Justice has also vehement presumption that he should have been by the Erles followers (especiallie the gallowglas) sent as a pledge into Spaine for perfourmance of such promises that have been made by them to Doctor Saunders.[53]

Drury was about to set out on his final journey towards Waterford. It was a moving encounter between the dying, war-hardened soldier and the troubled countess, torn in two by her desire to protect her son and yet having to place him in the care of the very institution that sought to destroy his father. In their past dealings Drury had shown her a crusty courtesy and had come to respect her political and diplomatic abilities. Now he recognised her fear as a mother for her child's safety. It was a heart-rending scene as the tall woman bent down to embrace her small son and hold him close, aware that it might be for the last time. The pale, timid child, who since his birth in captivity had continued to be a captive of the tragic fates that buffeted his family, clung tightly to his mother, fearful of once again being condemned to a dark, menacing life behind locked doors, among strange, unfriendly faces. Drury reassured Eleanor, but as she looked into the haggard face, perhaps seeing death in his tired eyes, she felt a momentary stab of fear and begged him to do all he could to ensure that her child might be treated gently. With a breaking heart she lifted her son onto the saddle beside one of Drury's officers and watched the cavalcade slowly disappear down the narrow, rutted track.

Following the departure of Drury, Sir Nicholas Malby was appointed temporary governor of Munster. He instituted the final campaign of humiliation which was eventually to push the vacillating Earl of Desmond over the brink. A flurry of correspondence between the two sides preceded the action. Malby curtly summoned the earl to appear before him at Limerick, and sent him a proclamation against the rebels which he ordered Garrett to have posted throughout his lordship. Garrett haughtily replied to the effect that his service 'against the rebells would be more available than his presence . . . in

Limerick'.[54] Malby promised the earl 'much honour and favour . . . if he will get that papistical arrogant traitor Sanders to be arrested'.[55] Garrett reciprocated by giving Malby some useless information on the actions of his brothers. Malby, without recourse to the Crown or to the Council in Dublin, set out on his own initiative, ostensibly to flush out the rebels but, in effect, to plunder the earl's lands. On 3 October 1579 he was confronted near Monasternenagh by the forces of Sir John of Desmond in full battle array. A fiercely-fought pitched battle ensued until eventually the English pikemen penetrated the rows of galloglass and kern and the rebel army slowly gave ground. Sir John and Dr Sanders escaped into the woods along the Maigue river.

When news of the defeat reached Askeaton, the earl hurriedly forwarded his congratulations to Malby. But Malby was unimpressed. He was convinced that the earl was involved with the rebels: 'He is the onlie man that did seeke to cutt my throate,' he informed the English Privy Council, 'the onelie arch traytor of Mounster, his two brethren are but ministers to serve his vile disposition.'[56] Malby's accusations were, as yet, based on conjecture; tangible proof of the earl's active implication in the rebellion was more difficult to establish. But conjecture and rumour were sufficient for Malby, who despised all that Desmond represented.

Eleanor's abilities as mediator were powerless against such intense and irrational behaviour. There was no one in the Council in Dublin with whom she could intercede in order to call off Malby. Her husband had temporised with the administration for months, but the Crown had also violated agreements made with him. Fired by puritanical religious zeal, Malby now prepared to exact a terrible retribution. He burned and pillaged his way through the earl's estates up to the gates of Askeaton castle and pitched camp in the abbey across the river. From a window of the castle Eleanor watched the final act of violation and degradation perpetrated against her husband. The proud earl notified the English Privy Council of Malby's action:

The saide Sir Nicholas encamped within the Abbie of Asketin and ther most malitiosslie defaced the oulde monuments of my ancestors, fired both the abbie, the whole tower and all the countrie therabouts and ceased not to shote at my men within Askyten castle.[57]

The thoughts of the earl as he helplessly watched the very heart of his Desmond heritage being ravaged, the bones of his ancestors and of his first wife so dishonoured, have not been recorded. The once all-powerful Earl of Desmond had been rendered powerless to prevent the outrage committed by a lowly captain of the Crown within sight of his own castle. In his despair he even appealed to his bitter rival, the Earl of Ormond:

> *Your mother's grave hath beane most spitefully used by Sir Nicholas Malbye. It hath beene broken so that nowe there remaineth no monument thereof. I bescheche your consideraccion of my cause and howe I have ben persecuted by a Captain that hath no authoritie to do the like.* [58]

But whatever vague sympathy, or fear, Black Tom might have felt for his neighbour, the old wounds of their personal animosity were still too raw for him to intervene.

The final push came from Drury's successor, Sir William Pelham, who was appointed Lord Justice of Ireland in October 1579. One of his first acts was to appoint the Earl of Ormond military governor of Munster. He also issued a patent to Ormond, 'who having the keeping and custodie of the young Lord Girald [*sic*] sonne and heir to the erle of Desmond was by a warrant willed to deliver him to Captain Dachworth and he to bring or conveie him to the Castell of Dublin'. [59] During his journey in Drury's custody to Waterford the child had fallen ill. As Drury's own condition had worsened, it was decided to leave the Earl of Desmond's son in the care of the Earl of Ormond. Drury subsequently died at Waterford on 3 October without being able to discharge the undertaking he had given to Eleanor. Pelham was not only determined that Desmond's son would be placed well beyond the grasp of all factions in Munster, but was also planning to use the boy as a valuable bargaining counter against his father.

Rumours flew like sparrows from tree to tree across Munster that the Earl of Desmond had finally declared for the rebels. Pelham neglected to check the accuracy of the rumours, but summoned the earl to his presence. Secure in his stronghold at Askeaton, the earl declined to put his head into the lion's mouth. Pelham threatened to execute his son. There was no time to appeal to the Queen. If Garrett went to Pelham, there was every likelihood that he would promptly be imprisoned. It was decided that Eleanor should again intercede on his behalf. 'I have sent my wife to declare the causes of my present stay', the earl informed Pelham, 'and how my country has been burnt and spoiled, my castles taken and myself misused.'[60] Pelham received Eleanor coldly. He would not be hoodwinked by her or by her husband like previous Crown officials. Her husband, he was convinced, intended to rebel. Eleanor reminded him that they had voluntarily given up their only son as proof of the earl's good intent. She graphically described the outrages perpetrated by Malby on her husband's property and the provocative sacking of Askeaton abbey. Surely, as a subject of the Crown, her husband had the right to the Crown's protection.

Pelham momentarily drew back and agreed to give the earl one final chance. With perhaps spiteful intent he chose the Earl of Ormond to act as mediator and, through him, presented Eleanor with a set of unacceptable demands: that Desmond submit to the Lord Justice; that he deliver Dr Sanders into Crown custody; that he surrender Askeaton and Carraigafoyle castles to the Crown; and that he join in the campaign against his brothers and serve under the command of the Earl of Ormond. Pelham well realised that the Earl of Desmond had neither the power nor the will to comply with such demands.

Eleanor realised the futility of her mission and returned to Askeaton to be with her husband. Pelham moved his forces close to Rathkeale. He sent Ormond to negotiate with Desmond. But the latter's presence merely served to antagonise Garrett further. 'I will remain as true-hearted a subject to Her Majesty as any one that seeketh to undo me,' he informed Pelham and demanded 'that my servant may go with my complaints to Her Majesty and the Council, whose judgement I am contented to abide'.[61] But Pelham and his war-dogs now smelled blood and, knowing the Queen's penchant for pardons instead of costly war, reacted quickly. Without the permission or knowledge of the Queen or the Privy Council, Pelham had the Earl of Desmond 'with sound of Trumpett'[62] proclaimed a traitor, thereby forcing him, as one commentator noted, 'for his owne safety to run that course against his will',[63] into the arms of Dr Sanders. Significantly, the proclamation was signed by Pelham, the Earl of Ormond, his brothers and Eleanor's brother, the Baron of Dunboyne. Some of the lords of the Pale, Gormanston, Baltinglass and Delvin, refused to be signatories. On 2 November 1579 the proclamation was simultaneously announced in Dublin, Waterford, Cork and Limerick and in other towns and settlements throughout the country.

As news of the proclamation reached Askeaton, its significance momentarily numbed Garrett and Eleanor. Thoughts of confiscation, exile and execution flashed through their minds. But in a desperate bid to avert the disaster, Eleanor took to her horse, and, as was reported, 'within one houre after this proclamation, the Countess of Desmond came to the campe but the campe was before dislodged'. [64] Pelham had already let loose his dogs of war and, almost gleefully, he reported the outcome to the Queen. 'Desmond has been proclaimed a traitor,' he wrote. 'Ormond has already drawn blood and kindled the fire in the midst of Desmond's country . . . I have left the prosecution of the war to him.' [65]

Soon the traditional adherents of the House of Desmond, client lords and chieftains, retainers, galloglass and swordsmen, combined with the promoters of the Counter-Reformation, descended on Askeaton to claim their leader. Despite her efforts Eleanor watched her worst nightmare unfold as her husband was borne headlong into rebellion. Both realised the outcome should the rebellion prove unsuccessful: execution and dispossession. There were to be no farewells between Eleanor and her husband. For the following four desperate years, wherever the Earl of Desmond hid or lay down to rest, in woodland, marsh or mountain, his wife was not far from his side.

Under a sombre sky, slowly and painfully, the fourteenth Earl of Desmond limped from his castle into the November evening. A hundred hands lifted the crippled earl onto his horse. The papal banner was unfurled over his head. The centuries-old Desmond war-cry, '*Shanid Abú*' gave way to '*Papa abú*' as the Geraldine leader rode out from Askeaton castle, the reluctant champion of a crusade he neither believed in nor understood.

Chapter 7
Rebellion

The wrathful skies
Gallow the very wanderers of the dark,
And make them keep their caves: since I was man
Such sheets of fire, such bursts of horrid thunder,
Such groans of roaring wind and rain, I never
Remember to have heard: man's nature cannot
*   carry*
The affliction nor the fear

KING LEAR, III, ii

As news of the Desmond rebellion spread across the country, initially it seemed likely to provoke a wider conspiracy among the Gaelic and gaelicised lords. In Connaught the clans of Mayo and Galway rose in support. Scots mercenaries poured into Ulster. In Leinster James Eustace, Viscount Baltinglass, a determined Catholic, conspired with the Wicklow chieftain, Fiach MacHugh O'Byrne. There was unrest in Limerick city, and the mayor was taken prisoner by insurgents. Sir John of Desmond plundered Kerry and burned the town of Tralee. The rebels attacked the lands of a grantee, John Rowly, and left him nailed to his castle door as a warning to others. Dr Sanders exhorted the leaders and promised more assistance from the Pope and the Most Catholic King of Spain.

But solitary in the Escorial palace the black-garbed lay leader of the Counter-Reformation, God's lieutenant on earth, Philip II, gloomily contemplated a batch of despatches from his spies in England. They were proof of the distinct lack of progress being made against his heretic sister-in-law and her godless kingdom. But the blame could be squarely laid at Philip's own door whose predilection for deliberation and detail made progress virtually impossible. Every despatch was scrutinised, every emissary personally interviewed, every detail gleaned was methodically stored in the dispassionate mind of the anointed head of the greatest and most Catholic leader in the world. Now that the House of Guise in France had become part of his orbit, and that his control over the Netherlands was restored, there was time to contemplate how best to resume the crusade against Elizabeth and to fulfil his 'gossamer vision of a Europe purged of heresy and united in the ample bosom of mother church'.[1] Had not Elizabeth blatantly aided and comforted his rebellious and heretical Dutch subjects? Now with news of a crusade in Ireland against her, led by an Irish leader who sought his help, the King pondered over the direction his religious zeal and political revenge might take against his sister monarch.

While the banner of rebellion, emblazoned with the cross of the crusade, had been placed in the hands of her reluctant husband, Eleanor was yet hopeful that Garrett's slide into ruin could be reversed. She had not been included in the Lord Justice's proclamation and was therefore free to negotiate with the authorities and put her diplomatic skill to use on her husband's behalf. But she had no trustworthy contact in the Dublin Council. Her only remaining recourse was to gain direct access to the Queen and her Council in England. Elizabeth must be made aware of the conduct of her officers in Ireland who, for reasons other than duty, had alienated her husband from the Crown. Eleanor well knew that many servants of the Crown, both in Ireland and in England, had greedy eyes fastened on the fertile acres of her husband's estates. A push towards rebellion rather than a pull towards loyalty presented the prospect of rich reward for such energetic and ambitious officials. Her letters to England were liable to be intercepted by the self-same officials, determined they did not reach their destination. But there was another, albeit desperate, way. On 4 November 1579, two days after her husband was publicly proclaimed a traitor, a despatch, signed by Pelham, Ormond and Malby to the Queen's secretary, Sir Francis Walsingham, made the startling announcement: 'To be a solicitor that in respect since the proclamation, the Countess of Desmond hath left her husband that she may enjoy her jointure.'[2]

Even as Garrett was hustled away into rebellion and as the great wood of Clonlish swallowed him and his followers, Eleanor put her plan into action. She obtained a meeting with her kinsman the Earl of Ormond, to whom she revealed her intention to divorce Garrett, ostensibly because of the shame and ruin his actions had brought on her and on his family. She asked that her marriage portion or dowry be returned to her in order that she might sustain herself. Initially her request was taken at face value. It was on record that the Countess of Desmond had long endeavoured to keep the earl loyal to the Crown, and she had letters from a grateful Queen to prove it. Divorce was common among the Gaelic and gaelicised aristocracy. Ormond himself had been recently divorced. Aware of Eleanor's long devotion to Garrett, Ormond became suspicious of her sudden desire to obtain her jointure. Her real reason, he suspected, was to obtain funding to enable her to take her husband's case to London. And Eleanor was forced to admit her real intent. 'Now that it hath pleased God to wrap my husband into these late troubles,' she wrote to Ormond, 'I wish to repair to Her Majesty's preserve and desire you to send me a passport. I mind to take shipping at Cork or Kinsale.'[3]

As Ormond deliberated over her request, desperate to attain her goal before Garrett, by some precipitate action, could put himself totally beyond all help, Eleanor had some cattle rounded up and asked Ormond 'to make sale of such kine as I sent to your country to bear my charges in England for that both my husband and I have incurred certain debts in England, it is needful that you send me a protection to pass with my stuff and goods until I shall come to Her Majesty without any molestation'.[4] Ormond informed her that he had not the authority to issue her with a pass, but that he would forward her request to Lord Justice Pelham. However, he took care to forewarn Pelham: 'I have had a letter from my Lady of Desmond. It is thought, I dare say, by those that wrote it to be cunningly penned and devised but the intent is easy to understand.'[5] Pelham, in any event, had no intention of allowing the Countess of Desmond access to the Queen. Elizabeth had sounded the first notes of disquiet about the peremptory way he had proclaimed the Earl of Desmond. Desmond's wife pleading her husband's case, with the support of the Cecil faction at Court, might well mean dismissal or even imprisonment. Pelham wrote his reply to the Earl of Ormond: 'I have considered of my Lady of Desmond's letter. Pray you stay your hand from these her vain petitions till our meeting and answer her letter with silence.'[6]

But Eleanor refused to accept silence as an answer. She demanded and received an audience with the Lord Justice. She asked him to suspend the proclamation against her husband until she could further negotiate with him. Pelham refused but granted her permission to go to her husband and promised her 'that grace would be showid to her husband if he would consent to ye delivery of his brother and Doctor Saunders'.[7] Pelham warned her that she must return 'within certaine daies to live in the Pale or with the barron of Dunboine her brother'.[8] Eleanor realised that Pelham would never permit her access to the Queen or retract the proclamation, short of Garrett's unconditional surrender. Gathering her few belongings, she fled to join her husband, and failed to return within the allotted time. To damage whatever credibility she might have with the Queen, Pelham informed Sir Francis Walsingham 'that there is not any emonge the conspiratours that more encouradgeth the disloyaltie of them than she. And therefore I believe that her messadge is but collorable . . . to gaine intellegence for purpose.'[9]

By now, however, the Queen's disquiet over the proclamation of the Earl of Desmond and the continuation of the war in Munster had changed to anger. She ordered Pelham to explain his actions. Pelham protested that Desmond had been covertly involved in rebellious conspiracy since the time of James FitzMaurice. To sting her princely pride, Pelham further informed the Queen that 'in all his skirmishes and outrages since the proclamation, Desmond crieth *Papa aboo*, which is the Pope above even above you and your imperial crown'.[10] But Elizabeth was not satisfied. Rebellions cost money, while pardons, particularly on conditions favourable to the Crown, cost nothing. She had learned of the attempts of the Countess of Desmond to gain her royal ear and also of Pelham's efforts to prevent her. Elizabeth demanded further explanation from her Lord Justice.

But before Pelham could compose an excuse, the Earl of Desmond, as Eleanor feared, put himself beyond redemption by an inexplicable attack on the town of Youghal. The town was in a state of total unpreparedness for the assault. In the middle of a thunderstorm the rebel army, with Garrett at its head, entered through a breach in the walls. Then, amid scenes of wanton carnage and cruelty, Youghal was sacked. Houses were set on fire, citizens put to the sword, women ravished, while the Desmond hordes, with wild exultant cries, ransacked buildings and stuffed their clothes with gold and silver from the town's coffers. It was reported that the Earl of Desmond, Sir John and the Seneschal of Imokilly tore down the emblem of the Queen's coat of arms from the courthouse and hacked it asunder with their daggers. For four days and nights the rebels looted the town. Laden with booty and prisoners, the Earl of Desmond and his 'crusaders' marched away, leaving Youghal in flames.

Eleanor's reaction to the sack of Youghal was one of disbelief that her husband would allow his own town to be destroyed. But religious fanaticism had by then fuelled the flames of rebellion. Dr Sanders ardently preached the message of the Counter-Reformation and exhorted the earl that his secular struggle against the Queen in Ireland was part of a glorious international crusade against heresy. The Pope and King Philip would soon come to his assistance, Sanders assured him. The Earl of Desmond listened and felt uplifted, no longer hamstrung by his physical deformities or political deficiencies. Religion elevated him to his true status as the great rebel Geraldine fighting the just cause of faith and fatherland. His letters to the Gaelic chieftains and to the Catholic lords of the Pale reflected his belated conversion to the crusading cause. Writing to Viscount Baltinglass, Garrett now maintained:

It is so that I and my brothers are entered into the Defence of the Catholick Faith, the overthrow of our Country by Englishmen which had overthrown the Holy Church and go about to over-run our country and make it their own and make us their Bond men. [11]

Messengers and letters of support flowed into his base at Newcastle from Turlough Luineach O'Neill, Fiach MacHugh O'Byrne, Baltinglass, and lords and chieftains from every province. They made extravagant promises of Scottish galloglass and Gaelic kern. But promises were easily made, and the Earl of Desmond had yet to prove how much support his cause commanded abroad before the effusive pledges of his erstwhile allies in Ireland could be translated into practical assistance.

As the mournful winter winds howled around Newcastle, Eleanor realised that she was powerless to stem the fast-flowing tide which bore her husband and his house steadily towards their doom. She looked across the dimly-lit room to where Garrett, seated with Dr Sanders, dictated to a secretary the now interwoven words of religion and rebellion. She observed the almost skeletal features of her husband, his sickly pallor and hunched shoulders. The winter campaign had taken further toll on his health. She thought of her son, alone in his dark cell in Dublin Castle. The servants she had sent to care for him had been dismissed, and Pelham had ordered 'that the constable of the Castle shall provide for his diett and wantes and that his nurse shall onely attend him there'. [12] Yet she was satisfied that even Dublin Castle was a safer haven for her child than his native Munster over which the storm was about to break.

For the hunt was on—one of the greatest manhunts in history—for the most feeble prey that ever went to ground. While the Queen dithered to finance an all-out offensive against the Earl of Desmond, the Earl of Ormond took matters into his own hands. Passing between Askeaton and Newcastle, he burned and looted right up to the foothills of Slieve Logher, on a mission of vengeance on his ancient enemy until, hampered by appalling weather conditions and lack of supplies, he reluctantly returned to Ormond, hopeful that in the new year Elizabeth might loosen the purse-strings and he could continue the campaign against his step-father.

Towards the end of January 1580 two well-appointed ships arrived off Dingle. They carried letters for the Earl of Desmond and his brothers from the King of Spain. Garrett hurried to Castlemaine to confer with the king's messengers. Both the success of the rebellion and his own fate depended on help from Philip. He told the messengers to urge their master to send the long-awaited assistance without delay. He promised support from all the lords of the country and confidently declared that he would have a substantial army at his disposal. And during the early months of 1580 many hitherto undecided lords wavered to the cause. The Earl of Clancar was either compelled by Garrett or exhorted by Dr Sanders to join the rebellion. It was even rumoured that Edmund Butler, the Earl of Ormond's brother, who was married to Garrett's sister, had 'stood a little wavering and was to be doubted', [13] before being pulled back into line by his brother, Black Tom. But since the sack of Youghal, militarily Garrett had accomplished little. Ever fearful for his safety, like a shadow he flitted from Newcastle to Aherlow, to Adare, to Carraigafoyle on the Shannon, until he finally came to rest at the more secure fortress of Castlemaine. His landless adherents, while they awaited action against the enemy, looted and ravaged the countryside. The peasants, as ever, bore the brunt of their excesses and sought protection in the woods and mountain foothills. Eleanor also momentarily disappeared from view. There was no one with whom she could negotiate, and little reason for her to do so. She spent the winter months with her daughters between the fortresses of Castlemaine and Castleisland deep in her husband's territory.

In the spring of 1580 the war recommenced with a vengeance. It was reported that King Philip had troops and ships massed at Spanish ports, ready to sail to Ireland to support the rebel Earl of Desmond. Elizabeth's nightmare, that Spain would use Ireland as a backdoor into England, seemed likely to become a reality. The English court factions closed ranks and united to repel the foreign threat. The hitherto divided coteries led by Cecil and Walsingham were now of one voice. They urged the Queen to back Ormond and Pelham and to provide the means for an all-out offensive against the Earl of Desmond. Cecil, Ormond's one-time adversary, admitted:

> So must I merely say with others, Butler aboo against all that cry as I hear in a new language Papa aboo. God send you your heart's desire, which I know is agreeable to mine, to banish or vanquish those cankered Desmonds and to plant again the Queen's Majesty's honour and reputation.[14]

And finally, with the approval of the Privy Council and a reluctant nod from Elizabeth, the armed might of the Crown was unleashed on the Earl of Desmond. In March 1580 Ormond joined forces with Pelham at Rathkeale, and together they commenced a dreadful war of retribution. They divided their forces: Ormond moved towards the Shannon; Pelham kept inland, towards Newcastle. It was said that they each kept track of the other's progress by the billowing clouds of smoke they left in their wake as they burned and pillaged their way west.

The country people fled for their lives before the new fury. But to Pelham every peasant or tenant who resided within the Desmond lordship was deemed a rebel and the English scouting parties indiscriminately sought out and slew panic-stricken men, women and children. His despatches to the Privy Council unashamedly detailed acts of remorseless barbarity and deprivation committed against a largely defenceless peasantry. Exultantly describing a typically punitive raid, he wrote:

The people and cattle flying before us in the mountains were followed by some horsemen and light footmen. There were slain that day by the fury of the soldiers above 400 people found in the woods; and wheresoever any house or corn was found, it was consumed by fire. [15]

The unfortunate people who were subjected to such treatment were shamelessly abandoned by their overlord and left to stand defenceless before his enemies. The Desmonds, Dr Sanders and their swordsmen were far removed, safe in their remote castle outposts, out of range of the pitiful cries of the abandoned peasantry. In vain the people waited for the banner of their hereditary protector to appear and save them from their doom. But the great Geraldine lord did not come to their rescue, and Pelham's soldiers and Ormond's galloglass found nothing to obstruct them. Steel fell on unprotected bone and hacked its way over the mutilated bodies of its unresisting victims. From the branches of the Munster oaks the putrefying corpses hung in gruesome proof of Pelham's progress. The once lush Desmond pasturelands were reduced to a blackened heath as Ormond sated his revenge on his old enemy and Pelham, one of the new breed of Puritan military commanders, merely did his job.

But Munster was not ravaged just by the armies of the Crown. As the Earl of Desmond and his army withdrew into remoter areas, they too burned and looted everything in their path. Every fortress between Castleisland and Tralee was demolished to prevent its use by the enemy. Cattle were seized and driven into secret valleys and hidden recesses in the mountains to provide sustenance for the fighting men. The peasantry were left to fend for themselves as best they could, and any who remonstrated were summarily dealt with.

Some of the stronger Desmond castles, such as Askeaton, Newcastle, Adare, Glin and Carraigafoyle, directly in Pelham's path, remained intact, secure in the impregnability of their thick stone walls. Carraigafoyle on the Shannon was considered one of the most formidable and its destruction was to open a new chapter in military warfare in Ireland. The castle commanded a strategic position at the entrance to the Shannon estuary. It was garrisoned for the Earl of Desmond by a mixture of papal and Irish troops under the command of captain Julian. In view of the aid expected from Spain, defence of the castle took on a new urgency. Unable to risk the journey himself, Garrett sent Eleanor to convey plans for the defence of the castle to the garrison. With a small escort she set out on the hazardous journey. Although not technically a wanted rebel like her husband, nonetheless she could not afford to fall into the hands of the Crown forces. Successfully eluding English scouting parties from the armies of Pelham and Ormond she delivered her husband's instructions. Great earthworks were immediately constructed on the estuary side of the castle to provide additional protection for the ships expected daily from Spain. On the landward side two separate ditches with a wall and a further earthwork were erected. Every chink and cranny in the outer walls of the castle was filled with masonry to prevent potential besiegers obtaining a foothold. In Garrett's estimation, and indeed by the military convention of the day, Carraigafoyle was thus rendered impregnable.

When English ships, under the command of Sir William Winter, however, anchored off the castle with a cargo of siege guns, Garrett's defensive modifications, earthworks, ditches and smooth masonry proved useless as for two days the guns pounded the defences of Carraigafoyle. On 29 March a breach was finally made in the barbican. Pelham's troops poured into the castle and spared none of the defenders. As the cannon and culverins boomed their relentless message of victory across the Kerry countryside, Pelham next prepared to move against the heart of the Desmond lordship. The siege cannon were pointed at Askeaton. But there was little need to fire even one shell. On learning about the destruction of Carraigafoyle and the fate of the defenders, Garrett's garrison at Askeaton fled for their lives and, as they departed, set fire to the magazine, which blew the greater part of the castle asunder. Pelham appointed a garrison under Sir Peter Carew and Sir Henry Wallop in the ruins of Askeaton, while Sir George Carew and Captain Hollingworth encamped in the adjacent abbey.

Reports of the destruction of Carraigafoyle and the partial destruction of Askeaton were brought to the earl, who, with Eleanor, was at Tralee. The fall of Askeaton must have been a severe blow, being not merely a place of great significance in the Desmond heritage and history, but also the home in which they had snatched a few brief years of happiness and contentment.

As Pelham's army closed in, Garrett's followers, who had so vociferously and eagerly prevailed upon him to lead the great crusade, began to desert in numbers. There was still no sign of the Spanish aid promised by Dr Sanders. With the exception of a brief, isolated uprising by Richard-in-Iron Bourke in Mayo, Connaught too had failed to rise in support of the crusade. There was a shortage of food and supplies, and Garrett's swordsmen preyed far and wide over the impoverished land. To stem the tide, Garrett was reported to have told his followers 'that yf aid from Spaine and the Pope cam not before Whitsontide he would leave them to make their composition with the Englishe as well as thei colde'. [16] Numbed by the ferocity of Pelham's tactics, few could envisage such a course of action. The English forces pressed ever closer, and the list of garrisons established by them grew. Captain Bouchier occupied Kilmallock and captain Wilks held Adare. The hunt was on for the Earl and Countess of Desmond, Dr Sanders and the earl's brothers. Each day scouting parties from the various garrisons scoured the forests, mountain foothills and the secret recesses of Aherlow for the fugitives. Even Eleanor's brother, the Baron of Dunboyne, joined in the hunt for his sister and brother-in-law.

As the net tightened, the Desmond fugitives flitted from place to place. Everything now depended on Spain. Garrett became suspicious that Dr Sanders intended to desert him, and kept a close watch on the cleric who, for better or worse, had become his one remaining hope of salvation. In his present position there seemed little possibility of reconciliation with the Crown and restoration to his title and estates. Only from a position of strength could he hope to negotiate with Elizabeth. In the large rambling fortress of Castleisland the earl and Eleanor waited. The winter had been difficult with severe frost and snow. The earl could scarcely walk. His personal physician, Maurice Lee, deserted him and sought Pelham's protection. Aqua vitae was now the only medicine with which the earl could obtain relief from the pain that racked his feeble body, and with which he could deaden his mind to the reality of his dreadful predicament.

Eleanor sent their daughters to be cared for in the few remaining friendly houses. She entrusted her children to the protection of her half-brother, Donal MacCarthy of Carbery, and her brother-in-law, Owen MacDonagh MacCarthy of Duhallow, both of whom were subsequently imprisoned by Pelham when they refused to divulge the whereabouts of their charges. Eleanor sent another daughter to the care of her sister, the Countess of Clancar. The strain, both physical and mental, had taken its toll. She had been sucked into the morass against her better judgement. Her husband had succumbed to the pressures exerted on him from both sides. She had her opportunity to desert him and chance her luck with the English authorities. But the persistence and constancy that were the hallmarks of her character were difficult to shed, even if she had wished to do so. Her influential position in the Desmond household even yet attracted the attention of the English administration. In an attempt to reduce English unease at the ruthlessness of his campaign in Munster, Pelham sought, through Eleanor's brother, to involve her in a government plot 'for ye apprehencion of John of Desmond and Saunders'[17] in return for Garrett's pardon. While there was little love lost between Eleanor and Sir John and Sanders, she had even less trust in the Lord Justice. She too had come to the conclusion that in the present situation the only solution to their dreadful dilemma was a Spanish one.

But the strain of watching and waiting had begun to affect the relationship between the fugitives at Castleisland. Sir John bitterly accused the earl of cowardice and inaction. After heated exchanges the brothers separated. Sir John led his followers on a series of wild forages, while Garrett made a short sortie into Limerick, where he was surprised by the ward out of Adare castle. In the ensuing engagement his horse was shot from under him, and it was only with considerable difficulty that his followers managed to hustle him back to the safety of Castleisland.

In June 1580 Pelham and Ormond combined once more for an offensive against the Earl of Desmond. They drove the MacCarthys and O'Callaghans, together with their cattle herds, before them and advanced along the Blackwater on a long, energy-sapping trek into the palatinate of Kerry. News of their progress reached Eleanor and Garrett belatedly. With Pelham at their heels, there was little time for an orderly withdrawal from Castleisland, and, as Pelham reported, 'the erle of Desmond being ther with his ladie was forced to forsake his horse and betwixt some of his gallowglass to take to the bogg.'[18] Eleanor had to abandon several items of clothing from her personal wardrobe, which, together with some vestments belonging to Dr Sanders, were derisively torn to shreds by Pelham's soldiers. Aided by the strong arms of the galloglass, the Earl and Countess of Desmond fled into the night. Splashing and stumbling through the bogs and marshes around Castleisland, the cries of their hunters in their ears, they ran for their lives. Garrett fell down exhausted, unable to continue, and had to be carried on the shoulders of his galloglass to the safety of the mountains. Here the fugitives took a brief respite, then separated.

With a small escort, Eleanor set out for Newcastle to lead the pursuers away from her husband. On her journey she encountered the admiral of the English fleet, Sir William Winter. Since the fall of Carraigafoyle, Winter's fleet remained anchored in the Shannon estuary but, following a rendezvous with Pelham, he had taken the fleet around to Dingle Bay. On his return he encountered the Countess of Desmond. Eleanor informed him of the sequence of developments that had forced her husband into rebellion. She begged him to take a letter to the English Privy Council so that she might negotiate directly with them for her husband's pardon and for a cessation of the war in Munster. The pitiful sight of the dishevelled countess touched Winter, who agreed to forward her letter to England.

Eleanor sat down to compose the most honest and poignant letter of the entire tragic saga. It is at once a powerful and compelling document. It demonstrates her knowledge and understanding of the minds of those she sought to change. She gives an objective analysis of her husband's shortcomings, but also her conviction that he had been pushed by Pelham and Malby into a rebellion he did not want. 'My husband and his countrie have bene bled by persons who are in authoritie here,' she wrote, and reminded the Council of her husband's loyal conduct until the death of Sir William Drury. Then, Eleanor contends, Sir Nicholas Malby was allowed free rein in Munster and 'the place of Justice was void. Malbie', she asserts, 'marched therewith into my husbands countrie, murdered certaine of his men, toke and spoyled certaine of his castles, burned within houses old men and children and within churches bourned certaine monuments of his ancestors and, a thinge which', as Eleanor asserts, 'greeved him most, openlie called him a traytor within the cytye of Lymerick.'

Eleanor grasps the opportunity to explain how both she and her husband had been denied access to the Privy Council by English officials in Ireland. Despite her husband's promise to disassociate himself from those whom she describes as 'his unnaturall biethern and the traitor Saunders', and the delivery of their son to the Crown, her husband had been left with no option but to join in the rebellion or be overrun. For her own part, she declares that after her husband had been publicly proclaimed a traitor, she had indicated to Pelham and Ormond that she wished to leave Munster and go to the Queen, but this had been denied her. She puts on record her suspicions concerning the evil intent of her brother-in-law, Sir John of Desmond, who, she claims,

> *since the tyme I was married and especiallie settens yt shall be please God to send my husband a sonne . . . hathe allwaies enveyied the prosperitie of my husband and by all meanes sought both in Englande and here to throwe him into some action, wherebie he might incure her Maties indignaction hopinge thereby (as nowe he doth manifest havinge shott at the marke which longe he desired) to come by the Erledome as with hope he hathe ben alwaies prevented by my meanes and the actions of those that loved my husband.*[19]

In her letter Eleanor fearlessly apportioned the blame for her husband's rebellion, as she adjudged it, on both sides: on the provocative actions of Pelham and Malby on the one hand, and on the greed and jealousy of her husband's brothers on the other, while in between lay the devious aspirations and plots of Ormond, Sanders and the rest. Winter accepted her missive for the Privy Council and promised, when the opportunity arose, he would have it delivered. Eleanor later rejoined her husband, determined to keep him alive until either the hoped-for Spanish aid arrived or her letter produced a pardon from Elizabeth.

Meanwhile the hunt continued unabated. There was to be no respite for the rebel Irish earl and his adherents. From the sod cabins of the lowliest kern to cold mountain caves, to the dens of wild animals, the Earl and Countess of Desmond crept stealthily. With a handful of faithful attendants, like 'deere they laie upon their keepings and so fearfull they were, that they would not tarrie in anie one place anie long time but where they did dress their meat, then they would remove and eat it in another place to lie'.[20] They ranged over the more mountainous and marshy parts of Munster. At times her husband had to be carried on a pallet while, ever watchful, Eleanor rode at the head of the band, ready to sound the alarm at the first sight of danger. She endured many narrow escapes from pursuing English scouting parties, on the watch for her in the hope that by finding her they might also discover the earl's whereabouts. 'We had the Countess of Desmond in chase two myles', captain Bouchier of the Kilmallock garrison reported, 'and myssinge her selfe took a great prey of three hundred kyne from her.'[21] It became too risky to travel by day. Too many eyes, both native and foreign, sought the fugitives, to secure the silver on their heads. Munster was pockmarked with English garrisons from which scouting parties daily emerged to scour the countryside, while the earl's own followers cursed their overlord and blamed him for the ruination of crops, the seizure of livestock and for their hunger. But the main thrust of their anger was directed against Dr Sanders. Even in the earl's company he became reviled by the people for his hollow promises of Spanish arms and gold. The earl's authority alone protected him, and now for reasons that had little to do with a religious crusade.

During the summer many of the Earl of Desmond's erstwhile allies, including the Earl of Clancar, O'Sullivan Beare and O'Sullivan More, O'Callaghan and O'Donoghue, submitted to Pelham. Rumours of the likely appointment of a new lord deputy began to circulate. Pelham redoubled his efforts in his attempt to capture the rebel earl and his family.

I give the rebels no breath to relieve themselves [he boasted to the Queen] but by one of your garrisons or other they be continually hunted. I keep them from their harvest and have taken great preys of cattle from them by which it seemeth the poor people that lived only upon labour and fed by their milch cows are so distressed as they follow their goods and offer themselves with their wives and children rather to be slain by the army than to suffer the famine that now in extremity beginneth to pinch them. [22]

As Pelham reported, the first signs of a serious famine had appeared, as the devastated land and terrified people succumbed to the awful consequences of the long war.

Suddenly the focus of political attention was diverted from Munster to the hitherto loyal English Pale, where James Eustace, Viscount Baltinglass, aided by Fiach MacHugh O'Byrne, raised the papal banner high over Leinster. This latest revolt was part of the wider intensification of the counter-reformation movement abroad. Jesuit agents, Parsons and Campion, had been smuggled into England and were actively exhorting English Catholics to rebel for faith and freedom. The objectives of the Counter-Reformation were espoused by Baltinglass who, unlike the Earl of Desmond, exemplified the true reforming zeal of the movement. Urged on by Dr Sanders, with whom he had been in contact, Baltinglass now displaced the Earl of Desmond and moved centre-stage in the revolutionary crusade. He exhorted Sir John and Dr Sanders to join him and move the thrust of the crusade to Leinster. Sir John had little patience or respect for his sickly brother, while Sanders had detected a marked falling-off in the earl's crusading fervour. The earl might well be the chosen receptacle for the seeds of the most holy revolution, but his true motives seemed to derive from more worldly and material considerations. The real crusading spirit of the Counter-Reformation appeared to Dr Sanders to be embodied in Viscount Baltinglass and Sanders secretly made plans to make his way to County Wicklow.

Despite the events in Leinster, there was no respite from Pelham in Munster. Deserted by both relatives and allies, Eleanor interceded again with Pelham, tracing him to Askeaton, where he received her amid the ruins of her castle home. The harrowing circumstances of her life during the past year had taken their toll on the haggard figure who knelt before the Lord Justice to again plead her husband's cause. But the resolute and pitiless faces of Pelham and his assistant, Geoffrey Fenton, were mirrored in Fenton's report of the meeting: 'The Countess came in . . . but with the same impudencie wherewith she hath covered her face since her last breaking out with her husband; yet taketh she uppon her to worke hym to submission.'[23] Pelham would not relent. Again he refused Eleanor permission to present her husband's case at court. There was no option but to keep the field, survive the winter and hope that the rumours that had begun to circulate about Pelham's impending recall proved true.

Meantime Pelham's harassment continued unabated as he sought to isolate the fugitives from their remaining supporters. It was rumoured that Sir John had secretly conspired with Sir Warham St Leger, the newly appointed provost-marshal of Munster, to betray his brother and secure a pardon for himself, while Rory MacSheehy, a captain of the Desmond galloglass, was urged by Pelham to capture Dr Sanders. Pelham warned Lord FitzMorris not to succour the fugitives. 'You have had in your country', he wrote to him, 'the traitor earl, his wife, his brother and Sanders, whom you might have apprehended if you had listed.' To ensure FitzMorris's future actions, Pelham informed him that his two sons were to be detained 'until I may see some service done by you in delivering up some of the principal conspirators above named, dead or alive'.[24]

While the whispers and rumours flew, Garrett's half-brother, Sir James 'Sussex', was wounded on a plundering raid in Muskerry and captured by the Sheriff of Cork. He was delivered in chains to St Leger and imprisoned in Cork goal. After two months of physical and mental torture, Sir James was executed in October 1580, as St Leger reported to the Privy Council: 'Sir James of Desmond who (by direction of the Lord Deputie) I caused to be hanged drawen and quartered at the gates of this town . . . who yeelded to godward a better end than otherwise would have don if he had not dyed to death.'[25] James had pleaded for summary decapitation. But the twenty-two-year-old rebel had instead to suffer the ignoble and gruesome form of execution reserved for traitors. He had faced his ordeal bravely. The English administration in Dublin noted his death and merely observed that 'the pestilent hydra hath lost another of his heads'.[26]

In September 1580 Arthur, Baron Grey de Wilton took office as Lord Deputy. Pelham reluctantly surrendered the sword of office in the knowledge that he had failed to complete his mission against the Earl of Desmond and that the methods he had employed in Munster had found little favour at Court. Moreover, Admiral Winter had kept his word to Eleanor, and her letter had eventually reached the Queen. Elizabeth had little time for the Puritan fanaticism of Pelham and his kind, particularly where such zeal cost her money. Where loyalty could be purchased, even for a time, Elizabeth was willing to overlook political and religious shortcomings. She had scant regard for the Earl of Desmond; she cursed him roundly for being a drain on her resources, and wished him dead or in exile. Yet the Countess of Desmond's letter made the Queen question the appropriateness of Pelham's precipitate actions against the earl and his subsequent policy of annihilation which had accomplished little but to devastate one-quarter of her Irish realm. Pelham felt bitter about the criticism. His companion and aide, Sir Nicholas Malby, protested to the Queen's secretary on his behalf. It was unjustifiable, Malby stated,

that the wordes of an infamous woman, the wyfe of a proclaymed traytor herselfe a nowtorious traytoress, the great worcker of these wicked rebellions in the popes behalf should cary their credyt to deface the faythfull service of a dutyfull and honest servant.[27]

But Pelham's day had come and gone. Elizabeth dismissed his protests as more urgent and disturbing events unfolded.

The new, untried but impatient Lord Deputy carried the fight to Baltinglass and Fiach MacHugh O'Byrne, deep in the recesses of the Wicklow mountains, and thereby paid the penalty. At Glenmalure the O'Byrne kern and galloglass decimated Grey's raw English recruits. The effects of the victory were instantaneous. In the north O'Rourke and O'Donnell rose in revolt, while Turlough Luineach O'Neill prepared to attack the Pale with an army of 5,000 clansmen. His rival, the English-educated Hugh O'Neill, the Baron of Dungannon, hid himself in the woods and loudly protested his loyalty to Elizabeth 'even if all the Irishry in Ireland should rebel'.[28] Sir John of Desmond besieged Maryborough and Ormond was attacked by the rebels. To add to the explosive situation Spanish aid arrived, undetected, at the ill-fated harbour of Smerwick.

The news of the uprisings and the arrival of the long-awaited aid from Spain spurred Eleanor and Garrett into action. The years of intrigue and subterfuge, of tears and humiliation, of deprivation, hunger and loss, seemed at last likely to be vindicated. The long, lonely vigil was over. The King of Spain had kept his word; the army of salvation had arrived. As they urged their horses over the steep mountain passes towards Dingle, the depression and misery of their situation momentarily lifted and Garrett swore to avenge the wrongs they had suffered. As they topped the last hill before the descent to Dún an Óir, the promontory fort standing stark and windswept against the sea, their elation turned to disbelief. Instead of the army of well-appointed troops promised by Sanders, they saw a force of 700 'poor simple bisognos, very ragged and a great part of them boys'.[29] Philip had sent aid to the crusaders in Ireland, but his interests in the Low Countries took precedence. It was significant that the majority of the troops were Italian. With the soldiers was Friar Mateo de Oviedo, the apostolic commissary, Friar Cornelius O'Mulrian, the papal Bishop of Killaloe, and some Jesuit preachers.

Ill-clothed and totally inexperienced in warfare, the soldiers quickly succumbed to the cold and damp of the Irish climate. Their leader, Sebastino di San Joseppi from Bologna, was equally incredulous to learn that the pale, sickly man who had to be lifted off his horse was the great Irish crusader who was to lead them to victory against the army of the English heretic queen. Philip had sent sufficient arms for the 4,000-strong army promised him by the Earl of Desmond and Dr Sanders. Where was this great army the Italians wanted to know? They were assured that over the hills the army waited. But San Joseppi would never know that beyond the high peak of Slieve Mish lay a people decimated by war and famine, too hungry and unwilling to bear arms in a cause they did not understand.

A massive confidence trick had been practised by both sides, for which each would pay a costly price. Sir John and Dr Sanders hurried to Smerwick and sent urgent messages back to Philip to the effect that nothing less than 8,000 well-equipped, experienced troops could ensure the success of the crusade. Rashly Garrett also outlined to the king the miserable circumstances of his situation, the seizure of his estates, his poverty, and how both he and his countess were daily driven from pillar to post in their own estates by the army of Philip's heretic sister-in-law. The effect of this plaintive tale on the cold, reserved king was no more than an indifferent shrug of the black-caped shoulders and a detached resolve to pursue Christ's crusade elsewhere, under the leadership of a less distressed leader.

Reports of the 'invasion' reached Dublin where Lord Deputy Grey, impatient to blot out the embarrassment of Glenmalure, joined forces with the Earl of Ormond and made for Dingle. The Golden Fort might yet provide him with the chance to restore his tarnished image. In Grey's army were Walter Raleigh, captains Zouche and Mackworth, while the poet Edmund Spenser acted as the Lord Deputy's secretary. At the beginning of November Grey pitched camp at Dingle. As the English army approached, the Desmond leaders and their supporters hurried away with empty promises of aid to the Italians. Admiral Winter sailed into Smerwick and cut off any chance of escape by sea. The siege of Dún an Óir commenced. Initially the Italians flew the papal insignia from the fort. As the siege intensified, it was replaced by a black and white banner, a signal to the Geraldine army to attack the English in the rear. No army materialised and the Geraldine leaders remained hidden. The Italians sued for terms, but Grey would only consider an unconditional surrender, to which, it was controversially reported, San Joseppi agreed. Grey, the hero of Spenser's *Faerie Queene*, the brave knight Artegal, then ordered Raleigh and Mackworth to implement, to the letter of the law, the prevailing rules of sixteenth-century warfare. The unarmed survivors of the siege, with the exception of a handful of officers, were mercilessly slaughtered.

Six hundred died at Smerwick, a dreadful indictment of the sub-human cruelty of warfare, and the tragedy of broken promises and incomprehensible and ineffectual alliances. San Joseppi and his inexperienced youths were the sacrificial victims of the deviousness of international politics, fuelled by the raging flames of religious fanaticism. The shame of Dún an Óir must rest on the Puritan shoulders of Lord Deputy Grey, but also on Dr Sanders and the Earl of Desmond, whose rash and empty promises had first lured and then abandoned the Italians to their fate. While Grey's action at Smerwick was sharply criticised by some factions at the English court, the Queen viewed it merely as a removal of another threat to the security of her realm. Accordingly she thanked and commended Grey for his endeavours. It is significant to note that there was no official remonstration by the Catholic powers, who, if the positions were reversed, would have probably acted likewise.

For Garrett Smerwick was the final, fateful step which placed him beyond all hope of redemption. His action made reconciliation with the Queen now virtually impossible. He had aroused the deepest anger in Elizabeth as he turned her greatest fear into stark reality by bringing England's most dreaded enemy into Ireland; for that the Queen would never forgive him. Garrett's great gamble had failed, and the fortunes of war were once again in England's favour. The risk of Spanish intervention in Ireland receded; the honour of the Crown had been bloodily restored; Turlough O'Neill no longer threatened the Pale; the Burkes of Connaught had been subdued; and Viscount Baltinglass, his cause clearly lost, was attempting to flee to the continent. Hope abounded that the tiresome Earl of Desmond might do likewise.

For Eleanor the débâcle of Smerwick proved her long-held misgivings. Dr Sanders and his religious crusade had pushed Garrett onto the wrong horse. But a strange change now occurred in her husband. After Smerwick the earl had parted company with Dr Sanders, each embittered by his brief association with the other. Released from the pretence of espousing a cause in which he had no real interest, Garrett reverted to the cause which was life itself to him, the defence of the power and privilege of his title. The Queen, who after Smerwick considered the earl to be of little consequence, was amazed when it was reported that the Earle of Desmond, who was thought to be either dead or fled, 'beginneth to appear and to show himselfe, having assembled a great companie.'[30] The foreign 'Pápa abú!' exhortation of the crusade was replaced by the native war-cry of 'Shanid abú!' as the Earl of Desmond prepared to lead his followers in the only real crusade he knew.

For Dr Sanders the long, dismal, aimless campaign in Ireland finally exacted its price. Totally disillusioned with the Gaelic leaders and their Gaelic ways, so different from the glorious crusade envisaged by FitzMaurice, the sodden woods and oozing bogs of Kerry had sapped the fiery zeal and burning energy of the scholarly agitator. While English steel for three long years had diligently sought his head, ironically it was the Irish ague and famine that eventually killed 'the supporting pillar of the Catholic faith'[31] somewhere among the briary thickets of Clonlish wood in the damp spring of 1581.

While Eleanor might well have been amazed at the change in her husband and his determination to continue the rebellion, her amazement was compounded by the policy of peace and reconciliation suddenly being preached by his bitter rival, the Earl of Ormond. For years Ormond had opposed and plotted against Garrett and aided officers of the Crown in the spoliation of his estates. The extent and ferocity of the expeditions perpetrated by the new breed of English officials and soldiers in Ireland now alarmed him. Munster had already suffered more than enough. But Grey and the avaricious freebooting captains in his retinue, eager for the spoils of war, would not be stopped. While the Earl of Desmond's estates and property were now easy pickings, Ormond could not help but wonder whether the greed and lust for land of the new breed of English military conquistadores would stop short at the lands of his enemy. Might equally greedy eyes be eventually cast on his own domain and questions raised regarding his extensive powers? Black Tom had to tread warily lest his hesitancy be interpreted as disloyalty and his estates subjected to the same fate as those of Desmond.

During the winter months of 1580–81 Eleanor lay low. Garrett was determined to continue the fight, and his rekindled resolution had also tended to make him stronger physically. Consequently when, in April 1581, the Countess of Desmond and her sister presented themselves to Ormond at Cork city, the reasons for their appearance were again open to conjecture. Ormond authorised protections for both women. Eleanor was examined before the Munster Commissioners, among whom was her former jailer in London, Sir Warham St Leger. Asked if she came on her husband's behalf, she replied 'that she was not authorised by him to sue for him but did it of her owne head'.[32] She was then escorted back to her lodgings with instructions to commit her petition to paper. Ormond permitted her sister to depart to live under the custody of her brother, the Baron of Dunboyne. The real reasons for Eleanor's unexpected appearance at Cork became apparent. Her husband was determined to continue a campaign in which she had suffered immeasurably and, it was reasonable to assume, she could take no more of the physical fatigue and mental anguish. But her written petition reflects a more likely reason: that she might find in Ormond, who now also wished for a cessation of hostilities, a likely means to achieve access to the Queen. Despite his new-found pride and determination, she realised that her husband could not hold out much longer.

In her letter Eleanor requested permission to take her case to the Queen so 'that my travell maye be a meanes to brede a generall quiet into this province and precure mercie to my husbande nowe driven to distresse'.[33] She did not directly request a pardon for her husband, as Garrett had forfeited that right by aligning himself with a foreign power. She merely requested that she be permitted to seek the Queen's mercy for herself and her husband. Her dilemma, she stated, was such that 'as nature tyeth me to the companie of my Lord my husbande (who so unhapely is fallen into her Maties heavie displeasure) yet', she assured them, 'my dutie remembered to her Matie'.[34] She pleaded for the welfare and safety of her daughters who had suffered considerable distress and want during the course of their young lives. 'I doe also beseche your wisdom', she asked, 'that I may take my daughters with me into England or els to leave them with my ffrendes untyll my retorne out of England . . . to remaine free and not as prisoners.'[35]

Ormond forwarded her petition to the Lord Deputy and Council in Dublin, where it was received and endorsed by Grey's secretary, Edmund Spenser. Spenser was influenced in writing his epic *The Faerie Queene*[36] by his term of service with Lord Grey in Ireland and, it is believed, he based the character of the evil temptress Radigund on Eleanor. Grey and his Council were unmoved by Eleanor's petition and recoiled in assumed horror at what they termed 'so arrogant a petition made without submission or confession of her husband's horrible treason and her owne'.[37] They accused her of *the treason of bringing in of strangers into this realme by the practize of her husband, and by all conjecture much furdered by her, hath in all reasonable opinion so aggravated her former offences as we see lesse cause nowe than before to graunt a matter so offensive to her highness.* [38]

Grey sought to continue the policy of his predecessor Pelham, to ensure that the Earl of Desmond would have no option but to continue in his rebellion, so that there could be no last-minute pardon from the Queen. Half a million acres of land was at stake, far too lucrative a prize to have snatched away by the tears of the rebel's wife. Grey ordered that Eleanor be sent back to her husband so that her presence might slow him down; otherwise, he argued, 'he maie go with as few companie as pleaseth him from wood to wood and from bogg to bogg or to Spaine or Scotland when to warrant further help ... but', Grey reasoned, 'having hir in his train he cannot chuse whether he leaveth or goe'. [39] It was Grey's opinion that the Earl of Desmond 'hath more care for the said Countesse and her traine to leave them than he hath of himself'. [40]

Eleanor's case was not helped by the actions of Sir Warham St Leger, already with a foothold in Desmond land which he hoped to extend. His differences with the Earl of Ormond at this time were common knowledge; any sign that Black Tom favoured the rebel's wife would likely be seized upon by St Leger as proof of his disloyalty. He wrote to Lord Burghley, the Queen's chief secretary, to add a further impediment to Eleanor's passage to the Queen:

In my simple opinion, ther can no good growe of her going thither. I vow to God ... I know her to bee as wicked a woman as ever was bred in Ireland and one that hath ben the chief instrument of her husband's rebellion. And if she bee licensed to go out, your lordship shall doo as good an act as ever you did in your life to this realme to cause hir hed to be stroken of or else to be kept in perpetuall ymprisonment. [41]

The cries of the avaricious became more strident against the slightest possibility which might deprive them of the prize so near their grasp. With the weight of official opinion firmly against her, Eleanor knew she was fighting a losing battle in her attempt to gain access to the Queen. Ormond was powerless, even if he wished, to help her and

Grey accused him of dangerous and suspicious tendencies and relieved him of his position as military governor of Munster. He also persuaded the Queen to exclude the Earl and Countess of Desmond and Sir John of Desmond from any amnesty. Thus, with Ormond sidelined and Eleanor barred from England, Grey ensured that the devastation in Munster would continue until the Earl of Desmond was taken dead or alive in rebellion. The scent of potential riches wafted stronger than the acrid stench of decaying corpses and scorched earth as the eager English bloodhounds leapt from the slips and tore after their prey.

Eleanor rejoined her husband in the wilderness for the final agonising phase of the war. She had done everything in her power to salvage something, anything, from the ruins. Stalked like wild beasts, she and Garrett went to ground. The long winter months of 1581–2 were, according to the annals, notable for 'great wind, constant rain, lightning and much tempestuous weather'.[42] Like demented spectres they flitted across the decayed Munster landscape. They were pursued without respite by captain Zouche, an eager, uncompromising officer in the Munster service. He reported that he had almost caught the countess on several occasions, but Eleanor had merely lured his posse away from where her husband lay, too exhausted to flee further.

To the English soldiers who pursued her, the Countess of Desmond became an obsessive figure, dominating their gossip and nightmares. Stories of her evil, devious ways were peddled from camp-fire to camp-fire. She became the object of their fear, hatred and lust; the she-devil, the mythical harpy, a wanton woman. Was it true that under the pretence of seeking pardon from the Lord Deputy she had spied for the rebels? Was it not whispered that she was a witch? What self-respecting woman—and a countess to boot—would willingly live like a wild animal in the woods and bogs of this godforsaken country? The soldiers savagely cursed her as the incessant rain soaked them to the skin and quenched their camp-fires. They swore at her as they spat the spoiled biscuit and chewed the tainted, uncooked meat of their rations. They cursed her and the country that gave her birth as they vomited their guts out and shivered uncontrollably with ague and dysentery amid the oozing marshes and frozen mountain passes of Munster. Was it true that she traded her favours easily? The red-rimmed, hungry eyes of the war-weary soldiers gloated at the prospect of her capture.

In the middle of a cold, misty November night the soldiers' desire was almost fulfilled. A scouting party from the nearby garrison at Kilmallock came upon an isolated wattle cabin hidden deep in a wood. Eleanor, her nerves as taut as the strings of a crossbow, heard the sound of movement outside. She roused her exhausted husband. There was no time to awaken the galloglass, who, shrouded in their great woollen cloaks, were asleep under the surrounding trees. Supporting her husband, Eleanor stumbled from the cabin and into the darkness. The clansmen sprang to arms and engaged the English soldiers in a fierce battle. Desperately Eleanor looked for an escape. Before her was the dark outline of a river, swollen by the winter deluges. Behind her the victorious shouts of the English as they put the galloglass to flight. There was no escape. Quickly she helped Garrett to the river bank and into the ice-cold water. The river rose almost to their chins which with difficulty they kept above the fast-flowing current. Hidden from sight by the overhanging bank, they waited. The soldiers surrounded the cabin, and captain Zouche entered to effect the capture of the wretched fugitives. A makeshift bed stood in the corner, the coverings still warm to the touch.

Zouche ordered a search for the occupants, convinced that they were still in the vicinity. The soldiers spread out. They came to the river and searched in the undergrowth above the bank. Beneath them Eleanor held the sagging body of her husband afloat, her body almost numb in the icy water. She could scarcely breathe. Finally Zouche called off the search, and in silent agony Eleanor waited until the last sounds of the English posse faded and the strong arms of the surviving galloglass came to her rescue to lift her from the river. Returning to the cabin, they found that Eleanor's clothing had been ripped to pieces and trampled into the mud by the frustrated soldiers. There was no time to recover. A voluminous Irish woollen mantle was wrapped about each of them, and they were carried into the night by the faithful Desmond retainers to seek another temporary shelter before sunrise.

While Zouche was to be again denied the capture of the elusive earl and countess, it was he who was destined to draw first blood in the renewed campaign at the beginning of 1582. Since the massacre at Smerwick, the subsequent death of Dr Sanders and the flight to the continent of Baltinglass, Sir John of Desmond had remained in Munster. In early January he set out to rendezvous with the Seneschal of Imokilly near Castlelyons, County Cork. On information received from a spy, Zouche lay in wait and, in the ensuing struggle, Sir John was killed by a spear thrown by his former servant named Fleming. Thus the life of a turbulent, unscrupulous and bold Geraldine was brought to a bloody end. Sir John was the most active leader of the Geraldines and, while he could be accused of many dark deeds and even darker designs, there was a certain decisiveness about his actions, in marked contrast to the vacillations of his elder brother. His antagonism to Eleanor and the deep mutual dislike that existed between them stemmed from many causes. Her Butler origins perhaps aroused his Geraldine prejudice; he resented her influence over Garrett; furthermore, she had borne his sickly brother an heir, thereby eliminating his own chances of succession.

The decapitated body of Sir John of Desmond was hung in chains over the main gate of Cork city. There it remained for almost three years, a grisly spectacle, until the skeletal remains were blown away into the river by a storm. Zouche despatched the head as a new year's gift to Grey in Dublin, while the Queen was presented with Sir John's 'fair torquoise [ring] set in gold'.[43] His estates in County Cork were later granted to captain Thomas Norris and Sir Walter Raleigh, while the poet Edmund Spenser received the castle and lands of Kilcolman. The war-mongers and war correspondents of the long campaign were amply rewarded for their efforts.

The Earl of Desmond alone remained to carry on the resistance. It was confidently expected that he would capitulate. But the earl rarely did what was expected of him. There was to be no surrender on his part. Moreover, the remaining Geraldine supporters clung to him as their sole means of salvation. If the earl received a pardon, it would be conditional, and preserve his life only. The estates of his dependent lords and clansmen were likely to be expropriated and parcelled out to the land-hungry English freebooters as payment for their services. The earl had no option but to continue the rebellion, or at least stay alive, until aid came from abroad or until Elizabeth relented. Garrett had become a prisoner of his heritage and during 1582 his liegemen and followers once more flocked to his banner. There was growing unease at the continued policy of spoliation being pursued in Munster. Even former perpetrators of the destruction, hardened campaigners like Raleigh and St Leger, now echoed the Earl of Ormond's reservations for which they had previously condemned him. They expressed concern over the scorched-earth policy of Grey when it seemed likely that the Desmond estates might be forfeited and divided among themselves. Elizabeth swore at her Lord Deputy who, despite the resources she had given him, had accomplished little. Desmond, the 'arch-rebel', still roamed free, and Munster was desolate.

The earl still held out and, as one observer noted, 'he continued still in his old accustomed spoiling and wasting the countries and trusting to no house nor castell did shrow himselfe in woods and bogs'.[44] From his hiding-place, deep in the Glen of Aherlow, the earl reverted to attacks on his hereditary enemy, raiding the nearby lands of Ormond and skirmishing occasionally with the English patrols sent to track him down. Eleanor continued to accompany him and, as late as June 1582, Zouche reported yet another running encounter with the Countess of Desmond, whom he claimed he had 'distressed'.

Although not named with Garrett in the original proclamation of 1579, Eleanor had loyally shared his hunted existence and had been on the run with him for over two years, enduring the greatest hardships imaginable. Her physical and mental health was near breaking-point. Her devotion and loyalty had been tried and tested in the icy waters of Munster's marshes and rivers, on the cold floors of huts and caves, in hunger and in the countless sleepless nights, when every rustle and stir in the dark heralded the end. She had faced the wrath and vengeance of the Crown as she strove to intercede and negotiate on her husband's behalf. Whether physically unable to bear the strain any longer, or, as is more likely, in yet another effort to intercede and seek some terms by which Garrett might yet surrender and survive, Eleanor appeared before Lord Deputy Grey at the English camp near Maryborough on 15 June 1582. Grey was moved by the emaciated woman who, in dirty ragged clothing, courageously stood before him to plead her husband's case. But with his usual self-righteousness and sense of duty, 'yet weighing the nature and quallitie of her actions and howe farre she might participate in the trayterous councelles and conspiracies of her husband', he had her conducted 'to the house of an honest merchant of Dublin there to remeine in estate of a prysoner untill . . . we might be directed how to dispose of her further'.[45]

In semi-captivity in Dublin, Eleanor awaited her chance to intervene on her husband's behalf. But by now Elizabeth and her Privy Council wanted an end to the war, and an end to the troublesome Earl of Desmond. There were to be no further negotiations or time-wasting interventions. Walsingham instructed Grey to withdraw the protection he had given Eleanor and ordered that she was 'to retourne back agayne to her said husband within a certain tyme', after which 'if shee happen to bee taken she must then bee subject to such punishment as the laws will laye uppon her for her conduct'.[46] The Crown demanded the unconditional surrender of the Earl of Desmond so that his estates and property could be used to pay the expenses incurred by the war. His death, however, would also bring the same result. In the somewhat naïve belief that Grey shared his desire for rapprochement, Walsingham advised him:

> *You should appoint some such person to delyver unto the countesse by wave of friendly advice that if she could persuade the said Earle her husband to come in and submitt him selfe simplie to her Maties mercie, the only waye hee can nowe take for his safetie, the Queen might then consider not only to leave him his liefe but also to use some further clemencie towardes him.* [47]

But Grey neglected to put the Queen's offer to Eleanor, who was unaware that it had been made until some time later. Neither Grey nor his administration wished for any last-minute chances of reconciliation. Fortunes and reputations were at stake.

During the summer months of 1582, while Eleanor awaited her fate in Dublin, she was allowed to visit her son, still incarcerated in Dublin castle. James was now eleven years of age, and Eleanor was greatly distressed at the conditions under which he was being detained. She wrote to Lord Burghley and reminded him that she had voluntarily placed her son in the Crown's care, but that the 'boy now remaineth in the Castell of Dublin, without any kynd of learninge or brenginge upp or any to attend uppon him. . . . In consideracion of his innocency and tender yeares',[48] she asked that he should be transferred from the unsuitable environment of the Castle and sent to England where, she hoped, someone in power might take a friendly interest in his welfare and future. As her husband had forfeited his chance of retaining his title and estates, it was an appropriate time to remind the Crown of the existence of his son. If her husband's estates were attainted Eleanor hoped the Queen might agree to restore at least part of them, together with the hereditary Desmond title, to his son when he came of age, as she had done in the case of his kinsman the Earl of Kildare. An English education and upbringing, as with Hugh O'Neill, might be the way to ensure her son's eventual succession to his inheritance. Her request for her son's removal to England was subsequently granted.

Forced to rejoin her husband on the run, Eleanor protested to the authorities against the decision which, she maintained, 'above all things in this world she abhoreth and ever hath and the greatest thing against her nature and bringing upp'.[49] She again asked to be allowed to plead her case before the Queen, but the stern, immovable faces of Grey and the Council gave her her answer. The unconditional surrender of her husband was the only outcome they were prepared to accept. Wearily Eleanor returned to Garrett with the 'offer' of the Lord Deputy and Council. Infuriated, Garrett stepped up the tempo of his campaign against the Crown. He had now simply nothing to lose. A demonstration of power might yet induce the Crown to offer better terms to bring an end to the conflict. Moreover, the old Geraldine pride had been once again ignited, as he mounted his horse to instil the fire of battle into his war-weary liege lords and famine-stricken followers. All Geraldines who defied his call to arms were summarily dealt with. When informed that four of them had accepted Crown pardons, he ordered their arrest. They were brought before him and, it was reported, 'calling them traitors, he had them stripped naked and slashed to death by his kinsmen, every sword in the band taking part in their death'.[50] 'So shall every Geraldine be served who shall not follow me,'[51] the rebel earl decreed. His actions shed the last vestiges of the pseudo-ideologies that had motivated him previously. The age-old aspirations for supremacy and independence resurfaced as the Earl of Desmond mustered his hereditary men-at-arms in a final attempt to halt the march of time. 'Misery had given the man courage. . . . English ruthlessness threw him back into the life mould of the Gaelic captain.'[52]

Significantly, as he had begun, Garrett took the fight to the territory of his rival, Black Tom of Ormond, and plundered Tipperary along the Suir valley to the borders of Waterford. At Knockgraffon, near Cahir, he soundly defeated Ormond's brothers to put a winning touch on the age-old Desmond-Ormond feud. He was supreme in the palatinate of Kerry, where the English garrisons cowered for cover. Garrett's old ally, the Seneschal of Imokilly, plundered east Cork and west Waterford and looted the Earl of Ormond's grand new house at Carrick-on-Suir.

The starving kern and weary galloglass flocked to the Earl of Desmond's standard in one final furious drive in defence of the archaic world that had bred and sustained them. Their overlord for the first time assumed the dignity and stature of a hero and, as such, was destined to become a legend in folk memory.

By now Eleanor's term of protection from Grey was drawing to an end. She had failed—perhaps she had not wanted to succeed—in persuading Garrett to seek a conference with the Lord Deputy and Council, who were now agreeable 'to meet the erle 20 myles from Dublin if shee by any persuasion may drawe her husband thither'.[53] Eleanor requested an extension of her protection, and this was granted. She also asked for a ten-day truce for Garrett and his followers, but this was denied. Eleanor brought three of her daughters, Margaret, Joan and Katherine, into Cork city and obtained Crown protection for them. There she was enveloped in a web of intrigue and double-dealing. She obtained an interview with Sir Warham St Leger, who informed her that Garrett's life might be spared but that his restoration was not negotiable. St Leger knew better than anyone that such terms were repugnant to the earl, and, in any event, he had no desire to see the earl reconciled with the Crown and risk losing a slice of the Desmond estates.

At the same time as his offer to Eleanor, St Leger warned the Privy Council in England: 'Desmond if received to mercy, will ever be a hollow-hearted subject.'[54] He informed the Queen that Desmond had embarked on a new conspiracy with Spain and was planning another invasion. But Elizabeth was weary of the long campaign and was still susceptible 'to have the rebellion ended without blood'.[55] She urged that Desmond be induced to surrender. But too much blood had already been shed, and the Queen's hopes were frustrated by her officers' greed, as well as by the earl's new-found enthusiasm for the fight.

It is ironic that the saga of the fall of the House of Desmond should be terminated by the self-same feud with which it had started. While Elizabeth had run out of money, ideas, and patience regarding the Desmond rebellion, the old rivalry between two Irish lords would achieve what her best administrators and military men had failed to do. And thus she left it to her old friend, Black Tom, to bring the bitter war to an end. Despite the misgivings of her officials in Ireland, she appointed him Lord General, with a force of a thousand soldiers and power to grant pardons to all rebels in the Earl of Desmond's camp. By this time the plight of Munster had become desperate. The famine raging there for many months now spread across the country to the walls of Dublin city. In Munster, particularly towards the west, the situation was beyond belief. 'The lowing of a cow or the voice of a ploughman was not heard from Dingle to the Rock of Cashel,'[56] the annalists recorded.

Ormond's plan was to confine the Earl of Desmond to one locality, preferably within Kerry, which had suffered particularly severely from famine. From Clonmel, Ormond drove Garrett, Eleanor and their followers before him westward, while the English garrisons of Limerick and Kilmallock attacked Desmond's seneschal. One by one the earl's allies deserted him and accepted the pardons offered. The Baron of Lixnaw submitted, as did lords Roche and Barry. The greatest blow to the Desmond cause came when Garrett's long-time ally, the Seneschal of Imokilly, fearful for the welfare of his only son, then in the custody of St Leger, made his submission to the Earl of Ormond.

Deserted, but for a few galloglass and retainers, Garrett and Eleanor made the exhausting journey once more over the mountains into Kerry and were hunted day and night without respite. Eleanor's female attendants were captured by the soldiers while, aided by a heavy fog, Eleanor and Garrett barely effected their escape. Garrett's health had further deteriorated, and the galloglass now took turns to carry their lord on their shoulders to evade the relentless hunters who sniffed the scent of the kill. Eleanor sought to negotiate for terms, but Ormond would not agree to anything less than Desmond's unconditional surrender. Ormond had also joined the ever-increasing pack who clamoured for the anticipated spoils. Claiming all the Desmond estate, on the grounds that his mother was the sole heir of the eleventh Earl of Desmond, his enemies sought to discredit him at court. 'The Lord Generall', it was said, '. . . sometime useth speech of a title he hath to all Desmond's lands and seemeth to think he hath well deserved the same, though he had no title thereunto.'[57]

The extent of the despair and the hopeless sense of isolation of the Earl of Desmond was revealed in his unprecedented appeal for help to his bitter rival Ormond. Abandoned in the wilderness by his friends, he now turned to his enemy as a last resort:

As I may not condemn myself of disloyalty to her Majesty, [he wrote to Ormond] so cannot I excuse my faults, but must confess that I have incurred her Majestie's indignation; yet when the cause and means which were found and devised to make me commit folly shall be known to her Highness, I rest in an assured hope that her most gracious Majestie will both think of me as my heart deserveth and also of those that wrung me into undutifulness, as their cunning devise deserveth.[58]

As Black Tom qualified for the latter category, he refused Desmond's offer to parley without first receiving his total surrender. In vain Eleanor pleaded Garrett's abhorrence to be 'destrainte of libertie, a thing' which she well knew 'he can not indure for he acounteth it more greyvous than death'.[59] But Ormond's reply was to pursue the campaign with increased ferocity. The tally of 'traitors put to the sword'[60] mounted. Captains, galloglass, constables and kern fell at the hands of Ormond's army. Rumours reached Ormond that Desmond intended to escape by sea to Spain and he tracked him deep inside the palatinate of Kerry. Through Castleisland, Castlemaine and on into Dingle, Ormond's forces encountered little resistance from a people beaten by war, want and hunger and whose lord, like a wild animal, had been reduced to live in the wastelands of his once vast lordship.

Finally, towards the middle of June 1583, Eleanor came before the Earl of Ormond and submitted unconditionally. Ormond reported to the Queen that the countess 'put her self holye to your majesties mercye', and added: 'This poer lady lamenteth greatlye the follye and lewdness of her husband whome reason could never rule.'[61] While Eleanor might well have lamented, it was, perhaps, not for the reason which Ormond felt obliged to report to Elizabeth, but because she had said her final farewell to Garrett. In the wild wastes of Slieve Logher, where they had taken a last refuge together, they had decided to part. He had become hampered by her presence and needed total freedom of movement if he was to continue to evade his pursuers. At least that was the excuse he chose so that she might be spared the fate that hourly awaited him. She was the mother of his heir, whose future safety would require all her energy and intelligence, if something was to be salvaged from the ruins. Her health was beginning to feel the effects of the long years of hardship. Her durability and resilience could only be marvelled at. She had withstood, without protest, hunger and deprivation. She had shared her husband's brief glory and long humiliation. More politically able than he, she had never openly criticised his oftentimes inexplicable behaviour and actions; instead she had worked to expose the devious plots of his relatives and Crown officials; and in her dealings with the Crown she had shown no little diplomatic skill. As Garrett watched his countess disappear from view, the fighting spirit must finally have evaporated from his emaciated body. Without her, it would be as much as he could do, to hide from the bloodhounds that were fast following behind him.

The long hunt finally came to an ignoble end within the recesses of Garrett's treasured palatinate. At the beginning of November 1583 he was run to ground with about twenty of his followers in the wood of Glanageenty in the parish of Ballymacelligot, about eight kilometres east of Tralee. Ironically, in view of what was to occur there, it was the country of the O'Moriartys, among whom Garrett had been fostered as a child. His remaining galloglass captain, Goram MacSweeney, had been captured and executed by Ormond. The Earl of Desmond now lay exhausted, 'concealed in a hut, in the cavern of a rock',[62] while his followers scoured the barren countryside for sustenance. On the southern shore of Tralee Bay they seized a number of cattle, the property of Maurice O'Moriarty, pillaged his house and assaulted his wife. The O'Moriartys were incensed and sought the assistance of the English garrison at Castlemaine.

Accompanied by six English soldiers, the O'Moriartys tracked the cattle to Glanageenty. They fanned out, and one of them, Owen O'Moriarty, climbed a hill which overlooked the steep glen below. A fire flickered in the distance. As the first light of dawn on 11 November gleamed fitfully through the swirling morning mists, they attacked the camp in the glen. The guards ran for their lives. The attackers entered the cavern, where an old man was asleep on the ground beside the fire, attended by two frightened young boys and a woman. The old man roused himself. A soldier of the garrison, Daniel Kelly, lunged with his sword at the slowly rising figure, almost cutting off his arm, while another hit him a glancing blow to the head. 'I am the Earl of Desmond,'[63] the old man cried out. The attackers were astounded. They had stumbled across the most wanted fugitive in memory. Visions of the bounty offered for his capture, dead or alive, spurred them into action before the earl's followers could regroup and return. Kelly bound the earl and they tried to drag him through the woods. But Garrett could not walk and the wound in his arm was bleeding profusely. After a hurried conference, Kelly raised his sword a second time and decapitated the earl. With the grisly trophy clutched in his hand, Kelly and the rest hurried back to Castlemaine to claim their reward.

The head of the Earl of Desmond was sent to Kilkenny, from where Ormond forwarded the prize to the Queen.

God of his goodness who be praised for ever hath answered your L. expectations [he wrote to the Privy Council] by cutting of that wicked member whose head I have thought good to send by this bearer to her Matie as a profe of the happie ende of his rebellion.[64]

Elizabeth eyed the head of the Earl of Desmond in death as coldly as when alive and ordered it to be impaled on London Bridge. Ormond ordered a search for the earl's body, but loyal Desmond retainers concealed the remains and later interred them in a small chapel at Kilnamanagh near Castleisland. The 'old' Earl of Desmond was in fact just fifty-one years of age at the time of his death.

Eleanor received the news of Garrett's death at Kilkenny where she resided with her daughters under the protection of the Earl of Ormond. Whether she was shown the ghastly trophy as it was prepared for despatch to England is unknown. Perhaps, despite the cruel and often barbaric customs of the time, she was spared the ultimate anguish. The sense of inevitability about the outcome of the long struggle against both time and the Crown, and the future daunting role to salvage something for herself and her family from the wreckage, perhaps helped ease the pain and sense of loss at Garrett's cruel end. She had done everything in her power to avert the catastrophe. Her wayward husband had become a prisoner of his pride, of his heritage and of the past, with dreadful consequences for himself and his family. As yet Eleanor had only begun to reap the bitter harvest he had sown.

'And thus', a contemporary chronicler recorded, 'a noble race and ancient familie descended from out of the loines of princes is now for treasons and rebellions utterlie extinguished and overthrowne.'[65] The dead earl had bequeathed a terrible legacy to Munster, to his wife and children, and to his dependent followers. 'And as for the great companies of souldiers, gallowglasses, kerne and the common people who followed the rebellion,' the chronicle continues,

the numbers of them are infinite, whose blouds the earth dranke up
and whose carcases the foules of the aire and the ravening beasts of the
feeld did consume and devoure. After this followed an extreme famine,
and such as whom the sword did not destroie, the same did consume
and eat out.[66]

The death of the Earl of Desmond closed the final chapter in the
history of medieval Munster. In death Garrett inadvertently attained
the greatness and prestige that eluded him during his life. For
tradition and literature chose to depict him as one of the great
symbolic patriotic figures of history. In a perceptive comment on the
process, Seán O'Faolain has written:

Natural tradition, reaching above individual human weakness,
translated him into one whose equal was not in nobility, honour and
power. It is fantastically untrue, and yet in its truth is the power and
poetry of Ireland, and in its untruth her indifference to all her children
whom she sacrifices ruthlessly to her needs.[67]

But the facts reveal the personal ambitions and the defects that
motivated Desmond in his campaign against the Crown. The absence
of any ideological stimulus does not detract from his actions. On the
contrary it helps us sympathise and identify with the basic human
urge to retain power and patrimony and to survive, an urge that
compelled him to strive against the tide of time and give meaning to
the tribalistic war-cry of his house, 'Shanid abú!'

Chapter 8

The Pauper Countess

I and my childrin have tasted of so moche myserie
thattt I protest unto your honnor I knowe no waye
howe to preserve me and them from perishing by
famyne except her Matie do nott relieve us.

ELEANOR, COUNTESS OF DESMOND, TO LORD BURGHLEY,
4 SEPTEMBER 1585

The death of the Earl of Desmond and the end of the rebellion were causes for public celebration in Cork, Waterford, Limerick, Galway and Dublin. Garrett's death was hailed as a joyful deliverance from years of turmoil and devastation. If a sense of loss and sadness was felt by the adherents of the House of Desmond, it was expressed in secret. The earl's allies, one by one, submitted and accepted the pardons offered them by the Earl of Ormond. The galloglass and kern hid their weapons and lay low until a new leader might emerge from the ruin and require their services in a new conflict. The terrified tenantry and peasantry crept out of the woods and mountain refuges and returned to the plough to till the despoiled land and to await the arrival of new masters. 'Munster had suffered a violent upheaval, and time was needed to organise the new departure which, from the viewpoint of the state as beneficiary of the FitzGerald collapse, the occasion demanded.'[1] The Earl of Desmond, possessor of a great estate, had been slain *in flagrante bello*, and this 'was deemed and constitued an immediate attainder, in which instance the heir was irrevocably bound'.[2] Desmond's rebellion and subsequent death 'threw into the hands of the Crown the vast tracts forfeited by the earl and his adherents and which were now to be parcelled out to new possessors'.[3] But before the spoils of victory could be distributed among the waiting freebooters and adventurers, a commission of survey was first established to determine the precise title and extent of the lands claimed by successive earls of Desmond. The potential prize, over half a million acres of Munster, was worth the brief delay.

While the legal wrangles regarding the appropriation of her late husband's property got under way, Eleanor attempted to pick up the broken pieces of her life. She was thirty-eight years old, in the prime of life, yet with the vicissitudes and deprivations of a lifetime behind her. But her agony was not over. Her circumstances were difficult and her future uncertain. As the wife of a rebel, she could expect little sympathy for her plight. As an active participant in the rebellion, she knew that her life could yet be in jeopardy should the full force of the law be brought to bear. She rested for a time with her daughters, under the protection of the Earl of Ormond at Clonmel, and waited for the dust to settle. She was accompanied by a few female attendants, some Desmond retainers and her confidant and friend, Morris Sheehan. Her son was still a prisoner in Dublin Castle, but arrangements to have him transferred to the Tower of London were in train—and for reasons other than the furtherance of his education, as Eleanor had initially requested. The rightful heir to the Desmond estates might be more easily forgotten if concealed in the tombs of the Tower, where his sequestered existence might be less likely to trouble the conscience of those about to perpetrate one of the greatest frauds in history. The prospect of salvaging something for her son from the ruins of his inheritance seemed remote, but Eleanor never dismissed a chance, no matter how slim, in the cause for which she had fought and schemed so desperately.

Despite the antagonism of the Butlers towards her husband, Black Tom was content to allow her and her daughters remain in sanctuary in Ormond. He also urged the Crown to adopt a policy of reconciliation and to honour the pardons he had granted the rebels. 'Deal earnestlye with her highness', he asked Burghley, 'that no new devices be wrought to thrust those into a new rebellion, whiche have beehaved them selfes dutifullye and done service sins their submissions.'[4] Ormond's concern, however, arose not merely from a desire for reconciliation but from a deep-rooted sense of self-protection.

Eleanor hoped that the reconciliatory policy preached by Ormond would enable her to recover something from the wreck of her husband's estate. With this in view, in December 1583 she solicited Ormond's assistance to secure a formal pardon for herself and her family and to lodge a claim to part of the forfeited estates. Ormond was willing to secure her a pardon and wrote to the Lords Justices in Dublin on her behalf: 'My very good LLs. the Countess of Desmond hath beene an ernest sutor unto me to writt to your LLs for pardon.'⁵ However, regarding her intention to secure part of her husband's estate, Ormond was less enthusiastic. 'She clameth', he wrote, 'to have a great porcion of therle of Desmond's lands for her joyntor.'⁶ In an attempt to prohibit her from making a claim to her husband's estate, the Irish Privy Council curtly signified to Ormond 'their disapproval of any pardon to the Countess of Desmond'.⁷ But Eleanor refused to be deterred and persuaded the earl to plead her case for a pardon directly to the Queen. In January 1584 she met with qualified success when the Queen notified the Dublin administration:

> We are also content that the lady of Desmond shall have her pardon with some such conditions annexed thereto as shall be thought convenient for her quiet behaviour.⁸

Elizabeth could well afford to be magnanimous in victory. A pardon was an insignificant exchange for one of the greatest prizes that had ever fallen into her lap.

By now the clamour of claims to the escheated estates had reached a crescendo, and Eleanor's tentative approaches were pushed aside. The hordes of undertakers, adventurers, Crown administrators and soldiers who queued up for the great pay-off were joined by the remnants of the House of Desmond, seeking their share of the spoils. Garrett's elder half-brother, Thomas Roe FitzGerald, whose claim to the earldom had been disallowed in 1558 in favour of Garrett, now came forward, together with his son James. They petitioned the Queen to restore them to the Desmond estates, which they claimed were rightfully theirs. They further argued that since neither had supported the Earl of Desmond in the late rebellion, there was no impediment to their case. Their pleas, however, fell on deaf ears. Eleanor again entered the fray with a claim to lands in Limerick. Ormond notified the Crown of her intent. 'She claymeth', he wrote, 'to have had a conveyance from her husband afore his entering into rebellion for the most part of his land in the County of Limerick.'⁹ Whether the conveyance was actually produced or not is uncertain, but her claim was taken so seriously by the Irish Privy Council that they withheld her pardon until the matter could be satisfactorily resolved in favour of the Crown.

Eleanor and her daughters were still living on charity, and their future position and welfare in Ormond had become precarious. They could not remain there indefinitely. Already Eleanor's persistent claims to the forfeited estates of her husband had embarrassed her current protector and threatened his own claim to the lands. Consequently, during the early months of 1584, the Council in Dublin brought pressure to bear on Eleanor to forfeit whatever claims she was reported to have to her late husband's estate. 'Before I could receive my pardon', she later testified, 'I was fayne to enter into recognizences of £10,000 that neither my self nor eny other to my use shall make tytle, challenge or entrye, to any dower, jointor or thirds of eny parte of my husband's lands.'[10] She was further obliged to agree that neither she 'nor eny of my five comfortles children shall nott departe this realme, neither can I obtayne licens to go in to England to be a petitioner to her Matie'.[11] The policy of alienation implemented against her husband was to be continued against his widow and children lest the Crown relent and deprive the waiting hordes of avaricious entrepreneurs of even the smallest part of the great prize. Denied the restitution of her dowry price she was condemned to live on the charity of others. Ormond was ordered to provide 'a diet of 10d per diem for her self her daughters and weeman',[12] and on this meagre subsistence the Countess of Desmond and her household were expected to exist.

She was abandoned by the Gaelic world whose cause her husband had sought to champion. Few of his Gaelic and gaelicised allies wished to associate with or be seen to assist the traitor's wife. Her brother, the Baron of Dunboyne, also deserted her in her need. The English-educated James Butler had matured in the mould of his overlord Black Tom. He had little sympathy or tolerance for the Gaelic world that had absorbed his brother-in-law and brought about his downfall. He had become a prominent member of the 'Old English' aristocracy, loyal to the Crown and more concerned with matters of land and title than attempt to hold back the tide of time in defence of an outmoded way of life. For Dunboyne the enemy was not the Crown but the new breed of English adventurers whose appetite for land and wealth might not be appeased merely by the acquisition of the attainted lands of his rebel brother-in-law. To succour a rebel's wife and children, even one's own sister, might well be used by the enemy to discredit him with the Crown. Moreover, Eleanor had quarrelled with her brother over his refusal to give up lands bequeathed to her by her father as part of her dowry and which she had entrusted to her brother before the rebellion. As ever, Eleanor was left with little option but to rely on her own efforts and wits in the continuing battle to survive.

For almost a year Ireland had been administered by two Lords Justices until, in June 1584, Sir John Perrot eventually assumed the office of Lord Deputy. On his departure from England, the Queen imparted to him her usual impossible requirements for 'good' government in Ireland: 'to increase the revenue without oppressing the subject, to reduce the army without impairing its efficiency, to punish rebels without driving them to desperation, and to reward loyal people without cost to the Crown'.[13] The most pressing issue facing Perrot was the settlement of the Desmond estates; and the knowledge of Munster that he had acquired during his term as President there made him a suitable candidate for the job. In June a commission to survey the escheated lands was established under the Vice-Treasurer Sir Henry Wallop, Sir Valentine Browne, Surveyor-General Ashford and two auditors. Wallop was an able property administrator, and the work of the commission progressed steadily. It is significant that, like many of his fellow-administrators in the Irish service at the time of the Desmond collapse, Wallop was richly rewarded from the escheated estates, being later granted the ancient Geraldine seats of Askeaton, Adare and Croom.

Perrot's attention was initially diverted to Ulster where he took the field against a force of Scots mercenaries whom he suspected of being part of a plot concocted by the king of Scotland against Elizabeth. After a brief but ineffective campaign, which elicited a sharp rebuke from Elizabeth against 'such rash unadvised journeys',[14] Perrot returned to Dublin and prepared to summon the first parliament to be held since 1569.

Eleanor had alerted the Lord Deputy to her plight, and initially Perrot seemed well-intentioned towards her. He ordered that she and her family should be removed to his custody and that provision be made for them in Dublin. But he was in some doubt as to what to do about her long-term future. 'We think her estate to be verie bare,' he informed the Queen, 'and much she lamenthed and desyreth to be sent over to your Matie. We have no warrant to proceide against hir by lawe, to send her over, to bayle her or relieve her.'[15] He requested the Queen 'to geve some direction concerninge her'.[16] While he awaited instructions he had Eleanor and her entourage brought from Clonmel and housed within the precincts of Dublin Castle. Eleanor's plight was indeed pressing. Without money or means, abandoned by friends and relations, she had been reduced to the status of a beggar.

> *So as I and my children have lived in such calamitie than if my lo: Deputie had nott taken pittie of me and them in relevinge us owtte of his Lops: kitchin we might have starved with honger: for in my necessitie all my kinsmen and frends have utterly forsaken me.*[17]

In Dublin Castle Eleanor visited her son, then awaiting his imminent transfer to London. Now thirteen, James was old enough to comprehend the enormity of the tragedy that had befallen his house, with such disastrous consequences for his own future. For a fleeting moment Eleanor was reunited with her pitiful son, to whom she could give no tidings of freedom or hope, and whose future she could only expect to be as miserable as his short past, a life of captivity and exploitation. As the day of his departure loomed nearer, Eleanor pleaded with Perrot that her son should be accompanied to London by his nurse and one of his sisters. Little attention was given to the fate of the heir of Desmond. In Ireland men were too busy in a fierce struggle for land to concern themselves about the fortunes of a child whose patrimony had evaporated, whose legitimate place was taken by another, and who would have been—even had he a lordship to succeed to—'equally set aside as from his youth unfit to command in troubled times so powerful a sept'.[18] The dark vaults of the Tower of London closed over the child who was fated to spend sixteen long years in captivity, forgotten and ignored by the powers to whose care he had been entrusted. Eleanor and her daughters continued their life of humiliation and despair in Dublin Castle, defenceless and destitute, fed by the morsels that fell their way from the Lord Deputy's table.

Perrot convened a parliament in April 1585. Twenty-seven counties were represented, mainly by the 'Old English' group. While some Gaelic chieftains were present in both houses, and others were invited to attend as observers, most Gaelic-held areas were not represented. Dublin was *en fête* for the occasion, and the narrow cobbled streets were thronged with lords, chieftains and their retinues. Eleanor looked on with the rest at the parade of Gaelic chieftains and anglicised lords dressed in their obligatory English apparel. She saw her husband's old fellow-conspirator, Turlough O'Neill, choking in the doublet and hose of his new-found allegiance, yet prepared to put on the loyal show to preserve his interests. Beside him rode the greatest single threat to his position in Ulster, his second cousin, the English-educated Earl of Tyrone, Hugh O'Neill, who had been well rewarded for his contrived loyalty, his help in suppressing the rebel Earl of Desmond, and his participation in the savagery that had subdued and despoiled Munster. Thither came Eleanor's brother, her brother-in-law the Earl of Clancar, and the former friends, allies and liege lords of her husband, as they trooped into Perrot's parliament to vote for the formal attainder of their former overlord. But Eleanor could scarcely blame them for their sudden conversion. As she had long counselled her husband, survival was the key, and adaptation was the means to survive. Loyalty to an antique and doomed world was a luxury which could no longer be afforded.

The parliament was an acrimonious one. Perrot was thwarted by antagonistic officials in his own administration and by the lords of the Pale, who continued to oppose the Crown's intent to replace the old system of cess by a land tax. Perrot was opposed and failed also in his attempt to enact a measure suspending Poynings' Law which, if successful, would have enabled legislation to be passed by the Irish parliament without recourse to England. Religion, for the first time, began to emerge as a divisive political measure. Until then the Crown had been prepared to tolerate religious divergence in Ireland because it feared that any attempt to impose the reformed religion would lead to even greater civil unrest. 'It was more important that the Queen should rule Ireland than that Ireland should abandon the Pope.'[19] But now, with the ideological struggle between Catholicism and Protestantism encroaching on the political issues of the day, and with the power of Spain threatening her throne, Elizabeth was forced to change her ambivalent attitude. Catholic Ireland was a danger to Protestant England's security. By their intervention in the Desmond rebellions Philip II and the Pope had already attempted to capitalise on this fact. While the more radical Puritan elements in both the Irish and English administrations sought the implementation of laws against recusants in Ireland, Perrot well realised that, for the moment, sheer strength of numbers alone ensured 'the impossibility of coercing the majority into conformity',[20] and plans for the introduction of penal legislation were, for the moment, postponed. But Perrot's temporising attitude and generally pacific policy towards the Gaelic lords and chieftains, combined with his public antagonism to the more radical elements within his own administration, provoked the latter's enmity and were eventually to lead to his downfall.

In the second session of the new parliament the long-awaited bill of attainder against the late Earl of Desmond and his adherents was introduced. Whether Eleanor was involved in the subsequent attempt to prevent the attainder of her husband and to have the Desmond estates returned to her, in trust for her son, is uncertain. However, given her astute political knowledge and her ability to negotiate and intrigue as well as the next, it is likely that she plotted and was party to this final attempt to secure that for which she had endured and sacrificed so much. To thwart her potential claims to the estates, a measure was first pushed through parliament by the government. It stipulated 'that all conveyances made, or pretended to be made, by any person attainted within thirteen years before the Act, shall be entered on record in the Exchequer within a year, or be void'.[21] Before the bill of attainder could be introduced, however, Sir John FitzEdmund FitzGerald rose in the chamber and submitted the original feoffment 'by which the late Earl of Desmond had placed all his estates in trust for his wife and son, at a time when he was wholly free from all taint of rebellion'.[22]

There was uproar in the house. Panic-stricken potential grantees clamoured for an explanation. Sir Henry Wallop was speedily despatched to determine whether the late earl's deed of association with his adherents, signifying his intention to rebel, had been signed by him *before* the execution of the enfeoffment of his lands. If it had, then by the terms of the new act, the earl was deemed to have forfeited his estate. If, however, the date of the feoffment preceded that of the document containing the deed of association, then the Crown's claim to the Desmond estate was invalid. 'In the entire collection of the State Papers of England, no document exists that was of equal importance as to its absolute correctness of date, as this one, for on none other ever depended the transfer of estates so vast and so valuable.'[23]

The feoffment, as preserved among the Carew Papers in Lambeth Palace, bears the date of 10 September 1574, while the deed of association is dated 18 July 1578, four years later. Wallop claimed that the deed of association bore the incorrect date and should have read 18 July 1574, thus putting it 'seven weeks earlier than the execution of the feoffment'.[24] He based his conclusion on the contents of the first sentence of the deed of association, which reads: 'Whereas the earl had assembled his kinsmen and others after his coming out of Dublin . . .'[25] This, he contended, referred to the earl's escape from detention in Dublin in November 1573.

Given the fortune that depended on the issue, as well as the anxiety of the Crown and the avaricious expectations of the waiting undertakers and speculators, it is not beyond the bounds of reason to suspect the authenticity of Wallop's evidence. It certainly seems strange that the matter was only raised in the first place because Sir John FitzEdmund FitzGerald, who had been a signatory to the deed of feoffment, was convinced that a miscarriage of justice was about to be perpetrated against the Countess of Desmond and her son. Throughout the duration of the Desmond rebellion FitzEdmund had been a model of loyalty to the Crown and had dissociated himself completely from the rebellion of his kinsman. He explained his actions regarding the feoffment to Sir Francis Walsingham as having no ulterior motive other than a sense of justice and fair play: 'I thought it my parte to tell, onely in discharge of my conscience and honestie before God and the worlde, not as a thinge I wished allowed.'[26]

FitzEdmund's efforts were doomed to failure. Parliament accepted Wallop's theory. The final attempt to prevent the forfeiture of her husband's estates and title came to nought, leaving Eleanor and her children ostracised. Had she succeeded then 'the vast estates of the earl must have slipped through the fingers, matchless for their tenacity, of Her Majesty, and a multitude of enterprising English gentlemen must have returned home'[27] empty-handed. The act of attainder of the Earl of Desmond and his chief supporters 'and the vesting of their lands, without inquisition, in the Crown',[28] was passed without a whisper of protest from the Gaelic and gaelicised chieftains and lords present, much to the relief of the potential colonists who lined up for the division of the spoils.

After the attainder of her husband and the confiscation of his estates, the fortunes of Eleanor and her family rapidly deteriorated. Perhaps to punish her for attempting to prevent the forfeiture, Sir John Perrot withdrew his assistance, and Eleanor and her daughters were thrown onto the streets of Dublin and on the charity of anyone touched by their plight. Most of her acquaintances resolutely turned their backs. However, she still retained her astute insight into the political arena and her ability to exploit the many factions and coteries that it comprised. She turned for help to Perrot's implacable enemy, Adam Loftus, the Archbishop of Dublin, who agreed to alert the Crown to the extremity of her circumstances in Dublin.

> *I assure you [he wrote to Burghley] hir case (being chargid with childrin) is so miserable that seldom the lyke hath bene sene in a woman of hir calling. All hir frends . . . have quite forsaken hir: so as if yor L, with the rest of that honorable board, be not a mean to hir Matie, to grant unto hir some portion to releive hir and hir childrin, there is no doubt but that shortly they all will goo a beginge.*[29]

But the government was reluctant to come to her aid. As the winter drew near, the cold, unfriendly streets of Dublin held more terror for Eleanor than the wastelands of Munster. She was heavily in debt to merchants and traders in the city and her credit was fast running out. The desperation of her plight as she scrounged food and clothing for her needy children she conveyed in a letter to Burghley:

> *I and my childrin have tasted of so moche myserie thatt I protest unto your honnor I knowe no waye howe to preserve me and them from perishing by famyne except her Matie do nott relieve us.*[30]

But winter came and went without any assistance from the Crown. With her ragged, frightened children clutched around her, she tramped the streets of Dublin in search of sustenance. In a city that had recently felt the effects of famine, for which her husband was blamed, few doors were opened to her, and the faces of the citizens were as cold as the icy winds that blew through the narrow streets. Once again she wrote to remind Burghley of her wretchedness and poverty:

> *At the present time my miserie is such that my children and myself liveth in all wante of meat drinke and clothes, having no house or dwellinge wherin I with them may rest, neither the aid of Brother or kinsman to relieve oure necessitie which is so myserable that I see my poore children in manner starve before me.*[31]

The memory of her husband's rebellion and of her personal involvement in it were, however, still vivid at court. Walsingham had never favoured the Earl of Desmond or his house, and his dislike of Garrett was transferred to his widow. Memories of the effects of the rebellion were constantly recalled, as in December 1585, when the Crown rewarded the Earl of Desmond's executioner, Daniel Kelly, 'in consideration of his having slain the traitor Desmond'.[32] The Queen incessantly bemoaned the vast amounts expended in the suppression of the rebellion. And as the extent of the damage and devastation of the forfeited Desmond estate became apparent, there were growing doubts as to whether the land would ever recompense the Crown for the outlay it had expended in securing it.

But Elizabeth was also confronted with more urgent and important issues in England which diverted her attention from Ireland and from the pleas of an impoverished Irish countess. Around her the tempo of national and international intrigue had reached a crescendo. Plots against the security of her realm and conspiracies against her life daily ebbed and flowed. A plot among English Catholic gentry, aided and abetted by the Spanish ambassador to England, to assassinate her, had earlier been uncovered. The plot hinted at the involvement of the Queen's cousin, Mary Stuart, who despite being kept under close confinement in Sheffield, continued to scheme against her cousin with unrelenting enthusiasm, conspiring with the King of Spain, the Pope, the Duke of Guise, and her son James VI of Scotland. Mary attracted the attention of the international conspiracy which sought Elizabeth's overthrow. Every scheme had hitherto been unsuccessful; nevertheless, Mary, who 'seemed to thrive on adversity and derived renewed hope from every defeat',[33] persevered. As the prospect of war with Spain grew ever more likely, and the plots against Elizabeth grew more desperate, Protestant feeling in England, both among the people and in the parliament, against Mary Stuart and her foreign Catholic fellow-conspirators, grew. Puritan opinion demanded her head, and Elizabeth's counsellors cautioned that she was sheltering within her kingdom 'the daughter of sedition, the mother of rebellion, the handmaid of iniquity and the sister of unshamefastness'.[34] But Elizabeth had constantly refused to permit the execution 'of a divinely ordained sovereign . . . it set a dangerous precedent'.[35] During 1586, however, Mary exceeded her previous indiscretions in a reckless new plot against the Queen. This time the wily Walsingham had baited the trap and gathered the necessary evidence. Elizabeth was left with little option but to sanction the trial and execution of her cousin.

Before that event Philip of Spain finally made up his mind 'that the retribution of heaven upon the heretic and monstrous Queen of England had been too long deferred'.[36] He considered Elizabeth's imminent downfall God's expressed will, and himself the chosen instrument to put that will into effect. Elizabeth and her subjects, on the other hand, believed that England was the final bastion of hope for the world against the insidious incursions of the Catholic confederacy led by the Pope, the King of Spain and the Catholic faction in France, driven by the lust for power of the Medici and their Valois dynasty. 'The odds had been taken, the sides drawn, and Europe waited and speculated on which of them, Elizabeth of England or Philip of Spain, was the shining messenger of the Lord.'[37] It was not surprising that the welfare of an Irish countess, no matter how destitute and deprived, received little attention at the English Court.

For Eleanor the crisis facing herself and her children, however, was to her as important as Philip's designs on England. Rebuffed at every level, in May 1586 she again solicited the help of Archbishop Loftus, who agreed to write to the government on her behalf. The archbishop's appeal was blunt. He could himself vouch for the countess's extreme necessity, he told Burghley, and

> *could not resonably denye, being an eye witness of her extreme mysery ... to make knowne ... how in truthe she standeth at this prsnt: being not hable to sustaine her selfe or her poore children with necessary foode, but are ... lyke to famishe if her Matie do not grant bestowe some portion upon her for her relayfe.*[38]

But, as before, the archbishop failed to get a response.

Eleanor was now at her wits' end. She faced the prospect of prison as her bills mounted and the merchants and money-lenders clamoured for payment. Secretly she prepared to embark for England in a last-ditch attempt to plead her case personally at court. But she was prohibited by law from leaving Ireland without special licence from the Lord Deputy. She had, moreover, signed bonds which had been guaranteed by members of the Munster aristocracy to that effect. Undeterred, however, during the latter months of 1586 she begged and borrowed from every available source to fund her mission. But some of the lords who had guaranteed her bonds, such as Viscount Roche of Fermoy, who was bound for the sum of £100, grew uneasy about her intentions. They urged her to reconsider her proposed flight to England. She refused. Finally Lord Roche alerted Lord Deputy Perrot to Eleanor's plans. He begged Perrot that, in view of his dutifulness, his own bond of £100 should not be forfeited. Perrot's cryptic reply did little to relieve his anxiety. 'Touching the countesse of Desmonds going into England,' the Lord Deputy wrote, 'yt is more than I knowe, neither can she goe without licence from me so to doe, which she is not like to have.'[39]

But before Eleanor could attempt her escape to England in early 1587, her plight was finally brought to the attention of the Queen, who decided that 'the Countess of Desmond should have a pension of one hundred pounds Irish'[40] and ordered Sir John Perrot to pay her. On the strength of the promised pension, Eleanor obtained additional credit from the Dublin merchants to feed and clothe herself and her children, though, as she later divulged, 'I owe duble for everything I hadde.'[41] Her indebtedness to the merchants increased when Perrot declined to pay her the pension out of his administrative costs. Her situation was again desperate. 'Her creditors (being not paid of their former debt) would no further lett her have meate, drinke nor any other necessaries.'[42] Eleanor could take no more. Towards the end of 1587 she managed to obtain a passage to England, leaving her daughters in care in Ireland.

She made her way to London, and for the following twelve months she followed the court in the same state of abject poverty and debt as she had endured in Ireland. Even if she had the means to influence or bribe those in power to gain access to the Queen, political developments made an audience virtually impossible. Throughout the early months of 1588 rumours of an imminent invasion by Spain preoccupied Elizabeth and her Privy Council. After months of speculation the great Spanish Armada lumbered into the English Channel 'to visit the censure of God upon a middle-aged female'.[43] Despite ample warning, England was ill-prepared to meet the challenge. All through the summer, as Elizabeth moved her court from place to place, Eleanor followed patiently in her wake. She had to maintain a low profile. Passions and prejudices had been aroused in England against the new Spanish threat to which her name, in the past, had been linked. The court bustled with activity as messengers brought despatches with reports of the sea battles in the Channel, and the Queen and her counsellors held lengthy meetings on matters of state security. But Eleanor persistently and patiently waited her chance. She had become used to isolation, hostility, humiliation and poverty and the quiet resignation that such conditions induce. She had been somewhat encouraged by Burghley, who had looked on her presence kindly enough, though he could, as yet, spare little time to examine her case in detail.

She meanwhile contrived to visit her son in his cell in the Tower. Memories came flooding back as she traversed the stone passages to be reunited with him as she had with his father some twenty years previously. She found James in distress from an ear ailment which was being treated by the prison physician without success. His general health had, not surprisingly, remained fragile. The damp, stale air of the Tower did little to relieve the general malaise that had afflicted him since birth. He had become both institutionalised and anglicised, a passive prisoner of his unnatural surroundings, nervous and apprehensive lest he incur the displeasure of those in charge of his welfare. His later correspondence is proof that Eleanor's concern regarding his lack of a formal education had been rectified. A schoolmaster, with a salary of £13-13s per annum, had been appointed to educate him, and he was taught to express himself well and to write in a bold, clear hand. His literary style, taking into account his youth and lack of experience of the world, was frequently 'very superior to that of the statesmen to whom his letters were mostly addressed'.[44] There was little else Eleanor could do for her son who seemed lost to her and to the world.

When the Spanish Armada finally disappeared towards the North Sea, to be battered and broken on the jagged, unfriendly rocks of the Irish coastline, Elizabeth resumed her more mundane duties. She agreed to receive the Countess of Desmond and hear her petition. Eleanor had her audience with the Queen at St James's Palace in early October 1588. Elizabeth wore her fifty-five years well. After the repulse of the Spanish threat she appeared every bit the

Goddesse Heavenly Bright,
Mirror of grace and Majestie divine,
Great lady of the greatest Isle, whose light
Like Phoebus lampe throughout the world doth shine[45]

of Spenser's *Faerie Queene*. Elizabeth could still dazzle her subjects
into love and loyalty by the very radiance of her attire. It was irrelevant
to her adoring subjects that the famous red hair was now a wig; her
ruddy complexion was liberally aided by the application of rouge and
rice powder. The regal presence that emanated from her slight frame
owed much to the sheer opulence and weight of her wardrobe. Good
Queen Bess had saved her subjects from a fate worse than the fires of
the Inquisition, and now, more than ever, 'she could still marshal
words and command emotions'.[46] And there was little competition or
threat to her looks, wardrobe or majesty from the gaunt, tattered,
dispirited countess who knelt before her to beg for sustenance to
provide herself and her family with the bare necessities of life. Sheer
pity alone would have moved Elizabeth to loosen her purse-strings. As
Eleanor explained the extremity of her situation in Ireland and how
the Queen's previous pension of £100 had been withheld from her,
Elizabeth's sympathies were aroused and she forwarded new
instructions to her Lord Deputy:

> *Wee having compasson of hir unhappie and miserable estate*
> *whereunto she is fallen, rather by hir said husband's disloyaltie, than*
> *by anie hir owne offence, are pleased for hir owne reliefe to bestowe on*
> *hir a yearely pension of two hundreth pounds sterling to be paid to hir*
> *quarterly out of our excheqr of that realme.*[47]

But past experience had made Eleanor suspicious of the Crown's
servants, and she reminded the Queen that her previous order to the
Lord Deputy and Council in Ireland for the payment of her pension
had gone unheeded. Elizabeth consequently despatched a personally
signed and sealed letter to her officials in Dublin, commanding the
prompt payment to Eleanor of her pension so that, as she stated, 'she
may have no just cause to complayne for want of payment of the
same'.[48] But bureaucracy seemed destined to thwart even the orders of
the Queen. For an addendum to the Queen's letter subsequently noted
that payment of the pension was, for some months, 'stay'd upon a
doubt moved by Mr Soliciter'.[49] Meanwhile, her mission accomplished,
Eleanor unsuspectingly returned to Ireland in high expectations of
some measure of respite from her state of misery and misfortune.

On her return to Dublin she found Sir John Perrot had been
recalled and that Sir William Fitzwilliam had succeeded him as Lord

Deputy. But the change in personnel brought little relief, for she found Fitzwilliam's administration as reluctant as its predecessor to comply with the Queen's instruction. By December 1588 she had received only part of her pension from the Council in Dublin. She therefore decided on a different course of action. She requested the English Privy Council that she might be paid her pension out of the English rather than the Irish exchequer. The Queen was agreeable, and accordingly in early 1589 Eleanor, accompanied by her daughters, Morris Sheehan and a small retinue, departed once more for England and settled near Westminster. But there were other reasons than the payment of her pension behind her decision to move to England.

The dispersal of her late husband's estates had begun. The lands to be planted were among the richest in the country. It was originally the intention of the Crown that seignories or chief grants, not exceeding 12,000 acres, were to be created for the principal grantees, or undertakers as they became known. But wily lawyers contrived to extend the grants on behalf of their clients beyond the proposed limits. Many grantees, notably Sir Walter Raleigh, ultimately became owners of estates of over 40,000 acres, much more than had been envisaged by the Crown. The grants were made in socage with a head or quit rent payable to the Crown. The plantation was widely advertised in England as an opportunity to acquire an estate at little cost. The native Irish were prohibited from becoming tenants or undertenants of the new proprietors. However, the initial aims of the Munster plantation were gradually distorted and undermined. The majority of the undertakers became absentees. Their estates were managed by agents who readily employed Irish tenants. Ireland's reputation for political unrest deterred the more suitable English farmers, who refused to be lured by promises of wealth to such a wild and unstable country. But the hardened veterans of Grey's expeditionary force showed little such hesitancy and eagerly grasped the spoils of war. In counties Waterford and Cork Sir Walter Raleigh and Sir Christopher Hatton received large estates. Sir Edward Denny, Sir Warham St Leger, Sir Thomas Morris, Hugh Cuffe and the poet Edmund Spenser, all received attainted Desmond land and property in County Cork. In County Limerick the main beneficiaries were Francis Berkeley, Sir William Courtney, Richard and Alex Fitton and Sir George Bourchier, while Edmund Fitton received over 11,000 acres in counties Waterford and Tipperary. The long hunt to extinction of the former proprietor had been vindicated as the pursuers reaped the rewards without regard for the widow and heir of the attainted earl.

However faint, Eleanor had not given up hope to salvage some part of the forfeited lands. Residence in London would enable her to petition her case directly rather than have to negotiate with the antagonistic administration in Dublin. She also sought more regular access to her son. While the conditions of his confinement allowed him 'the libertie of the Tower . . . and accesse of all his friends',[50] his health was again giving cause for concern. As well as a physician, he now required the services of a surgeon, while the list of medicines supplied by the Tower apothecary grew:

> *ii Bottels of serope of iii pints apeace*
> *ii pourgatives*
> *iiii ownces of perfumed lossengis for his nostrells*
> *iiii ownces of serope for his nostrells*
> *iiii ownces of Unguente for his eare*
> *iiii ownces of Implaster for his eare*
> *iiii ownces of pilles of Masticgini*
> *ii drames of pillemics*
> *i drame of Trossecs deterra sigillata.*[51]

The list was just part of the long catalogue of pills and potions prescribed for the various maladies that wracked his unhealthy physique.

In London Eleanor first made the acquaintance of the man who was to be central in her future life. Donogh O'Connor Sligo was also at court to petition for the restoration of his title and estate as the heir of his uncle. Sir Donal O'Connor Sligo had died in January 1588 and his estate had been subsequently seized by the President of Connaught, Sir Richard Bingham. In their past misfortunes and present straitened circumstances, Eleanor and Donogh had much in common.

The family of O'Connor Sligo were a branch of the royal O'Connor house of Connaught. The earliest historical references to the O'Connor sept of Sligo occur at the time of the Norman invasion. In the succeeding centuries, following a series of dynastic feuds, the O'Connor clan split into three divisions: O'Connor Roe, O'Connor Don and O'Connor Sligo. The O'Connor Sligo sept eventually settled in the area roughly equivalent to present-day County Sligo. A member of the sept bore the title King of Connaught between 1318 and 1324. By the sixteenth century the O'Connor Sligo was the acknowledged overlord of the area. But O'Connor dominance in Sligo became dependent on the O'Donnell chiefs of Tyrconnell, who also claimed a suzerainty over Sligo. Through alliances with the O'Donnells' enemies, the O'Connors constantly sought to cast off the shackles of O'Donnell dominance. To the south-west of Sligo lay the lordship of the former de Burgos—the Lower MacWilliam of Mayo and the Upper MacWilliam of Galway. The latter had been created Earl of Clanrickard by Henry VIII.

Sligo occupied a strategic position between Ulster and Connaught. Donogh's lordship incorporated the barony of Carbury, with Sligo castle as its central point. He also claimed the castles of Ballymote and Collooney. To protect themselves from the heavy exaction of the O'Donnells, the O'Connors had turned for help to the English. In 1568 Donogh's uncle, Sir Donal, made an indenture with the Queen which he interpreted as a reaffirmation of his overlordship of Sligo but which the Crown later claimed related only to the overlordship of the barony of Carbury. However, the grant allowed him to maintain his rights to the overlordship of the county, and the Crown tended to support him in his struggle against the O'Donnells. The agreement between O'Connor Sligo and the Crown worked well until jeopardised by a dramatic change in the political climate, marked by the arrival in Connaught of Sir Richard Bingham as President of the province in 1584.

A stern military campaigner, Bingham carried out his orders to the letter to extend English law into all parts of Connaught in the shortest time possible, allowing little scope for the Gaelic chieftains to adapt. Bingham began his campaign in Connaught by seizing the O'Connor Sligo castle of Ballymote, ostensibly as a precaution against an invasion by supporters of Mary Queen of Scots. Bingham recognised the advantage of securing a strong foothold in Sligo to control the pass from Ulster into Mayo and thus into the rest of Connaught. Sir Donal appealed to Sir John Perrot in Dublin. The Lord Deputy issued letters patent officially confirming the original agreement with the Queen, though excluding Ballymote and twelve quarters of land.

In the following year Perrot concluded the famous Composition of Connaught whereby, in lieu of cess, a rent of ten English shillings, or one Irish mark, was to be charged on every quarter of arable land in the province. Certain lands were allowed rent-free to principal lords. Their positions as elected heads of their traditional dependent clans were abolished, and each chieftain was made responsible for his own sept and had to hold his estate under the English law of primogeniture instead of the Gaelic custom of election. In relation to Sligo, the Composition 'merely put into formal feudal language the terms of the earlier agreement'[52] between Sir Donal and the Queen. Sir Donal continued to hold his estate in the manor of Ballymote and was granted all his lands free of the Composition rent. On his death in 1588, despite the seizure of Ballymote and Sligo by Bingham, his heir, Donogh, seemed likely to inherit the entire lordship.

Sir Richard Bingham, however, refused to recognise Donogh as his uncle's legal heir. 'The heir is base born and illegitimate,' he wrote to the Earl of Leicester, 'and the land, especially Sligo itself, by descent and lawful inheritance is now thrown into the lap of Her Majesty.'[53] Although a commission of inquiry subsequently found Donogh to be the legitimate heir, Bingham persisted in his opposition and moved his brother, George Bingham, into Sligo castle. While the dispute raged, ships of the Spanish Armada came crashing onto the Sligo coastline. Rumours reached the English court that the Spaniards who had survived were planning to invade Connaught in support of the Ulster chieftains. Possession of Sligo castle took on an added significance, and the question of Donogh's right to inherit was once again investigated. In an attempt to persuade the Crown to reinstate him and to repudiate the accusations of Bingham, Donogh took his case directly to the English court. There he became acquainted with the widow of the rebel Earl of Desmond.

The similarity of their situation, coupled with the fact that the success of both their petitions depended on the patronage and influence of Lord Burghley, was perhaps instrumental in establishing a friendship between them. Both were exiles, political outcasts, in poor circumstances and without friends. Of the two, Eleanor's position was the more extreme, especially in terms of her future financial and political expectations. Donogh, while currently regarded as politically dispensable by the English interest in Connaught, could become a vital factor to the Crown—and this possibility increased as the situation in Ulster deteriorated. But meanwhile both had to endure the tedious court protocol regarding their petitions. With little money to speed or influence the process, they had no option but to assume the patience and humility of the penniless and the powerless.

Both initially made little progress. Eleanor's pension was not forthcoming from the tight-fisted administration, while Bingham continued to press against the reinstatement of Donogh in Sligo. Unable financially to continue to follow the court, Eleanor settled near Westminster, under the care of a widow, Alice Pynnock, who, it was recorded, was paid the sum of £85 'for the diet of the Countess of Desmond'.[54] Together with her pension, Eleanor also sought further concessions from the Queen. By her entry without licence into England she had, in effect, transgressed the conditions of her pardon and had 'therby forfeited certain bonds wherein she is entered for the performance of the clause'.[55] The Queen eventually agreed to overlook the transgression and ordered the Lord Deputy to ensure that any future bonds made for her continuing good behaviour 'should not be hurtful or prejudicial unto her for that which is past'.[56] Slowly, Eleanor was beginning to experience some semblance of toleration, if not favour, in court circles. Her old enemy Walsingham was dead, and Sir Robert Cecil had joined his father, Lord Burghley, at the forefront of Elizabeth's administration. The younger Cecil was willing to extend a little sympathy and understanding to the long-suffering countess from Ireland and this brilliant, delicate, hunchbacked statesman became Eleanor's main refuge and hope.

While Eleanor's fortunes at court seemed likely to improve, the expectations of her friend, Donogh O'Connor Sligo, also seemed likely to bear fruit. In 1596, as the political situation worsened in Ireland, the Crown considered it expedient that Donogh should return to Ireland and be restored to part of his inheritance. England's supposedly loyal earl, Hugh O'Neill of Tyrone, from the fastness of his Ulster kingdom, noted Bingham's savage chastisement of Connaught, where the Mayo Bourkes, after three unsuccessful attempts to restore their ancient rights, had been ground into submission and their hired Scottish mercenaries butchered and drowned on the banks of the Moy. O'Neill noted too Bingham's advance into Sligo and his unrelenting campaign against O'Rourke of Breffny, who had sheltered some Spanish castaways from the ill-fated Armada. Alarm-bells sounded in the cunning, pragmatic mind of the Ulster chieftain as Bingham attacked Maguire's lordship of Fermanagh, the last remaining bastion of O'Neill's hitherto impregnable kingdom of Tyrone. The ghost of the dead Earl of Desmond might well have returned to remind him of the bitter fate he had helped inflict on Desmond and which now faced him in Ulster. But it was still too soon to show one's hand. There were too many intangible obstacles to be overcome before O'Neill's great plan could be put into operation. Despite the suspicions of the English administration in Dublin, he must continue to appear Elizabeth's loyal Irish earl. Consequently he bawled like a child before the Council in Dublin and tearfully protested his loyalty on old Fitzwilliam's shoulder to stifle suspicion that he was involved in a conspiracy with Spain and Scotland against the English Crown. But in December 1591 he helped to effect the dramatic escape of his relative and future ally, the young Red Hugh O'Donnell, whom Perrot had imprisoned in Dublin Castle. O'Neill sought to mould the lust for revenge of the young Tyrconnell chieftain, as well as the seething discontent of the Gaelic chieftains, into a calculating patience until the time was ripe for open confederacy and rebellion.

While O'Neill played a waiting game, his young ally attempted to reassert O'Donnell supremacy over Sligo, extend his power and influence into Connaught, and extract support for the forthcoming war with the Crown. Sligo was the key to success in the coming conflict, and both sides realised its strategic importance. The methods employed by Bingham were called into question as officials in the administration in Dublin, jealous of his success in Connaught, attempted to have him removed from office. Taking advantage of Bingham's misfortune O'Donnell raided unhindered through Sligo into Roscommon. In 1595 he seized Sligo castle, which was garrisoned by Bingham's brother. It was against this background that the English government, in a bid to stop O'Donnell's growing power in Connaught, decided that Donogh O'Connor Sligo should be reinstated 'in the hope that he could be used as a buffer against the commonwealth which O'Donnell appeared to be creating in Connaught'.[57]

Donogh returned to Ireland in 1596, while Eleanor remained on at her lodgings in Westminster. While Cecil had managed to have her pension restored, with directions that it should be paid at quarterly intervals, £200 per annum would hardly restore her to a lifestyle that befitted her rank and status. Furthermore, despite Cecil's intervention on her behalf, the pension continued to be paid sporadically at the whim of petty officials. Her petitions to Cecil continued in the same vein as before. 'My great wants and extremities, the daily dearness of victuals . . . urges me to be more troublesome,'[58] she wrote to him in May 1597 in an attempt to secure a more permanent cure for her financial straits. If Cecil could not secure her part of either her jointure or the estate of her late husband, Eleanor made the startling request that he act on her behalf as matchmaker. She explained that she was willing to extend her offer 'to any in England or Ireland that would be pleased to marry either myself or my daughters'.[59]

Her request was not as extraordinary as it might appear. She was now over fifty years old and had been a widow for fourteen years. The political stigma attached to her name was gradually receding, although her distinct lack of a fortune or a dowry did not enhance her matrimonial prospects. But fortune took a hand to find her a mate. By the establishment of a network of marriage alliances in Connaught, Cecil was seeking to create an opposition among the local aristocracy to stem the support for the Ulster confederacy. He had successfully concluded a marriage alliance between O'Connor Sligo's sister, Maeve, and the prominent chieftain of the Mayo Bourkes, Tibbott-ne-Long, the youngest son of the redoubtable sea-captain, Grace O'Malley, who had visited the Court in 1593. The marriage had produced satisfactory political results, and the former rebel chieftain looked set to adhere to the Crown in the coming conflict. It would appear that Cecil considered a marriage between Eleanor and Donogh would serve a similarly useful purpose, while having the additional advantage of removing from Court a persistent petitioner whose humbled means was a constant reminder of the Munster confiscations.

It was arranged that Eleanor would return to Ireland. Cecil secured the restoration of her personal estate in Munster which her brother had withheld from her. The Queen also wrote on her behalf to the Lord Deputy

> to signify unto you our good liking of the retourne into the realme of the Countess of Desmond, for the opinion we have conceived of her good and lawful behaviour, towards us and our state, so we have now bin pleased to confirme the same unto you by those our own letters. . . . We require you to yealde unto her your favourable assistance in all her lawfull good causes as she may from time to time stand in need thereof and agreeable to the degree she holdeth.[60]

Cecil also obtained freedom of movement for her between Ireland and England. His diplomatic wizardry and Eleanor's persistence had finally achieved a small but, from Eleanor's point of view, significant victory.

In September 1597 Eleanor and her daughters prepared to leave for Ireland. On her departure she acknowledged Cecil's kindness and showed her appreciation as best her circumstances would allow. She presented him with a gift of an Irish harp, 'humbly praying you to accept the same, the rather that the sending comes from a thankful mind'.[61] Then, with a lightened burden and the hope of better fortune, Eleanor set sail for Ireland and a new beginning.

Chapter 9
The Chatelaine

Hecuba: *Fortune veers: be brave,*
Sail with the stream,
Sail with the wind of fate.
Do not run your ship of life
Headlong into the billows of disaster.

EURIPIDES, *THE TROJAN WOMAN*

In 1595 casting aside the mask of loyalty and co-operation, Hugh O'Neill, Earl of Tyrone revealed his intent. Throughout his career his actions had been stimulated by his driving ambition for greatness and power—objectives which once had appeared attainable by loyalty to the Crown, but which now seemed more likely to be achieved by espousing the cause of Gaelic Ireland, a cause he had initially fought to destroy. In February 1595 he sent his brother Art to capture the Blackwater fort, which he had previously helped the Crown to establish. He was proclaimed a traitor in June, and on the death of the old chieftain, Turlough Luineach, he assumed the Gaelic title of 'O'Neill'.

Together with his ally, Red Hugh O'Donnell, he set about establishing unified opposition to England's expansionist designs in Ireland. To this end he re-established communications with the Spanish court, not merely for gold and ammunition, but for an effective Spanish force to support rebellion in Ireland against the English Crown. And Spain seemed eager to assist in the new campaign. But even as the ships and supplies assembled at Cadiz in June 1596, England's sea-dogs, Essex and Howard, in a daring attack, destroyed them. A further attempt in October fell foul of the weather. O'Neill had to buy time and opened negotiations with the Crown. The

Queen, ever anxious to pardon rather than become involved in expensive warfare, accepted the excuses he proffered. Secretly he and O'Donnell continued to conspire with Spain, and called on 'the gentlemen of Munster' to join the Ulster confederacy and to 'make war with us'.[1] The Munster patrimony of Eleanor's late husband and the lordship of her new husband were destined to become part of the concluding chapter in the long saga of Gaelic resistance.

On her return to Ireland from the English court, Eleanor married Donogh O'Connor Sligo. She was then fifty-two years of age, while her new husband would appear to have been a few years her junior. Donogh was a sober, solid chieftain, more concerned to consolidate his position and his estates than engage in active rebellion against the Crown. While socially it could be said that she had married beneath her status, her marriage to O'Connor Sligo was a welcome respite from the years of misery, loneliness and ignominy she had endured since Garrett's rebellion and death. Moreover, from a personal point of view, the marriage seems to have been a happy one. She continued to be referred to as the Countess of Desmond and adhered to the active and independent role she had adopted throughout her life. She obtained possession of the small estate in Tipperary, which her brother had earlier sought to withhold from her, and together with her new husband, she journeyed to Munster to inspect her domain.

Her new home was to be her husband's lordship of Sligo, which the Queen had restored to him, with the exception of the castle and lands of Ballymote. But on their arrival there they found the lordship had been overrun by Hugh O'Donnell, who retained possession of Sligo castle. Eleanor and her husband initially settled at Collooney castle, from where Donogh made vain attempts to stem the ravages perpetrated on his estates and on the estates of his tributary lords, such as the O'Harts and the various O'Connor septs, who expected his protection against the exactions and rapine of O'Donnell. Donogh, in turn, depended on the Crown and, in particular, the English administration in Connaught, to protect him from O'Donnell. But after Bingham's suspension in 1596 the administration there had virtually collapsed and was unable to meet its obligations to the allied Gaelic lords. Consequently, many of the lords who had sided with the Crown, and were willing to administer their estates by English law, were now forced to align with O'Donnell.

In December 1596 Sir Conyers Clifford was appointed Chief Commissioner of Connaught (he was subsequently promoted to the vacant post of President of the province in September 1597). Donogh was acquainted with Clifford at court and was at hand to welcome him to Galway and accompany him on a tour of the province. His friendship was rewarded when Clifford recaptured Sligo castle and installed Donogh there with a garrison. Donogh reciprocated by inducing his brother-in-law, Tibbott-ne-Long Bourke, the most powerful chieftain in Mayo, to make terms with the Crown. Tibbott had become disenchanted with O'Donnell's bid for supremacy in Mayo, and as captain of a fleet of galleys, previously operated by his mother, Grace O'Malley, his sea power made him a formidable ally.

The new Lord Deputy, Thomas Lord Burgh, carried the fight against the Gaelic confederacy into Ulster. He recaptured the Blackwater fort and established a garrison there. Clifford, meanwhile, with the assistance of O'Connor Sligo, simultaneously attacked Ballyshannon castle, but was forced to retreat to Sligo. Clifford could do little more but establish Donogh at Sligo castle and hope to hold out against O'Donnell until further assistance could be had from England.

While her husband strove to hold his position in Sligo, Eleanor was embroiled in a legal battle with her brother, the Baron of Dunboyne, over possession of the disputed estate in Tipperary. Despite the Crown's grant, the baron still contested his sister's right. During the course of 1598 Eleanor journeyed to Dublin and to Tipperary to prepare her case against her brother. In the intervals she resided at Sligo and became acquainted with her husband's political friends, foes, family and relations. Once more she found herself surrounded by intrigue and conspiracies. The political situation was moving to a climax. Messengers from O'Donnell and from Clifford each sought her husband's support in the coming conflict, while spies from both sides reported their every move. No one could be trusted. Allegiances changed as quickly as the tide, and today's friend became tomorrow's foe. Eleanor met her husband's sister Maeve and her enterprising husband, Tibbott-ne-Long, the son of her late husband's former prisoner, Grace O'Malley. The famous female sea-captain still lived on in Mayo and, like Eleanor, had successfully petitioned the Queen for sustenance and protection. At the present time both she and her son favoured the Crown as a less evil option than the exactions of

O'Donnell. But, as Eleanor well realised from bitter experience, the loyalty of the minor lords and chieftains was transitory and depended on the ebb and flow of the political tide. Just as Garrett had expediently, for his political survival, sacrificed Grace O'Malley to the Crown, so had he a few months later eagerly sought and obtained the support of her husband in his rebellion against the Crown. But such was the political reality of sixteenth-century Ireland, where survival was the spur.

Clifford recommended to Sir Robert Cecil that Donogh should be restored to the castle and lands of Ballymote. Consequently Eleanor accompanied him to Dublin, from where he embarked for London, while Eleanor remained to prepare for the impending lawsuit against her brother. The baron demanded that her claim to the disputed estate should be tried by common law, but, as she explained in a petition to Sir Robert Cecil, 'to be tried by a jury of the citizens of Dublin where her brother is more favoured than she,'[2] could hardly be deemed justice. She requested instead that her case should be determined by the Irish Privy Council or heard in the Court of Chancery. Cecil agreed to have the matter further investigated. But political events intervened as Ireland was plunged into a rebellion that again threatened to engulf the entire country.

In August 1598 Sir Henry Bagenal, with an army of over 4,000 men, was sent north to relieve the fort on the Blackwater. O'Neill, O'Donnell and Maguire combined to defeat him decisively at the battle of the Yellow Ford. The result of the battle transformed the campaign of the Ulster chieftains. 'A wave of feeling that was like one vast geyser of long-suppressed discontent', as Seán O'Faolain wrote, 'gushed up and smothered the colonists until within a few months Tyrone was virtual master of Ireland and could see the outline of a rapidly forming confederate army.'[3] But if the exultant feeling was to beget effective results, it would take time for the unfamiliar notion of nationhood to penetrate the mind-set of the multitude of chieftains and lords who regarded the aims and ambitions of O'Neill and O'Donnell as merely an attempt to subjugate them. Already in Sligo and Mayo the peremptory actions of O'Donnell had alienated the principal lords there. It was difficult for O'Connor Sligo or Tibbott Bourke to see any exalted nationalist motivation in the plundering raids made by O'Donnell on their territories.

In Munster, however, the effects of the victory at the Yellow Ford were instantaneous and opened a new chapter in the struggle of the

House of Desmond. And Eleanor, wife and co-conspirator of the last Earl of Desmond, could not fail to become implicated as the survivors of her late husband's family grasped the life-line thrown to them by O'Neill. Garrett's nephew, James, the son of his disinherited half-brother Thomas, rose out of the ashes of defeat to lay claim to the estates and title of his uncle. Eleanor's reaction to the claim was antagonistic as it threatened her son's inheritance. The adherents of her late husband shared her view and referred contemptuously to James FitzThomas as the 'Súgán' (straw-rope) Earl. But with the support of O'Neill, the cowed and dispossessed liege lords of Desmond rose up, if not in support of the claims of FitzThomas, then in support of the only apparent means to wreak vengeance on the usurpers of their former lands and to regain their hereditary patrimony. With the assistance of O'Neill's captains, they ravaged and plundered the terrified colonists. The confederacy spread. O'Neill's son-in-law, Viscount Mountgarrett, together with the Earl of Thomond's brother, the Baron of Cahir, and the Kavanaghs of Leinster, joined with O'Neill. The former Geraldine fortresses of Newcastle, Shanid, Adare, Pallas and Tarbert were hastily abandoned by their new owners, who fled bag and baggage back to England, some never to return. Edmund Spenser, burned out of his estate at Kilcolman, conveyed the sense of horror and misery of the colonists:

> Out of the ashes of desolation and wasteness of this your wretched Realm of Ireland, vouchsafe to receive the voices of a few most unhappy ghosts of whom is nothing but the ghost now left buried in the bottom of oblivion.[4]

And there was no immediate relief forthcoming from the Crown, as the Desmond adherents, after sixteen years of repression and confiscation, took a bitter and bloody revenge, showing the planters little mercy. Black Tom, Earl of Ormond was, once again, given the task of suppressing the new Desmond revolt. He warned FitzThomas:

> We need not put you in mind of the late overthrow of the earl your uncle, who was plagued with his partakers by fire, sword and famine; and be assured, if you proceed in any traitorous actions, you will have like end.[5]

But the new Geraldine leader had grown tired of waiting for the Crown to reward him for his long loyalty and for his opposition to his late uncle. Ambition made him a willing ally of O'Neill and, in the terminology of the rebellion, he replied to Ormond: 'Englishmen were not contented to have our lands and livings but unmercifully to seek our lives by false and sinister means under colour of law.'[6]

Events in Desmond had repercussions for Eleanor and her son. The Súgán Earl claimed the estates, as the heir of Garrett's disinherited brother, but the Crown had previously recognised Garrett as the legal heir. In the field of politics, recognition of legal title was, however, a matter of expediency. If the rebellion in Munster got out of control, Elizabeth might well consider the restoration of James FitzThomas as the least expensive way to end the conflict. The claim of Eleanor's son, the legal heir, under lock and key in the Tower of London, might consequently be easily ignored. On the other hand, if O'Neill could be convinced that her son, if free, could more effectively unite the Geraldine factions in rebellion, then her son's restoration might be better realised by supporting the rebellion. It was said that O'Neill had employed the services of some of the Munster aristocracy, loyal to the late Earl of Desmond and who had access to his son in the Tower, to effect the boy's escape. The Privy Council acted on the rumour and apprehended Maurice FitzGibbon, the eldest son of the White Knight, and confined him to the Gatehouse in Westminster. Eleanor was drawn towards the complicated web of intrigue and subterfuge that tantalisingly held out hope of her son's restoration.

On his return from court in the late summer of 1598, Donogh O'Connor Sligo joined his wife in Munster. Amidst the intrigue and turmoil, their presence sounded alarm-bells in Dublin Castle. The Irish administration protested to the English Privy Council:

> We understand that O'Connor Sligo . . . is aryvid in Mounster and remayneth here with his wife the Countess of Desmond. We cold have wished that he had have staid longer in England consideringe the general unsoundness of the Irishry here and how apt they are to run with each other into disloyaltie.[7]

But, in the event, O'Neill settled for what was attainable in Munster and backed the claims of the Súgán Earl as the most expedient way to extend rebellion in Munster. Meanwhile, in Sligo, O'Donnell took advantage of Clifford's inability, through a serious lack of supplies and an insufficient army, to extend his control over Sligo. He captured and established his headquarters in Donogh's castle of Ballymote. On their return home Donogh and Eleanor settled instead at Collooney castle to await developments.

Since the death of Lord Burgh in October 1597 Ireland had been without a Lord Deputy. Elizabeth deliberated long over the appointment of a successor. The situation required a steady, trustworthy military leader. But in an ill-advised and impetuous personal decision, the Queen conferred the even more prestigious position of Lord Lieutenant on her current favourite, the temperamental second Earl of Essex. The young, headstrong earl considered the posting an opportunity to enhance his reputation at court and to display his military ability to an infatuated sovereign. On 15 April 1599 he arrived in Dublin with an army of 14,000 soldiers to confront the rebels, who were said to have a force of over 20,000. Accompanied by Eleanor, Donogh hurried to Dublin to renew acquaintance with the Lord Lieutenant, who had befriended him at court. Donogh accompanied Essex on a hosting through Munster before returning to Sligo to try and hold his ground against O'Donnell. Eleanor remained on in Dublin. She succeeded in obtaining husbands for two of her daughters. Margaret married Dermot mac An Dubhaltaigh O'Connor Don, a mercenary leader of some repute from County Roscommon. Katherine, her third daughter, became the wife of her cousin Maurice Roche, Viscount Fermoy. [The late Princess Diana was a descendant of this union.] It was a considerable achievement on Eleanor's part to find suitable partners for her daughters, given the political taint on their pedigree and their lack of a dowry or marriage portion.

Donogh was besieged at Collooney by O'Donnell, desperate to expel him from the last remaining fortress commanding the pass into Connaught from Donegal. It was also vital to English interests in Connaught that Donogh should retain possession of the castle. Consequently Essex ordered Sir Conyers Clifford to relieve his friend and sent an urgent order to O'Connor's brother-in-law, Tibbott-ne-Long, to bring ordnance and supplies by sea from Galway to Sligo. Clifford, the Earl of Clanrickard, O'Connor Don and an army of 2,000 soldiers marched overland towards Collooney. On 5 August 1599 they attempted to cross the Curlew mountains but were defeated with heavy losses by O'Donnell. Clifford was killed in the battle and his body decapitated. O'Donnell came before Collooney castle, where the siege was still in progress, and displayed the head as proof to Donogh. O'Donnell promised that if Donogh surrendered the castle he would restore him to his chieftaincy and provide him with cattle and supplies. It was subsequently reported to Essex that Donogh O'Connor Sligo submitted to O'Donnell because he, being 'under the tyranny of the other, will think any bargain good for him if it bring assurance of life and recovery of lands'.[8] But Donogh had little option. The Crown had proved unable to protect him and, in his present difficult situation, discretion appeared the better part of valour.

Donogh's submission had not allayed the suspicion of the Ulster chieftains that both he and Eleanor were in league with the Crown. Eleanor's preference naturally favoured the side which proposed to advance her son's prospects; up to the present time O'Donnell seemed more inclined to back the cause of the Súgán Earl. The hostility between Donogh and O'Donnell was deep-rooted. 'I have never slept quietly since you came into Ireland', O'Donnell was reported to have said to Donogh, 'for fear of you and your draughts.'[9] O'Donnell monitored Donogh's every move, and it was only with extreme difficulty that he managed to maintain contact with Eleanor in Dublin. He secretly conveyed letters to her by way of his trusted servants James Crean and Mulroney Oge. 'I thought good to write these few lines to you', he explained to her in September 1599, 'to let you understand that I received no answer of the last letters I sent you by Mulroney Oge.'[10] He informed her that he was being closely guarded by O'Donnell, who, at a meeting with O'Neill at Lifford, had with great reluctance agreed that his ally could have temporary custody of Donogh.

During his sojourn with O'Neill, Donogh became godfather to the Ulster leader's son, Shane. But despite the attempts of the Ulster chieftains to cajole or intimidate him into aligning with them, Donogh would give no commitment. His preference continued to be for the Crown. However, the English administration in Ireland had become unable to protect him and the many other minor Gaelic chieftains who, one by one, fell under the dominating influence of O'Neill and O'Donnell. Donogh had little option but to play for time. Through his secret correspondence with Eleanor, however, he realised the Crown should be made aware of his continued loyalty. He pointedly sent her four blank sheets signed with his name which he asked her to deliver to the Lord Lieutenant and Council. He urged her to hurry to him at the first opportunity so that, as he stated, 'I might confer with you of matters that I dare not write, fearing the way'.[11]

As reports of her husband's capitulation circulated in Dublin, Eleanor requested permission from the Council to go to him, 'under pretence', as the officials recorded, 'to give him advice and to hold him sound in heart to the state'.[12] Permission was refused, and the Council instead proposed 'to let slip the bishop his uncle who hath been always fast to the state'.[13] The bishop in question was the unscrupulous chameleon of intrigue and double-dealing, Miler Magrath, the Archbishop of Cashel. Despite the suspicions of the Council, there was little reason for Eleanor to incline, at his juncture, towards O'Neill and O'Donnell. O'Neill seemed determined to espouse the cause of the Súgán Earl at the expense of her son. James FitzThomas unequivocally asserted his right to the title and estates, which he claimed 'of long time hath been wrongfully detained from me and my father who by right of succession was lawful heir to the earldom of Desmond'.[14] At the same time the Dublin administration was taking no chances that the Countess of Desmond, intentionally or otherwise, could be drawn further into the intrigue. Eleanor refused to be deterred in her quest for the restoration of her son, and secretly she slipped out of Dublin and made her way to her husband, to see if the convoluted political situation could be turned to their advantage.

The Earl of Essex spent twenty-one weeks in Ireland, and under his ineffectual leadership the power of the Crown reached its nadir, while the Gaelic confederacy grew from strength to strength. Totally unopposed, O'Neill toured Munster and propounded the more lofty aims of the rebellion as a struggle to the death for the liberty of all Ireland from the English Crown. Meanwhile his ally O'Donnell ran riot in Connaught and compelled the vacillating chieftains there to his side. From England, the Queen berated Essex and ordered him to confront O'Neill in Ulster. But apart from meeting in private with the rebel chief—an incident which was later to be used to discredit him in England—Essex achieved little. His many enemies at court made the most of his indiscretions as they plied the Queen with rumours about his disloyalty and intrigue with O'Neill. On hearing this, the impetuous Essex deserted his post and fled to the side of his

Gloriana. But where money and the security of the realm were concerned, there was no favouritism to be had from Elizabeth. She promptly imprisoned her errant protégé and then set her mind to the task with which she had temporised for so long—the reconquest of Ireland.

Her formula for success centred on two people: Charles Blount, Lord Mountjoy, a straightforward military man, who succeeded Essex as Lord Deputy, and Sir George Carew, a wily, political manipulator, who was appointed Lord President of Munster. Both arrived in Ireland in the early months of 1600. The military abilities of the one, combined with the deviousness of the other, were finally to bring Gaelic Ireland to its knees. Mountjoy contended that the total destruction, both economically and militarily, of O'Neill's lordship was the only way forward. Carew's job was to loosen O'Neill's grip on Munster by destroying the Desmond alliance. With this end in view, he was to bring his Machiavellian capacity for intrigue and subterfuge to bear on the complex political situation obtaining in the province. And he had rich and fruitful pastures in which to sow the seeds of discord and dissension. The pawn he chose to use was a young man who, as yet, lay unsuspectingly entombed and forgotten behind the walls of the Tower of London.

Many schemes presented themselves to the unscrupulous mind of Carew. He set about exploiting the unstable and divided Gaelic society he encountered by pandering to the greed, fear and ambition of the principal actors. 'We hold it a very good piece of policy', he wrote, 'to make them cut one another's throats, without which this kingdom will never be quiet.'[15] First he attempted to involve Eleanor in a plot against James FitzThomas, the Súgán Earl, before hastily abandoning this plan when it was rumoured that Eleanor and her husband were in league with O'Donnell. Carew then turned his attention to Eleanor's daughter, Margaret, the wife of the mercenary leader Dermot O'Connor Don. Dermot commanded an army of 1,500 men in Munster, supposedly in the pay of O'Neill. Carew learned of Margaret's opposition to the Súgán Earl and her determination that her brother should be restored to the title and estates of his father. He consequently enlisted her help in a plot whereby her husband, for the sum of £1,000, would capture FitzThomas and deliver him to Carew. To sow further dissension among the confederates, Carew was to write a letter to FitzThomas to make it appear that the latter had conspired with him to kill Dermot O'Connor. This letter was then given to Dermot on the pretext that it had been intercepted from Carew to James FitzThomas.

O'Connor subsequently captured FitzThomas, ostensibly in O'Neill's name, displayed the fraudulent letter, secured his prisoner at Castle Lishin, near Charleville, and secretly alerted Carew. But before Carew could take custody of the prisoner, a large force of rebels rescued FitzThomas and, when the plot was discovered, O'Connor was forced to flee into Connaught. But despite his dramatic escape, the Súgán Earl's supporters, one by one, gradually deserted him. With little hope of assistance from O'Neill, who was being harried by Mountjoy in Ulster, like his uncle before him, the Súgán Earl took to the woods and mountains of Munster to await the promised aid from Spain. To completely destroy the Desmond alliance Carew next conceived a crafty project which, if successful, would transfer the allegiance of the Desmond adherents from O'Neill to the Crown. In order to put his plan into operation, Carew produced both his trump and his pawn in the person of Eleanor's son, James.

Little had been heard about the young Geraldine since 1593 when, in a plaintive letter to Sir Robert Cecil, he described himself as

> *an unknowne stranger who though young in years, yet being old in miserye . . . being born the unfortunate son of a faulty father. I have never since my infancy breathed out of prison—the only hellish torment to a faithful hart to be houlden in suspect when it never thought upon offence.*[16]

His long prison confinement had left its mark on the Desmond heir. The feebleness of his physical constitution was mirrored in a timid and malleable personality. He had little fight or vision, nor any sense of personal destiny, only a nervous and ingratiating desire to do his captor's bidding. To further split the Geraldine alliance, Carew now planned to restore the Geraldine heir to the Desmond title and to a small portion of his father's estate. The plan was greeted with little enthusiasm by the Queen, who had expended so much to subdue and destroy his father. Cecil, although generally supportive of the idea, voiced the Queen's fears to Carew. 'Much ado we have had', he wrote, 'to persuade her to have him sent, because she feareth that when he shall be there, it is not unlike but he and his cousyn

[James FitzThomas, the Súgán Earl] may be reconciled.'[17] Cecil, however, used his influence with the Queen, and in the autumn of 1600 preparations were set in train for the return of the forgotten Geraldine to Munster.

There is no evidence to suggest that Eleanor was even aware of her son's return. She was at this time ill and in semi-captivity at Ballymote castle, when news of her son's arrival in Munster reached her. But the happy tidings were tinged with disappointment. To prevent the formation of a Carew-inspired conspiracy between her son and her husband, O'Donnell imprisoned Donogh on Lough Esk. There he was 'so cruelly kept in prison that were it not for my soul's safety I would wilfully have ended my days . . . my legs being almost rotted with the fretting of the irons'.[18] Eleanor waited expectantly for some communication from her son, but no letter or messenger arrived. Carew spied on his every move, and in any event James seemed unwilling to undertake anything that was contrary to the wishes of his handlers.

The complex political manoeuvrings eventually drew Eleanor into their net. A marriage between her daughter Joan to Red Hugh O'Donnell was proposed. Whether to effect her husband's release, or to have the Ulster chieftains back her son rather than the Súgán Earl, she agreed to the alliance. She subsequently sent her servant and confidante, Mary MacShee, 'who served her at and ever since the rebellion of her husband and in whom she reposeth her greatest trust',[19] with letters to her daughter Joan, containing O'Donnell's proposal. She told her daughter that she was to return with Mary MacShee by the way of 'Thomand to Clanrickarde to Tibbott-ne-Long and so to Sligo',[20] thus giving rise to speculation of a wider-based conspiracy. Mary MacShee duly made the journey to Limerick and delivered her mistress's letters to her daughter. But Carew had Eleanor's servant under surveillance and bided his time to see if his young Geraldine charge would reveal any knowledge of the messenger's visit to his sister and the contents of his mother's letter. And Carew was not disappointed, for 'at the end of three days the Earl related to the President that such a woman was in Towne',[21] though he insisted that she had brought no message to him from his mother, but only to his sister Joan.

Carew arrested Mary MacShee who, under interrogation, revealed 'that the especiall cause of her coming was to convey away the said

Lady Joane to her mother and from thence to O'Donnell who had promised to consummate a Marriage with her'.[22] Upon examination by Carew, Joan acknowledged the fact, but insisted that she had never intended to yield to her mother's command without the advice and consent of her brother whom, she vowed, she had been about to acquaint with the details of her mother's letter. To deter further intrigue, Carew had Joan committed under restraint to the house of an alderman in Limerick City, while Mary MacShee was made a close prisoner in Limerick jail.

The episode, from beginning to end, was testimony to the scheming and deception that shrouded the actions of both sides during the period, with Carew the principal manipulator of every cut and thrust of the political intrigue. The motivations of Eleanor and the other parties are difficult to ascertain, as the surviving records are mainly derived from sources close to Carew, who seemed, at times, to lose himself in the depth and extent of his own duplicity. In Carew's opinion, the entire episode masked a wider and more devious conspiracy against the Crown, involving not only O'Donnell but also the supposedly loyal lords of Connaught—Donogh O'Connor Sligo and Tibbott-ne-Long Bourke of Mayo. Of Eleanor's part in the affair, Carew reported to the Crown that

> *The old craftie Countesse, understanding that this complot was discovered, pretended that her indeavours in seeking to effect this Marriage tended to no other end but to reduce O'Donnell to be a subject, although indeed there was nothing lesse meant.*[23]

Eleanor's son was reported by Carew to have been 'grievously offended with his mother, that would deal in a business of that weight and so nearly tending to his subversion'.[24]

A further incident occurred during this time which added substance to Carew's suspicion of a wider conspiracy. When Carew ordered Dermot O'Connor Don, who since the abortive plot against the Súgán Earl had remained in Connaught, to return to Munster to support his brother-in-law, he issued O'Connor with a safe pass out of Connaught. As he moved south with a small armed force, O'Connor was apprehended and killed at Gort by Tibbott-ne-Long Bourke, who claimed that he slew O'Connor because he was a traitor to the Crown. Carew, however, accused Bourke of conspiring with O'Neill,

O'Donnell and O'Connor Sligo to extend the rebellion in Munster, either by compelling the Earl of Desmond to their cause or, failing that, by ensuring that there would be no Gaelic support forthcoming for him in Munster.

Amid the storm of accusations and counter-accusations that followed, Eleanor never actually met her son during his brief stay in Munster. In fact she was never to see him alive again. His initial reception in the province as the lawful Geraldine heir had been encouraging. As Carew anticipated, the presence of the young earl drew support away from the Súgán Earl. At Youghal people flocked in their thousands to welcome the rightful heir of Desmond. At Kilmallock he was greeted by a large multitude 'as if they came to see him whom God had sent to be that comfort and delight, their souls and hearts most desired'.[25] And, as was reported, 'they welcomed him with all the expression and signs of joy, everyone throwing upon him wheat and salt as a prediction of future peace and plenty'.[26] But when the anglicised Geraldine displayed his religious preference by attending a Protestant service, as Carew reported to the Crown, he soon became an alien among his own people and asked to be allowed return to England. 'So far is his humour and religion different from the Irish as he thinks all time lost which is spent among them,'[27] Carew assured Sir Robert Cecil. James's usefulness to the Crown's cause in Munster subsequently receded. Cecil ordered his return to England, with a promise to find him a suitable bride and to bestow on him a small allowance. But at the age of thirty in mysterious circumstances he died in the Tower. Notice of his death was brief. 'I have buried according to your direction my Lord of Desmond,' his doctor reported to Cecil in November 1601. 'His necessary charges for his lodging in my house, my counsel unto him, his physic taken and funeral charges I have in a bill ready to show.'[28] In death as in life the last Earl of Desmond, like his father, seemed destined to be a drain on Elizabeth's purse-strings, as bills for the services and necessities provided for him during the last months of his captivity continued to be submitted to the Crown long after his death.

Four of his sisters and his servant, William Power, remained at Cork and petitioned the English Privy Council for additional subsistence and for 'p'curing Her Majesty's most gracious goodness towards them for their reasonable matching there or here'.[29] Regarding the future of their sister Joan, still under restraint in Limerick, the Privy Council agreed in August 1601 'to set her at liberty again as she was before, referring the care of her well doing to some of her sisters that they may have an eye over her'.[30]

The final episode in the Crown's long war against O'Neill and O'Donnell, and in the even longer war between Gaelic Ireland and England, drew to a ominous close. While Carew schemed and bullied the Geraldine adherents into sullen submission in Munster, Mountjoy wreaked havoc against O'Neill and O'Donnell in Ulster. The policy of devastation and spoliation successfully used against the Earl of Desmond two decades earlier, seemed likely to succeed again in Ulster. 'Our only way to ruine the rebels', Mountjoy advised, 'must be to make all possible waste of the means for life, but', he warned, 'if we be not supplied out of England, we shall as well starve ourselves as them.'[31] The policy was carried on without respite throughout the year 1601, leaving the Gaelic leaders no possibility to harvest or to replenish their stocks. At the same time Mountjoy established well-provisioned forts in the areas he subdued and backed the land campaign with a naval operation, led by Sir Henry Docwra, who landed behind O'Donnell's lines with an army of 4,000 men in Lough Foyle. There was little O'Neill or O'Donnell could do but hold out and wait for the promised aid from Spain. In Munster the Súgán Earl was captured by his erstwhile ally, the White Knight, and delivered to Carew. He was sent to the Tower where, it was reported, in 1607 he died 'in his lunacy'.[32]

On 21 September 1601, 3,800 Spanish soldiers, under the command of Don Juan del Aguila, landed at Kinsale in County Cork where they awaited the arrival of their Irish allies. By the end of October the Spanish were surrounded by Mountjoy and his army, which comprised many 'royalist' Irish. On 2 November Hugh O'Donnell assembled his forces at Ballymote castle and set out on the long march to Kinsale, leaving Eleanor and her husband under guard in the castle, with no part to play in the coming showdown. After weeks of deliberation O'Neill finally threw in his lot with O'Donnell and, at the end of November, joined him at Kinsale. In Mayo, Donogh's brother-in-law, Tibbott-ne-long Bourke, after months of vacillation and intrigue, finally decided to ally with the side which seemed most likely to restore him to the power he had forfeited to O'Donnell's puppet MacWilliam in Mayo. Gathering his clansmen and tributary chiefs he too sailed south to fight with Mountjoy at Kinsale.

Eleanor and her husband could do little but await the outcome of the most significant battle fought for centuries in Ireland, the result of which had enormous implications for their future. For Kinsale was more than a mere military confrontation. With a victory for O'Neill and O'Donnell rested some hope of the survival of a Gaelic Ireland and freedom from the malevolent control of England. For Mountjoy victory would destroy the Gaelic confederacy and secure Ireland, once and for all, for the Crown. For the multitude of minor players like Eleanor and her husband, who made up the patchwork quilt of Gaelic leadership, they could do little to influence events. Their fate and future lay in the hands of whatever side emerged victorious from Kinsale.

Mountjoy's subsequent victory at Kinsale on 24 December 1601 brought the long and bloody Tudor conquest of Ireland to a close. O'Neill returned to an Ulster devastated by famine, and opened negotiations with the Crown. O'Donnell made for Spain in the hope of reviving Spanish interest and support in the cause of Gaelic Ireland. In the last years of her eventful reign, the aged Elizabeth had lived to see her ambition in Ireland fulfilled, though at immense cost both to her Crown and to Ireland.

News of the defeat trickled through to Eleanor and her husband at Sligo, as the remnants of O'Donnell's army, under the leadership of his brother Rory, made their way back to Ulster. Despite the defeat, the cause of Gaelic Ireland still held a strange and fatal attraction. Already rumours of O'Donnell's imminent return with help from Spain kept the fires of resistance aglow. Fearful that the government's policy was 'to dispossess the principall men of their lands and livings and to get the same unto her Majestie's hands',[33] Donogh and his brother-in-law, Tibbott-ne-Long Bourke, now conspired to oppose the advance into Sligo of an English army commanded by Sir Oliver Lambert. But Lambert evaded their planned ambush and reached the town, which he found virtually destroyed. In August 1602 Rory O'Donnell compelled O'Connor Sligo to join him in the last recorded victory of the long campaign, when they routed a substantial English army at the place of Clifford's defeat three years previously. But the collapse of the cause of Gaelic Ireland was too far advanced to be reversed by a single victory. And at almost sixty years of age Eleanor realised this better than most. She knew only too well the outcome of defeat in rebellion.

In late 1602 news of Red Hugh O'Donnell's death in Spain reached Ireland. It was reported that he had been poisoned at the castle of Simancas near Valladolid. In Ulster O'Neill made his conditional peace with the Crown to try to salvage his earldom from the wreckage. O'Connor Sligo made terms with Lambert, who brought him to Athlone to meet with Mountjoy. O'Connor Sligo made a good case to the Lord Deputy, stating that he had been made a virtual prisoner by O'Donnell and had no option but to align with the rebels. Anxious to bring an end to the hostilities in Connaught, Mountjoy pardoned him, and in 1604 Donogh received a knighthood from the Crown.

But peace and pardons aside, the financial fortunes of Eleanor, her family and her husband were still precarious. During the long years of turmoil Eleanor's pension from the Crown had been irregularly paid and her daughters had not received their allowances. Her husband's territory of Carbury had been wasted by the incursions of O'Donnell and by the retaliatory attacks of the Crown forces. O'Connor Sligo testified to the condition of Ballymote, the only habitable castle on his estate: 'It is also greatly defaced and the house burnt down by O'Donnell's people. . . . I will, if granted it,' he promised, 'repair the castle and house.'[34] During Donogh's long absence in England the English administration in Connaught, particularly under Bingham, had also devastated his estate. The focal point of Crown interest was Sligo castle which, after Kinsale, had been taken by Crown forces under Sir John King. Moreover, the rents normally forthcoming from Donogh's estate had been rendered negligible by the late unrest. Both Eleanor and her husband were, once more, near the poverty line. Finally Sir Donogh obtained letters patent to the ownership of Sligo castle. There he settled with Eleanor to confront the new 'war' that was about to erupt over ownership of the land of Ireland.

While English military dominance had been established over Ireland, the ownership of the land still remained largely in Gaelic hands. Under Elizabeth's successor, James I, the battle for possession of the land of Ireland intensified. It was a war waged by lawyers, adventurers, profiteers and officials who, armed with pens, parchment, obscure deeds and money, sought to acquire by illegal or quasi-legal means, the estates and property of the impoverished native aristocracy. In Sligo Sir James Fullerton, a Scottish spy of James I, was granted the castle of Ballymote and the valuable lands of Sligo abbey. The rents payable to Sir Donogh from these properties were consequently distrained from him and he was forced to contest the claims of the new planters in court. Some of his claims were admitted by the Crown and, 'subsidised with government money, Sir Donogh bought from Sir William Taaffe much of the land which the latter had acquired in Sligo'.[35] He successfully instituted legal proceedings in the courts of Chancery and Exchequer to protect his estates from avaricious entrepreneurs who sought flaws in his title, and also to have restored the rents and services due to him from dependent septs. He spent the remaining years of his life attempting to put his estate and property on a secure legal footing by right of English common law. His estate, however, failed to yield sufficient profit, and he was forced to mortgage much land and property, particularly to the merchant families of Galway, who had the means to exploit the reduced circumstances of the old native aristocracy on the collapse of Gaelic law.

While her husband strove to untangle the legal and financial web of his estate, Eleanor, together with her daughters Joan and Ellen, proceeded to England to attempt to extract additional maintenance from the new king, James i. Despite her advanced age and the long years of surviving on the meagre subsistence she had managed to extract from the English administration, and in the face of persistent misfortunes, her hope never waned that fate eventually would deal her a kinder hand. She arrived in London in the summer of 1603 and, as she attested, 'for nine months following the court at great cost',[36] petitioned the King and the Privy Council for the restoration of her pension and for some part of her late husband's estate in Munster. She told Sir Robert Cecil that, owing to the destruction wrought by the late rebellion on her second husband's lordship, she was, once again, 'destitute of a place of abode both for me and mine'.[37] Her daughters petitioned the King in similar vein and attested 'that the misery of our estate is such as we are ashamed to make it manifest to the world'.[38] They appealed also to Sir Robert Cecil because, as they stated, 'your lordship ever stood the best friend that either our brother or selves have had, we beseech you now to assign us some proportionable living to our estates and calling'.[39]

By now Eleanor and her daughters were familiar figures on the outer fringes of court circles, as they hovered in the background, without the money, means or political clout to assert their case, but entirely dependent on the pity and charity of Cecil and other court officials. They followed the royal court from place to place for as long as their meagre means allowed. Lodged in back-street boarding houses and inns, they starved themselves of food and necessities in order to appear in some suitable state at court, wherein lay their only chance to alleviate their plight. They could not afford to dwell on the humiliation and degradation of their position, for the alternative—that they might be denied access to the court to plead their case—was too frightening to contemplate. Eleanor's remarkable will to survive alone brought them through the ordeal.

After much hardship and rejection their mission seemed likely to be successful. In 1605 Cecil arranged to have Eleanor's pension and arrears sanctioned for payment. Eleanor contrived to have an advance of one year paid to her, which she used to clear the debts incurred during her prolonged stay in England. She assured Cecil that she had arranged with the Earl of Kildare that he 'will join her in bonds, that if she die within the year, to restore so much thereof as shall not fall due during her life',[40] for, as she informed him, 'I know no other means to rid me hence or bear my charges; otherwise I must stay longer than I meant, and run further in debte, so much as I shall be unable to go at any time.'[41] But the old campaigner would see many more decades and outlive those from whom she now begged and borrowed. Whether out of compassion for her age and position, or whether to rid himself of a wily and persistent petitioner, whose mental and physical energies defied her years, Cecil granted her demands. He instructed the Lord Deputy and Council in Dublin to deal favourably with the countess and her daughters 'now on their return from England to Ireland and particularly to take order that they be paid from time to time the pension granted them by His Majesty without unnecessary delay'.[42]

While Eleanor managed to have her material wants alleviated, on her return to Sligo with her daughter Ellen, she found Sir Donogh still deeply involved in the legal battle to secure his estates and property. His competitors ironically accused him of seeking to acquire too large an estate, of having 'a great living and cannot be contented',[43] to which he replied, understandably, in view of the encroachment on his ancestral estates by the self-same accusers, 'I bear the name but they have all the substance.'[44] During 1607 and 1608 Sir Donogh fought a series of lawsuits to defend his estate from avaricious entrepreneurs and ambitious former tributary septs who sought to establish claims on the strength of broken or faulty deeds to lands in the hereditary possession of his ancestors. The pressures and expenses of each successive case began to take their toll. 'I am since my coming into Ireland', he complained to Cecil, 'tossed and troubled in wronged lawsuits by my continual disturber Sir William Taaffe, with whom is joined Sir Lionel Guest.'[45] But Sir Donogh was fighting a losing battle. His most deadly adversary was the swelling tide of greed and sharp practice that was far more insidious and effective as a means of reducing the Gaelic aristocracy than the guns and cannon of the previous century. Against this onslaught, Sir Donogh's determined endeavours, even when aided by Eleanor's considerable diplomatic skill, had little hope of success. On 11 August 1609 the old chieftain died at Sligo castle; as Eleanor informed Cecil, 'The tediousness in withstanding the said causes did so weary and wear him out that in the end the grief finished his life.'[46]

Eleanor had every reason to grieve the death of her sober, well-intentioned second husband. He had been kind and considerate and had striven unceasingly to provide her with a lifestyle commensurate to her rank. When every back was turned in her years of greatest poverty and humiliation, Donogh O'Connor Sligo, whether motivated and encouraged by political considerations, or simply from a sense of affection for the abandoned countess, offered her his hand and protection. The inscription Eleanor later had carved over his tomb is testimony to the deep affection she bore him:

> Is your hand the martial hand that shone in war
> And yours the gentle one that shone in peace
> Turned to ashes . . . ?
> I . . . who with moistened cheeks stretch forth
> My arms in redoubled lamentation
> Will ever be mindful of your death.[47]

And the affection which Sir Donogh bore his wife was more materially demonstrated by the extraordinary inheritance which he bequeathed to her and which, inadvertently, was to complicate yet further the already tangled affairs of his estate. As part of her jointure, Sir Donogh bequeathed to his wife 'thirteene castles, one hundred messuages, ten gardens, four thousand acres of land, one thousand acres of pasture, one thousand acres of wood, one thousand acres of moor and three thousand acres of heath'.[48]

Eleanor was, for a second time, a widow, but this time under less traumatic and calamitous circumstances. In theory she was substantially well-off but, in practice, the revenue-raising power of the O'Connor Sligo estate had been eroded over the previous decades. It was impossible to extract rents and dues from tenants and tributary septs who were unable or unwilling to pay. Moreover, the land had been plundered by both sides in the late war and had been neglected in the succeeding years during which the legal war to its ownership raged. The estate required a substantial injection of capital if it was to survive the financial and legal difficulties with which it was encumbered. To ease the financial strain which again threatened to overwhelm her, Eleanor embarked on a matchmaking exercise. In an attempt to consolidate control of the O'Connor Sligo estate, she married her daughter Ellen to Sir Donogh's brother and heir, Donal, a widower of thirty-five years of age. Of Sir Donal and his impending marriage to Eleanor's daughter, it was reported to Sir Robert Cecil:

He speaks English well; he was bred up in the wars in France; the people have a great opinion of him and he is like to prove an honest man if his grafting upon a crabbed stock do not alter his proper nature.[49]

But Eleanor's hopes were destined to be thwarted. Sir Donal survived his brother by a mere two years. Ellen married secondly Sir Robert Cressey of Cong, a member of the English administration in Connaught. Her marriage jointure on her second marriage placed added strain on the viability of the O'Connor Sligo estate. Eleanor married off her youngest daughter, Ellis, to Sir Valentine Browne, son and heir of Sir Nicholas Browne of Kerry. She had initially attempted to arrange a marriage between one of her daughters with the heir to the neighbouring O'Connor Don estate, but for political reasons the Crown opposed 'two such great families joining together'.[50]

Having finally secured matches for her daughters, it was not unreasonable that Eleanor should expect to enjoy her remaining years in the peace and tranquillity that had evaded her all her life. But it was not to be. She was forced to embark on yet another legal battle to protect the lands and property bequeathed to her by Sir Donogh. On the untimely death of her late husband's brother and heir, the O'Connor estate was inherited by his son by a previous marriage, then a minor. The wardship of the young heir was granted by the King to Sir Faithful Fortescue. 'Alarmed by the extent to which the property was tied up in marriage jointures, Fortescue initiated an action in the Dublin courts to have the Countess of Desmond's jointure overthrown'.[51] because, he claimed, of defects in the wording of the conveyance.

During the course of the year 1613 Eleanor made frequent representations to the Irish Privy Council regarding the properties in dispute, which were situated mainly in the area of Sligo town. When the case was eventually scheduled to be heard, she pleaded inability to appear, on the grounds of illness and old age. After a further delay the Council ordered an official investigation into the dispute. The investigators found in her favour and recommended to the Lord Deputy that Eleanor, whom they described as 'growne aged and hath not long to live', should be shown 'as much favour as may be afforded to a lady of her years and quality . . . that shee may at length be freed of theise unexpected troubles'.[52] Eleanor played the part of the aged, feeble lady who, at the end of her days, found herself the victim of greed and circumstance; as such she successfully evoked the sympathy of the Lord Deputy and Council who ruled that she should hold the lands for the term of her life and that they would then pass to Charles, the king's ward.

The Council, not unnaturally, presumed and based their judgement on the premise that Eleanor's death was imminent. But she long outlived both her opponents and her advocates, and retained possession of her jointure to the end of her long life.

Epilogue

Is that Penelope, Elinor, that second chaste Judith,
Indeed buried beneath marble stones?
I, mother Ierne, who with moistened cheeks stretch
forth
My arms in redoubled lamentation,
Will ever be mindful of your death.

INSCRIPTION ON ELEANOR'S TOMB, SLIGO ABBEY

Eleanor resided at Sligo castle for the rest of her life. Her days of petitions and appearances at the English court were over. No further correspondence from her prolific quill appears among the state papers of the day. There are no more allusions to the presence of the 'Lady of Desmond' at the royal court. References to payment of her prized pension, which she had fought so diligently to obtain from the Crown, appear sporadically in the state despatches in the early decades of the seventeenth century. She doggedly fought her case in the law-courts and hung tenaciously on to every acre bequeathed to her by Sir Donogh O'Connor Sligo. She stood her ground despite the powerful and resourceful new breed of fortune-seekers, entrepreneurs and wealthy merchants who, in the years after Kinsale, flooded into Sligo to take advantage, by way of defective title, bribery and sharp practice, of the remnants of the old Gaelic aristocracy and, whenever possible, to replace them as the new masters of the land. It took courage and gumption for an aged widow, on her own, to defend her interests with such success against such able opposition. But her days of penury were at last behind her, and her remaining years were spent in the relative comfort and dignity which had eluded her throughout her early and middle life.

Her ability as a matchmaker for her daughters had paid dividends. Her daughter Joan, for whom she had plotted a marriage with Red Hugh O'Donnell, married Dermot O'Sullivan Beare of Cork. Her third daughter, Katherine, after the death of her first husband, Lord Roche, married Donal O'Brien, afterwards Viscount Clare. On the death of her second husband, Sir Robert Cressey of Cong, her daughter Ellen married her cousin Edmund Butler, who in 1629 had succeeded his grandfather as Baron of Dunboyne; by this marriage Eleanor's unhappy feud with her brother over the disputed estate was laid to rest. Her youngest daughter, Ellis, married Sir Valentine Browne of Ross castle, Killarney, and 'thus as the wife of an undertaker's son enjoyed some portion of the vast estates which had been forfeited by her father's rebellion'.[1]

Eleanor's only son, James, the 'Tower Earl', left no heir. Soon after his death the title was claimed by her first husband's old protagonist, Black Tom, Earl of Ormond, in right of his mother, Joan, as the daughter and heiress of James, the eleventh Earl of Desmond. When the only daughter and heiress of Black Tom was subsequently bestowed in marriage on a Scotsman, Sir Richard Preston, by King James I, the claim to the Desmond earldom was revived. Preston, in right of his wife, was created Earl of Desmond by patent dated 1619. The patent stipulated that if Preston died without male heirs, the earldom should descend to George, the younger son of William Fielding, Earl of Denbeigh, with whom a marriage was then contemplated with Preston's only daughter and heiress. While the marriage did not in effect take place, the provision of the patent was allowed, and the ancient Irish title passed into the Fielding family, who became the Earls of Denbeigh and Desmond. The spirit of Garrett FitzGerald would surely have rested uneasily had his prized title come to rest on the descendants of his bitter rival, the Earl of Ormond.

In 1624 Eleanor erected an impressive tomb for her second husband in Sligo abbey. It is an interesting monument built in renaissance style, and is in an excellent state of preservation to this day. Situated in the south wall of the abbey, adjacent to the high altar, it consists of two arched recesses in which are carved two kneeling figures in profile, representing Eleanor and Sir Donogh. 'Sir Donogh is clad in plate armour, his helmet being placed on the ground behind him. His wife is dressed in a loose flowing overmantle, with a close-fitting cap on which a coronet is placed. Round her neck is a large ruff and a string of beads which supports a cross of the Greek pattern with expanded ends.'[2] The monument is decorated with heraldic emblems of the O'Connor, Butler and FitzGerald families. In 1989 a headstone from the monument was found in Sligo during excavations for a new office block. With Eleanor and her husband is buried her daughter Ellis, who died in 1623. The date of Eleanor's own death is less certain.

Her will, however, is dated 26 November 1638. By it she appointed her sons-in-law, Sir Donal O'Brien and Sir Robert Cressey, her executors 'and willed them to pay all her debts, called her stated accounts, and her funeral expenses out of her moveable goods and chattels'.[3] She bequeathed to her daughter Joan a silver ewer and basin, and to her daughter Ellen all the remainder of her goods, including her plate and jewels. She left various legacies to her grandchildren, friends and servants. 'She bequeathed towards the building of a hospital in Sligo £100, and £200 more (both out of her arrears in England) to be laid out in an annuity mortgage, or land, so as to yield £20 a year towards the support of the poor residing in said hospital.'[4] Despite her traumatic life, Eleanor lived to the remarkable age of well over ninety years, over double the average life expectancy of the time.

That she lived so long is a tribute to her courage, her indomitable will and her superhuman capacity to withstand suffering, loss and deprivation. Her mental ability enabled her to overcome the Machiavellian political practices of her time which brought about the downfall of many greater and more powerful. She endured much personal hardship and tragedy, but with extraordinary resilience returned, time after time, to meet and contend with each successive challenge. She was both a witness to and a participant in a period of almost unparalleled upheaval and destruction which had sucked an entire civilisation into its maw. She had seen a fertile province scorched to a blackened and wasted heathland, its population starve to death, their pitiful cries mingling with the sound of war and the clamour of the victors. She herself suffered the pangs of hunger and the deprivation of a fugitive's life as she stoically stood by her outlawed husband. She knew the pain of being forced to part with her children as, on countless occasions, political necessity tore them from her side. She experienced humiliation, insult, isolation and friendlessness as she pursued her mission for survival alone and without means. But her innate will to survive and her ability to adapt to the new order was the spur that impelled her to overcome her adversity and gave her the strength to outlive her opponents.

Elizabeth, FitzMaurice, Sidney, Perrot, Drury, Sir John of Desmond, Pelham, Malby, Dr Sanders, Burghley, Raleigh, Black Tom, Essex, Red Hugh O'Donnell, Cecil, O'Neill, the list of great and colourful characters with whom she shared the stage, had all passed on. Eleanor alone remained, the last surviving participant in as great a tragedy that ever befell a family and a nation.

In the quiet ruins of Sligo abbey today the tomb she had erected stands as the only reminder of this extraordinary but unsung heroine. In life Eleanor received few bouquets, and her lot in death was total oblivion from written history and even from popular folklore, which preserved the memory of many of her contemporaries. Yet, in musty archives, her prolific correspondence, the script almost indecipherable on the age-darkened, brittle parchment, bears testimony to the life, aims and ambitions of this extraordinary woman, on whom fortune seldom smiled but who steadfastly refused to succumb to the dark shadows that relentlessly clouded her life.

Appendix
The 'Old' Countess of Desmond

While the life of Eleanor Butler, Countess of Desmond, has received little acknowledgement, that of another Countess of Desmond has been recorded by both contemporary and latter-day historians and writers. The countess in question was Katherine FitzGerald, daughter of John FitzGerald, second Lord of Decies in Waterford, and wife of her second cousin, Thomas FitzGerald, twelfth Earl of Desmond. Her main claim to fame was her great longevity, which resulted in her appellation as the 'Old' Countess of Desmond.

One of the earliest references to this paragon of longevity is contained in Sir Walter Raleigh's *History of the World*, in which he records that, while married in the reign of Edward IV, the countess was still alive in 1589. Presuming, as was the custom, that she was married at the age of fifteen, and that the marriage took place in the last year of the king's reign, that would leave her at the remarkable age of 121 years in 1589. But evidence of her continued existence, well into the seventeenth century, is recorded by many contemporary historians, among them the famous Elizabethan writer and traveller Fynes Moryson, who died in 1614. In his *Itinerary*, published in 1617, he stated:

> In our time the Irish Countesse of Desmonde lived to the age of about one hundred and forty yrs, being able to go on foot four or five miles to the market towne, and used weekly so to do in her last yeares and not many yeares before she died.[1]

A few decades later, Lord Bacon in his *History of Life and Death* claimed that she lived to be 140 years old and that during the course of her long life she grew two sets of teeth!

On the death of her husband in 1534, the Old Countess of Desmond settled at Inchiquin castle, a few miles south-west of Youghal, which her husband had assigned to her as part of her jointure for the duration of her life. On her death the castle and lands would automatically revert to the earldom of Desmond. There, it was not unnaturally expected, she would live out her few remaining years. But successive earls of Desmond came and went and Inchiquin remained in the possession of its elderly chatelaine.

It is likely that she and Eleanor met several times during their long lives, especially during 1575, when the controversial enfeoffment of his lands by Eleanor's husband, Garrett, was effected. By a deed dated 5 April 1575 the Old Countess enfeoffed the castle and lands of Inchiquin to the Earl of Desmond. He, in turn, enfeoffed them in trust to his servants, Morris Sheehan and David Roche, for thirty-one years. Whether she supported Garrett's rebellion is unknown, but she was witness to the devastation of Munster and his subsequent death and attainder. In the plantation that followed, Inchiquin castle and lands were part of the Crown grant to Sir Walter Raleigh, who, whether obliged by law or in deference to the age of its antique resident, allowed the Old Countess to remain undisturbed at Inchiquin. Raleigh too expected that her demise would be imminent, but she lived to see Raleigh depart and Inchiquin pass into the grasping hands of Richard Boyle, Earl of Cork. Boyle was less inclined to tolerate the now seemingly unending occupancy of his new property by an aged tenant who simply refused to die. But the Countess resisted his attempts to dislodge her from her perch and, when Boyle persisted, she took matters into her own hands.

In 1604, at the phenomenal age of some 136 years, this female Methuselah set out from County Cork, with her daughter, who was over ninety years of age, for the court of King James I. It was recorded that 'landing in Bristol she came on foot to London', while her daughter 'being decrepid was brought in a little carte, their poverty not allowing better means'.[2] While there is no conclusive evidence as to the outcome of her petition to the king, it does seem likely that the touching and incredible apparition of this ancient woman, who had lived through the reigns of seven monarchs and overlapped with two others, was suitably rewarded. For the Old Countess returned to Inchiquin, where her long life was only brought to an end in 1604 by a bizarre accident. Sir Robert Sidney recorded the circumstances of her death:

She might have lived much longer hade she not mette with a kind of violent death, for she must needs climb a nutt tree to gather nuts, soe falling down, she hurt her thighe, which brought a fever, and that brought death.[3]

So ended the incredible life of the Old Countess of Desmond, although another account places her death ten years later, in 1614. A portrait of a woman which once hung in Muckross abbey, County Kerry, purports to be a likeness of her, painted during her visit to the court of King James in 1604.

Whether she met her death in 1604 or in 1614, the Old Countess of Desmond has entered both legend and history, where she has continued to be considered an inspiration in the records of human longevity.

Older far than my grand-dam, indeed, aye, as old
As that Countess of Desmond of whom we are told
That she lived to much more than a hundred and ten,
And was killed by a fall from a cherry tree, then
What a frisky old girl.[4]

Genealogical Charts

1. The Family Connections of Eleanor, Countess of Desmond

James Butler = Joan
(Baron of Dunboyne) | (dau. of Piers Butler,
d. 1533 | 8th Earl of Ormond)

Honora = Peter Thomas Joan = Roland Eustace Ellen = David Sir
(dau. of James of Grallagh d.s.p. (Viscount Lord Roche Bu
FitzGerald, d. 1579 Baltinglass) (Viscount Fermoy) of C
11th Earl of
Desmond)

James
(Viscount Baltinglass)

Maurice
Lord Roche
d. 1600

Séan ai
O'Carro

Margaret (1) = James = (2) Margaret John = Ellen John Ellis
FitzPatrick (Baron of (dau. of Connor d. 1612 (dau. of
(dau. of Baron of Dunboyne) O'Brien, 3rd Earl Thomas
Upper Ossory) d. 1629 of Thomond) Purcell)

James = Ellen 5 Sons
of Kilconnell (dau. of Walter 2 daughters
d. 1619 Butler, 11th
Earl of Ormond) Garrett FitzGerald (1) = (Countess
14th Earl of Desmond) d.c
d. 1583

Piers Walter Thomas 4 John
d. 1626 daughters d. 1602

Edmund (3) = Ellen = (1) Sir Donal James Margaret
(Baron of O'Connor Sligo (15th Earl of
Dunboyne) d. 1611 Desmond; the
= (2) Sir Robert 'Tower Earl')
Cressey d.s.p. 1601
of Cong

Dar

The author is indebted to Dr K. W. Nicholls, of University College, Cork, for his assistance and his kind permission to use his research material in the compilation of this genealogy.

c Oge MacCarthy = Katherine
of Muskerry) | (dau. of John Lord Barry)
1536

Edmund (2) = Síle = (1) Sir Cormac   = (3) Ricard Saxanach Burke
(Baron of | MacCarthy Reagh   (div.) (2nd Earl of Clanrickard)
Dunboyne) | d. 1582
d. 1567

u.

Honora = Owen   Eleanor = James   Ellen = Dermot
MacDonogh   FitzGerald   MacCarthy
MacCarthy   (Lord of   of Iniskeen
(Lord of   Decies)
Donal   Duhallow)   d.1581
na
Píopaidhe
John Butler (1) = Katherine = (2) Theobald na Sidhéan
of Kilcash   Butler* of Derryluskan

s Walter Thomas Piers   = Eleanor   Richard   William Katherine = Turlough
d.s.p. d.s.p. of   (dau. of   of Blackcaple   Magrath
Rathgoole Oliver Grace   fl. 1578   (son of Miler
of Courtstown)   Magrath, Abp
of Cashel)

Sir John Magrath
of Aylevalane

(2) Sir Donogh O'Connor Sligo
=   d. 1609

An   Joan = Dermot   Maurice (1) = Katherine = (2) Donal   Ellis   = Sir Valentine
h   O'Sullivan Lord Roche   O'Brien d. 1623   Browne of
on   Beare   d. 1600   Ross,
Killarney

D'Dwyer   Donogh = Eleanor   Connor   Other sons
d.s.p. 1638 Southwell   (2nd Viscount Clare)   and one
d.c. 1670   daughter

* Tibbot na Sidhéan's father was John Butler, a brother of
James Butler, Baron of Dunboyne. Tibbot married secondly
Katherine Burke, widow of James FitzMaurice FitzGerald (d. 1579).

2. Earls of Desmond

Bracketed numerals is indicate earls who were not in *de facto* possession.

Asterisks indicate Lords of Decies.

3. Earls and Dukes of Ormond

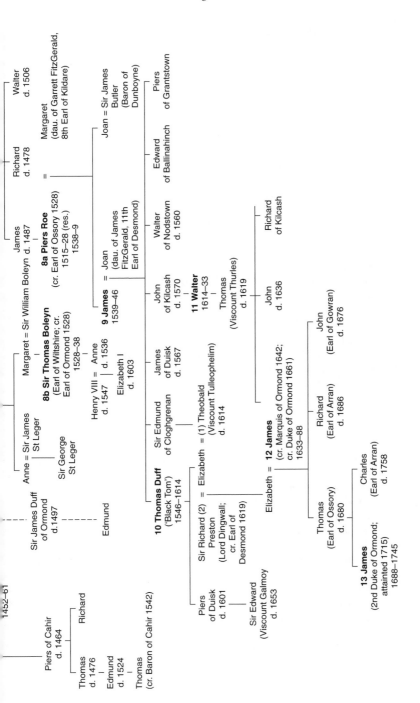

References

Chapter 1 (PAGES 6–21)

1. Maher, *Romantic Slievnamon*, 48.
2. *Cal. s.p. Ire.*, *1601–3*, 251.
3. Canny, *Elizabethan Conquest*, 22.
4. Nicholls, *Gaelic and Gaelicised Ireland*, 8.
5. Beckett, *Making of Modern Ireland*, 14.
6. Nicholls, *Gaelic and Gaelicised Ireland*, 73.
7. Ibid., 73.
8. Ibid., 78.
9. Joyce, *Social History of Ancient Ireland*, II, 120.
10. Butler, 'Peter Butler of Grallagh Castle', *Butler Soc. Jn.*, I, 3 (1970), 197.

Chapter 2 (PAGES 22–31)

1. Smith, *Elizabethan Epic*, 90.
2. 'The Housekeeping of Irish Chiefs', *Dublin University Magazine*, LIII (1959), 463.
3. Annals of the Four Masters, V, 1561.
4. N.L.I., MS 2289.
5. *Unpubl. Geraldine Docs*, I, 505.
6. Ibid.
7. N.L.I., MS 2289.
8. Ibid.
9. *Unpubl. Geraldine Docs*, I, 20.
10. Ibid.
11. Cox, *Hibernia Anglicana*, II, 392.
12. Nicholls, *Gaelic and Gaelicised Ireland*, 164.
13. Berleth, *Twilight Lords*, 76.
14. *Cal. Carew MSS*, I, 417.
15. Ibid., 416.
16. MacCurtain, 'The Fall of the House of Desmond', *Kerry Arch. & Hist. Soc. Jn.*, VIII (1975), 89.
17. Ibid.
18. *Annals of the Four Masters*, V, 1579.
19. Bagwell, *Tudors*, II, 48.
20. Ibid.
21. *Unpubl. Geraldine Docs*, II, 506.
22. Berleth, *Twilight Lords*, 81.

Chapter 3 (PAGES 32–52)

1. Berleth, *Twilight Lords*, 80.
2. FitzGerald, *Geraldines*, appx.
3. *Unpubl. Geraldine Docs*, I, 42.
4. Ibid., 56.
5. FitzGerald, *Geraldines*, 64.
6. *New Hist. Ire.*, III, 87.
7. *Unpubl. Geraldine Docs*, I, 61.
8. *Sidney State Papers*, 34.
9. Ibid.
10. Canny, *Elizabethan Conquest*, 32.
11. *Sidney State Papers*, 67.
12. *Cal. Carew MSS*, III, lvii.
13. Bagwell, *Tudors*, II, 114.
14. *Cal. Pepys MSS*, 47.
15. Ibid.
16. Wright, *History of Ireland*, 419.
17. Ibid., 422.
18. Gaughan, *Knights of Glin*, 29.
19. *New Hist. Ire.*, III, 88.
20. *Cal. Cecil MSS*, I, 349.
21. FitzGerald, *Geraldines*, 102.
22. *Unpubl. Geraldine Docs*, I, 23.
23. Ibid., II, 517.
24. Countess of Desmond to Munster Commissioners, 11 Jan. 1568 (S.P., 63/23/16 ii).
25. Ibid.
26. Munster Commissioners to Countess of Desmond, 13 Jan. 1568 (S.P., 63/23/16 iv).
27. L'Estrange, *Conna and Desmond*, 46.
28. *Cal. Cecil MSS*, I, 355.
29. S.P., various entries.
30. Desmond to Thomas FitzGerald, 10 May 1568 (S.P., 63/26/39).
31. *Unpubl. Geraldine Docs*, II, 515.
32. Bagwell, *Tudors*, II, 137.
33. Ibid., 138.
34. Canny, *Elizabethan Conquest*, 67.
35. FitzGerald, *Geraldines*, 259.
36. Bagwell, *Tudors*, II, 151.
37. *New Hist. Ire.*, III, 92.
38. Bagwell, *Tudors*, II, 154.
39. *New Hist. Ire.*, III, 93.
40. Bagwell, *Tudors*, II, 151.
41. *New Hist. Ire.*, III, 89.

Chapter 4 (PAGES 53–68)

1. FitzGerald, *Geraldines*, 262.
2. Ibid., 263.

3. Black, *Reign of Elizabeth*, 477.
4. *Unpubl. Geraldine Docs*, II, 484.
5. *Cal. Carew MSS*, V, 415.
6. *Unpubl. Geraldine Docs*, II, 415.
7. Ibid.
8. Ibid., 485.
9. Desmond to Cecil, 5 July 1570 (S.P., 63/30/69).
10. *Sidney State Papers*, 130.
11. St Leger to Privy Council, 17 Oct. 1570 (S.P., 63/30/87).
12. Ibid.
13. *Cal. Pat. Rolls Ire., Eliz.*, 546.
14. *New Hist. Ire.*, III, 99.
15. Berleth, *Twilight Lords*, 40.
16. St Leger to Burghley, 6 June 1571 (S.P., 63/32/54).
17. Ibid.
18. *Unpubl. Geraldine Docs*, I, 28.
19. Ibid., 62.
20. Ibid.
21. N.L.I., MS 2289.
22. *Unpubl. Geraldine Docs*, II, 485.
23. Ibid.
24. *New Hist. Ire.*, III, 91.
25. Lambeth Palace Library, MS 616.
26. Bagwell, *Tudors*, III, 210.
27. Ibid.
28. Ibid., 234.
29. *Cal. Carew MSS*, V, 430.
30. Bagwell, *Tudors*, II, 238.
31. Wright, *History of Ireland*, 437.
32. *Unpubl. Geraldine Docs*, II, 485.

Chapter 5 (PAGES 69–84)
1. *New Hist. Ire.*, III, 99.
2. Bagwell, *Tudors*, II, 248.
3. Ibid., 251.
4. Desmond to Lord Deputy and Council, 25 Nov. 1573 (S.P., 63/43/6 i).
5. Bagwell, *Tudors*, II, 487.
6. Justice Walshe to Lord Deputy, 24 Nov. 1573 (S.P., 63/43/6 III).
7. Bagwell, *Tudors*, II, 253.
8. Desmond to Lord Deputy and Council, 25 Nov. 1573 (S.P., 63/43/6 i).
9. Ibid.
10. Bagwell, *Tudors*, II, 263.
11. Ibid.
12. *Cal. Carew MSS*, I, 463.
13. Ibid.
14. *Cal. S.P. Ire., 1574–85*, 169.

15. Lord Deputy to Burghley, 18 Apr. 1574 (S.P., 63/45/72).
16. *Cal. S.P. Ire., 1574–85*, 27.
17. Ibid.
18. *Cal. Carew MSS*, I, 473.
19. Bagwell, *Tudors*, II, 281.
20. Ibid.
21. *Cal. Carew MSS*, I, 475.
22. *Cal. Pat. Rolls Ire., Eliz.*, 109.
23. *Cal. Carew MSS*, I, 480.
24. Ibid., 482.
25. Bagwell, *Tudors*, II, 284.
26. Countess of Desmond to the Queen, 12 Sept. 1574 (S.F., 63/47/55).
27. Ibid.
28. Ibid.
29. FitzGerald, *Geraldines*, 274.
30. *Cal. S.P. Ire., 1574–85*, 482.
31. *Unpubl. Geraldine Docs*, I, 25.
32. Ibid.
33. *Cal. S.P. Ire., 1574–85*, 65.
34. *Cal. Carew MSS*, II, 21.
35. Ibid., 22.

Chapter 6 (PAGES 85–113)

1. Canny, *Elizabethan Conquest*, 154.
2. *New Hist. Ire.*, III, 91.
3. Canny, *Elizabethan Conquest*, 3.
4. *New Hist. Ire.*, III, 100–1.
5. Wright, *History of Ireland*, 446.
6. MacCarthy, *Florence MacCarthy Mór*, 2.
7. Bagwell, *Tudors*, II, 314.
8. Wright, *History of Ireland*, 447.
9. Ibid.
10. Ibid., 448.
11. *Cal. S.P. Ire., 1574–85*, xxxv.
12. Perrot, *Chronicle of Ireland*, 141.
13. Ibid., 142.
14. *New Hist. Ire.*, III, 102.
15. *Cal. De L'Isle and Dudley MSS*, II, 60.
16. Ibid., 66.
17. *Cal. S.P. Ire., 1574–85*, xli.
18. Lord Deputy to Privy Council, 20 Feb. 1578 (S.P., 63/60/14).
19. Ibid.
20. Ibid.
21. *Cal. S.P. Ire., 1574–85*, xlii.
22. Chambers, *Granuaile*, 93.
23. S.P., 63/19/56.

24. Countess of Desmond to the Queen, 30 Sept. 1578 (S.P., 63/62/23).
25. Ibid.
26. *Cal. Carew* MSS, II, 140.
27. *Walsingham Letter-Book*, 161.
28. Ibid.
29. Ibid.
30. Lord Chancellor Gerrard to Burghley, 3 Jan. 1579 (S.P., 63/65/3).
31. Ibid.
32. Bagwell, *Tudors*, II, 365.
33. O'Faolain, *The Great O'Neill*, 76.
34. Curtis, *History of Ireland*, 198.
35. *New Hist. Ire.*, III, 104.
36. FitzGerald, *Geraldines*, 279.
37. Nicholls, *Gaelic and Gaelicised Ireland*, 73.
38. *Cal. S.P. Ire., 1574–85*, lvi.
39. Ibid.
40. Ibid.
41. Bagwell, *Tudors*, III, 21.
42. Ibid., 22.
43. *Walsingham Letter-Book*, 135.
44. *Annals of the Four Masters*, III, 3784.
45. *Unpubl. Geraldine Docs*, I, 30.
46. *Walsingham Letter-Book*, 168.
47. Ibid.
48. Ibid., 169.
49. Ibid.
50. Benvenuta, 'The Geraldine War—Rebellion or Crusade?', *Ir. Cath. Hist. Comm. Proc.* (1963–8), 17.
51. *Walsingham Letter-Book*, 195.
52. Desmond to Privy Council, 10 Oct. 1579 (S.P., 63/69/51).
53. *Walsingham Letter-Book*, 195.
54. *Cal. S.P. Ire., 1574–85*, 190.
55. Ibid.
56. *Walsingham Letter-Book*, 202.
57. Desmond to Privy Council, 10 Oct. 1579 (S.P., 63/69/51).
58. Desmond to Ormond, 10 Oct. 1579 (S.P., 63/69/50).
59. Archbishop Loftus and Sir Henry Wallop to Privy Council, 31 Oct. 1579 (S.P., 63/67/76).
60. Perrot, *Chronicle of Ireland*, 162.
61. *Cal. Carew* MSS, II, 162.
62. *Unpubl. Geraldine Docs*, I, 32.
63. Ibid.
64. Perrot, *Chronicle of Ireland*, 164.
65. *Cal. Carew* MSS, III, xvii.

Chapter 7 (PAGES 114–147)

1. Smith, *Elizabethan Epic*, 143.
2. *Cal. Carew MSS*, III, 164.
3. Ibid., 265.
4. Ibid.
5. Ibid., II, 207.
6. Ibid.
7. Pelham to Walsingham, 16 Feb. 1580 (S.P., 63/71/209).
8. Ibid.
9. Ibid.
10. *Cal. Carew MSS*, II, 190.
11. Cox, *Hibernia Anglicana*, II, 361.
12. *Walsingham Letter-Book*, 249.
13. *Cal. Carew MSS*, II, 225.
14. Berleth, *Twilight Lords*, 125.
15. *Cal. Carew MSS*, II, 236.
16. Pelham to the Queen, 1 Apr. 1580 (S.P., 63/73/28).
17. Pelham to Walsingham, 5 Apr. 1580 (S.P., 63/73/33).
18. Pelham to Wallop, 21 June 1580 (S.P., 63/73/68 i).
19. Countess of Desmond to Privy Council, 28 June 1580 (S.P., 63/73/67).
20. Wright, *History of Ireland*, 470.
21. Captain Golde to Walsingham, 17 Sept. 1580 (S.P., 63/70/51i).
22. *Cal. Carew MSS*, II, 292.
23. Fenton to Walsingham, 8 Aug. 1580 (S.P., 63/75/27).
24. *Cal. Carew MSS*, II, 297.
25. St Leger to Burghley, 9 Oct. 1580 (S.P., 63/77/24).
26. Perrot, *Chronicle of Ireland*, 170.
27. Malby to Walsingham, 24 Oct. 1580 (S.P., 63/77/52).
28. Bagwell, *Tudors*, III, 64.
29. Ibid., 69.
30. Perrot, *Chronicle of Ireland*, 172.
31. *Annals of the Four Masters*, v, 1761.
32. St Leger to Burghley, 15 May 1581 (S.P., 63/83/25).
33. Countess of Desmond to Lord General and Council of Munster, 29 Apr. 1581 (S.P., 63/83/6 ii).
34. Ibid.
35. Ibid.
36. Spenser, *Poetical Works*, ed. Smith and de Selincourt, 3.
37. Lord Deputy and Council to Lord General and Council of Munster, 10 May 1581 (S.P., 63/83/6 III).
38. Ibid.
39. Ibid.
40. Ibid.
41. St Leger to Burghley, 15 May 1581 (S.P., 63/83/25).
42. *Annals of the Four Masters*, v, 1779.
43. *Cal. S.P. Ire., 1574–85*, 339.

44. Perrot, *Chronicle of Ireland*, 178.
45. Lord Deputy to Privy Council, 22 June 1582 (S.P., 63/93/45).
46. Walsingham to Lord Deputy, 25 June 1582 (S.P., 63/93/53).
47. Ibid.
48. Countess of Desmond to Burghley, 28 Aug. 1582 (S.P., 63/94/104).
49. Countess of Desmond to Lord Deputy, 28 Aug. 1582 (S.P., 63/94/104 i).
50. FitzGerald, *Geraldines*, 289.
51. Ibid.
52. O'Faolain, *The Great O'Neill*, 81.
53. Captain Norris to Lords Justices Loftus and Wallop, 24 Sept. 1582 (S.P., 63/96/3 i).
54. *Cal. S.P. Ire., 1574–85*, 268.
55. Ibid.
56. *Annals of the Four Masters*, v, 1783.
57. *Cal. Carew MSS*, II, 364.
58. Desmond to Ormond, 5 June 1583 (S.P., 63/102/87 i).
59. Captain Golde to Burghley, 13 Apr. 1583 (S.P., 63/101/25).
60. *Cal. S.P. Ire., 1574–85*, 287.
61. Ormond to Burghley, 18 June 1583 (S.F., 63/102/88).
62. *Annals of the Four Masters*, v, 1793.
63. Bagwell, *Tudors*, III, 113.
64. Ormond to Burghley, 28 Nov 1583 (S.P., 63/105/83).
65. Perrot, *Chronicle of Ireland*, 182.
66. Ibid.
67. O'Faolain, *The Great O'Neill*, 83.

Chapter 8 (PAGES 148–70)

1. *New Hist. Ire.*, III, 111.
2. *Cal. Pat. Rolls Ire., Eliz.*, lxv.
3. Ibid.
4. Ormond to Burghley, 28 Nov. 1583 (S.P., 63/105/83).
5. Ormond to Lords Justices Loftus and Wallop, 16 Dec. 1583 (S.P., 63/106/13).
6. Ibid.
7. *Cal. S.P. Ire., 1574–83*, 484.
8. *Cal. Pat. Rolls Ire., Eliz.*, 94.
9. Ormond to Burghley, 26 June 1584 (S.P., 63/107/48).
10. *Unpubl. Geraldine Docs*, II, 67.
11. Ibid.
12. Lord Deputy to the Queen, 24 Oct. 1584 (S.P., 63/112/35).
13. Bagwell, *Tudors*, III, 123.
14. *New Hist. Ire.*, III, 112.
15. Lord Deputy to the Queen, 24 Oct. 1584 (S.F., 63/112/35).
16. Ibid.
17. *Unpubl. Geraldine Docs*, II, 68.
18. Ibid.
19. *New Hist. Ire.*, III, 113.
20. *Unpubl. Geraldine Docs*, III, 552.

21. Ibid.
22. Ibid., 553.
23. Ibid.
24. Ibid.
25. Ibid.
26. Ibid., 535.
27. Ibid.
28. *New Hist. Ire.*, III, 113.
29. Archbishop Loftus to Burghley, 18 June 1585 (S.P., 63/1 12/89).
30. Countess of Desmond to Burghley, 4 Sept. 1585 (S.F., 63/112/90).
31. Countess of Desmond to Burghley, 10 Feb. 1586 (S.P., 63/113/68).
32. *Cal. Pat. Rolls Ire. Eliz.*, 108.
33. Smith, *Elizabethan Epic*, 177.
34. Ibid., 175.
35. Ibid., 176.
36. Ibid., 181.
37. Ibid.
38. Archbishop Loftus to Burghley, 10 May 1586 (S.P., 63/124/8).
39. *Unpubl. Geraldine Docs*, II, 69.
40. *Cal. Pat. Rolls Ire., Eliz.*, 116.
41. Ibid., 70.
42. Ibid., 72.
43. Smith, *Elizabethan Epic*, 182.
44. *Unpubl. Geraldine Docs*, II, 72.
45. Spenser, *Poetical Works*, ed. Smith and de Selincourt, 3.
46. Smith, *Elizabethan Epic*, 203.
47. *Cal. Pat. Rolls Ire., Eliz.*, 186.
48. N.L.I., MS D.10028.
49. Ibid.
50. B.L., Lansdowne MS 65.
51. *Unpubl. Geraldine Docs*, appx, 567.
52. O'Dowd, 'Landownership in the Sligo Area, 1585–1641', 85.
53. Wood-Martin, *History of Sligo*, I, 323.
54. *Cal. S.P. Ire., 1596–7*, 325.
55. *Cal. Pat. Rolls Ire., Eliz.*, 479.
56. Ibid.
57. O'Dowd, 'Landownership in the Sligo Area, 1585–1641'. 111.
58. *Cal. Cecil MSS*, VII, 282.
59. Ibid.
60. *Cal. Pat. Rolls Ire., Eliz.*, 479.
61. *Cal. Cecil MSS*, VII, 378.

Chapter 9 (PAGES 171–92)

1. *New Hist. Ire.*, III, 123.
2. *Cal. Cecil MSS*, VIII, 248.
3. O'Faolain, *The Great O'Neill*, 203.

4. Ibid., 205.
5. Bagwell, *Tudors*, III, 303.
6. Ibid.
7. Lords Justices Loftus and Gardiner to the Privy Council, 31 Oct. 1598 (S.P., 63/202/3/135).
8. *Cal. S.P. Ire., 1599–1600*, 172.
9. Ibid., 158.
10. Ibid.
11. Ibid.
12. Ibid., 172.
13. Ibid.
14. *Cal. Salisbury MSS*, X, 67.
15. *Cal. S.P. Ire., 1600–1*, 424.
16. *Unpubl. Geraldine Docs*, II, 489.
17. Ibid., 492.
18. *Cal. S.P. Ire., 1601–3*, 572.
19. *Cal. Carew MSS*, II, 490.
20. Ibid.
21. *Pacata Hibernia*, 108.
22. Ibid.
23. Ibid., 109.
24. Ibid.
25. Bagwell, *Tudors*, III, 383.
26. Ibid.
27. *Cal. Carew MSS*, IV, 33.
28. *Cal. Salisbury MSS*, II, 491.
29. *Unpubl. Geraldine Docs*, II, 497.
30. Ibid.
31. Moryson, *Itinerary*, IV, 390.
32. Bagwell, *Tudors*, III, 391.
33. Moryson, *Itinerary*, IV, 214.
34. 'History of Ballymote Castle', *R.S.A.I. Jn.*, LVII (1927), 98.
35. O'Dowd, 'Landownership in the Sligo Area, 1585–1642', 240.
36. *Cal. Salisbury MSS*, XVI, 371.
37. Ibid.
38. Ibid., XV, 373.
39. Ibid.
40. Ibid., XVII, 587.
41. Ibid.
42. *Cal. S.P. Ire., 1603–6*, 568.
43. *Cal. Salisbury MSS*, XVIII, 291.
44. Ibid.
45. Ibid., XX, 136.
46. *Cal. S.P. Ire., 1608–10*, 760.
47. National Monuments Commission, Sligo Abbey.
48. Wood-Martin, *History of Sligo*, II, 12.

49. *Cal. S.P. Ire., 1608–10*, 298.

50. *Cal. S.P. Ire., 1606–8*, 197.

51. O'Dowd, 'Landownership in the Sligo Area, 1585–1641', 244.

52. Wood-Martin, *History of Sligo*, III, 11.

Epilogue (PAGES **193–6**)

1. Bagwell, *Tudors*, III, 384.

2. National Monuments Commission, *Sligo Abbey*.

3. Wood-Martin, *History of Sligo*, I, 257.

4. Ibid.

Appendix (PAGES **197–9**)

1. Rowan, *Olde Countesse of Desmonde*, 5.

2. Ibid., 12.

3. Ibid., 21.

4. Ibid.

Bibliography

1. MANUSCRIPT SOURCES

British Library
Cotton Titus MSS, BXIII, BXVIII, Papers on Irish affairs, 1559–1602. Lansdowne MS 65.

Hatfield House, Hertfordshire
Cecil Papers, 50/83; 51/30, 101; 55/15; 62/25, 86; 68/38; 75/46; 179/96.

Lambeth Palace Library
MS 616, ff. 157, 163, 165 (N.L.I. microfilm p 1701).
National Library of Ireland
MSS 2163, 2288–9, 2788, D. 2541, D. 2604, D. 2648, D. 2679, D. 10028.
State Papers relating to Ireland (microfilm; originals in Public Record Office, London): 63/19/56; 63/23/16, 16 ii, 16 iv, 32 VIII, 32 ix; 63/26/29, 39; 63/30/69, 87; 63/32/54; 63/34/33 i; 63/43/6 i, 6 III; 63/45/72; 63/47/55; 63/60/14; 63/61/53; 63/62/23, 24; 63/63/9, 58; 63/65/3, 4; 63/67/76; 63/69/50, 51, 76; 63/70/35, 51 i; 63/71/46, 209; 63/73/28, 33, 67, 68 i; 63/75/27; 63/76/51 i; 63/77/24, 52, 53; 63/80/39; 63/83/6 i, 6 ii, 6 III, 25; 63/87/7; 63/93/45, 53; 63/94/104, 104 i; 63/96/3 i; 63/101/11, 25; 63/102/86, 87 i, 88; 63/103/14; 63/105/83; 63/106/13; 63/107/48; 63/109/59; 63/112/35, 68, 89, 90; 63/113/68; 63/124/8; 63/150/39; 63/202/3/135; 63/207/1/32.

Glin, County Limerick
Papers and records in the keeping of the Knight of Glin.

Kiltinan Castle, Fethard, County Tipperary
Papers and records in the keeping of the late Mrs M. Ogden White.

2. CONTEMPORARY SOURCES

Annála Ríoghachta Éireann: Annals of the Kingdom of Ireland by the Four Masters, from the earliest period to the year 1616, ed. and trans. J. O'Donovan, 7 vols (Dublin 1851).
Annals of Loch Cé: A Chronicle of Irish Affairs, 1014–1590, ed. W.M. Hennessy, 2 vols (London 1871).
Carney, J., ed., *Poems on the Butlers of Ormond. Cahir and Dunboyne, 1400-1650* (Dublin 1945).
Cox, Sir R., *Hibernia Anglicana*, 2 vols (London 1689–90).
Davies, Sir J., *A Discovery of the True Causes Why Ireland Was Never Entirely Subdued until the Beginning of His Majesty's Happy Reign* (London 1612); facsimile reprint (Shannon 1969).

Derricke, J., *The Image of Irelande* (London 1581).

Holinshed, R., *Chronicles of England, Scotland and Ireland*, ed. J. Johnson, 6 vols (London 1807–8).

Moryson, F., *An Itinerary* (London 1617); 4 vols (Glasgow 1907–8).

O'Cleary, L., *The Life of Hugh Roe O'Donnell, Prince of Tirconail, 1586–1602* (Dublin 1893).

O'Daly, D., *Initium. Incrementa et Exitus Familiae Geraldinorum ac Persecution is Haereticorum Descriptio* (Lisbon 1655); trans. C.P. Meehan (Dublin 1878).

O'Sullivan Beare, P., *Ireland under Elizabeth, being portion of the History of Catholic Ireland by Don Philip O'Sullivan Beare*, ed. M.J. Byrne (Dublin 1903).

Perrot, J., *The Chronicle of Ireland, 1584–1608*, ed. H. Wood (Dublin 1933).

Spenser, E., *A View of the Present State of Ireland … in 1596*, ed. W.L. Renwick (Oxford 1970).

[Stafford, T.], *Pacata Hibernia* (London 1633); ed. S.H. O'Grady (London 1896).

Unpublished Geraldine Documents, ed. S. Hayman, 4 pts (Dublin 1870–81).

The Walsingham Letter-Book, or Register of Ireland, May 1578 to December 1579, ed. E. Hogan and N. MacNeill (Dublin 1959).

3. CALENDARS AND PRINTED MANUSCRIPT SOURCES

Calendar of the Carew Manuscripts, ed. J.S. Brewer and W. Bullen, 6 vols (London 1867–73).

Calendar of the Cecil Manuscripts, 8 vols (London 1883–99).

Compossicion Booke of Conought, ed. A.M. Freeman (Dublin 1936).

Calendar of the De Lisle and Dudley Manuscripts, 6 vols (London 1925–66).

Calendar of Fiants of the Reign of Elizabeth (Appendix to 12th–18th Reports of the Deputy Keeper of the Public Records of Ireland) (Dublin 1877–94).

Calendar of Ormond Deeds, ed. E. Curtis, Vols II–VI (Dublin 1934–70).

Calendar of the Patent and Close Rolls of Chancery in Ireland, Henry VIII to 18th Elizabeth, ed. J.C. Morrin (Dublin 1861).

Calendar of the Patent and Close Rolls of Chancery in Ireland, Elizabeth, 19 year to end of reign, ed. J.C. Morrin (Dublin 1862).

Irish Patent Rolls of James I: Facsimile of the Irish Record Commission's Calendar, foreword by M.C. Griffith (Dublin 1966).

Calendar of the Pepys Manuscripts (Dublin 1911).

Calendar of the Manuscripts of the Marquis of Salisbury, 23 vols (London 1883–1973).

Sidney State Papers, 1565–70, ed. T. Ó Laidhin (Dublin 1962).

Calendar of the State Papers relating to Ireland, 24 vols (London 1860–1912).

4. SECONDARY SOURCES: BOOKS

Anthologia Hibernica, Vol. I (Dublin 1793).

Bagwell, R., *Ireland under the Tudors*, 3 vols (London 1885–90).

— *Ireland under the Stuarts*, 3 vols (London 1909–16).

Beckett, J.C., *The Making of Modern Ireland. 1603–1923* (London 1966).

Berleth, R., *The Twilight Lords* (London 1979).

Black, J.B., *The Reign of Elizabeth, 1558–1603* (Oxford 1959).

Burke, Sir B., *Genealogical History of the Dormant, Abeyant and Extinct Peerages of the British Empire* (London 1883).

Canny, N., *The Elizabethan Conquest of Ireland: A Pattern Established, 1565–76* (Hassocks 1976).

Chambers, A., *Granuaile: Grace O'Malley—Ireland's Pirate Queen* (Dublin 2009).

— *Shadow Lord: Tibbott-ne-Long Bourke, First Viscount Mayo (1567–1629)* (Dublin 2007).

Clare, W., ed., 'The Testamentary Records of the Butler Families in Ireland' in *Genealogical Abstracts* (Peterborough 1932).

Cogan, A., *The Ecclesiastical History of the Diocese of Meath, Ancient and Modern*, Vol. I (Dublin 1874).

Curtis, E., *A History of Ireland* (London 1936).

Dunboyne, Lord, *Butler Family History* (Kilkenny n.d.).

Falls, C., *Elizabeth's Irish Wars* (London 1950).

FitzGerald, B., *The Geraldines: An Experiment in Irish Government, 1169–1601* (London 1951).

Gaughan, J.A., *The Knights of Glin: A Geraldine Family* (Dublin 1978).

Joyce, P.W., *Social History of Ancient Ireland*, Vols I–II (Dublin 1913).

Knox, H.T., *History of the County Mayo* (Dublin 1908).

Leask, H.G., *Irish Castles and Castellated Houses* (Dundalk 1972).

L'Estrange, A.G., *Conna and Desmond* (Dublin 1897).

Lodge, J., *Peerage of Ireland*, Vol. VI (Dublin 1789).

McCalmont, R.F., *Memoirs of the Binghams* (London 1915).

MacCarthy, D., *The Life and Letters of Florence MacCarthy Mór* (Cork 1975).

McClintock, H.F., *Handbook on Old Irish Dress* (Dundalk 1958).

— *Irish and Highland Dress* (Dundalk 1950).

MacCurtain, M., *Tudor and Stuart Ireland* (Dublin 1972).

McGurk, J.J., *The Fall of the Noble House of Desmond, 1579–85.*

Maher, J., ed., *Romantic Slievenamon in History, Folklore and Song* (Tipperary 1955).

Moody, T.W., and Martin, F.X., *The Course of Irish History* (Cork 1967).

Morley, H., ed., *Ireland under Elizabeth and James I* (London 1890).

National Monuments Commission, *Mainistir Sligigh* (Sligo Abbey) (Dublin n.d.).

New History of Ireland, Vol. III: *Early Modern Ireland, 1534–1691*, ed. T.W. Moody, F.X. Martin and F.J. Byrne (Oxford 1976).

Nicholls, K.W., *Gaelic and Gaelicised Ireland in the Middle Ages* (Dublin 1972).

— *Land Law and Society in Sixteenth-Century Ireland* (Dublin 1976).

O'Brien, B., *Munster at War* (Cork 1971).

O'Dowd, M., 'Landownership in the Sligo Area, 1585–1641' (M.A. thesis, University College, Dublin, 1979).

O'Faolain, S., *The Great O'Neill* (London 1950).

Ronayne, C. O'L., *History of the Earls of Desmond* (London 1929).

Rowan, A.B., *The Olde Countesse of Desmonde* (Dublin 1860).

Sainthill, R., *The Old Countess of Desmond* (Dublin 1861).

Smith, L.B., *The Elizabethan Epic* (London 1966).

Spenser, E., *Poetical Works*, ed. J.C. Smith and E. de Selincourt (London 1912).

Tower of London, Official Handbook (London 1984).

Wood-Martin, W.G., *History of Sligo, County and Town*, 3 vols (Dublin 1882).

Wright, T., *The History of Ireland from the Earliest Period of the Irish Annals to the Present Time* (London n.d.).

5. SECONDARY SOURCES: JOURNALS AND ARTICLES

Butler Society Journal, I, 3 (1970): Butler, T., 'Peter Butler of Grallagh Castle'.

— I, 5 (1973–4): Butler, G., 'The Battle of Affane'.

Clonmel Historical and Archaeological Journal, I (1968).

Cork Historical and Archaeological Society. Journal, 2nd series, III, 28 (1897): Butler, W., 'The Division of South Munster under the Tudors'.

— 2nd series, XXVI (1920).

Dublin University Magazine, LIII (1959): 'The Housekeeping of Irish Chiefs'.

Irish Catholic Historical Committee. Proceedings (1962): Mooney, C., 'The Irish Church in the Sixteenth Century'.

— (1963–8): Benvenuta, Sister M., 'The Geraldine War—Rebellion or Crusade?'.

Irish Genealogist, II, 3–6 (1945–8): Ward, M., 'The Barony of Dunboyne'.

Irish Geography, V, 3 (1966).

Irish Monthly, LIV (1926).

Kerry Archaeological and Historical Society, Journal, II (1969): Culhane, T.F., 'Traditions of Glin and its Neighbourhood'.

— VIII (1975): MacCurtain, M., 'The Fall of the House of Desmond'.

Limerick Field Club Journal, I, 2 (1897).

Meath Archaeological and Historical Society, Records, VI, 2 (1976): Ward, M., 'Townland Names in the Barony of Dunboyne'.

Royal Historical and Archaeological Association of Ireland, Journal, 4th series, V (1878–9).

Royal Society of Antiquaries of Ireland, Journal, XXXIII (1903): Westropp, T.J., 'Notes on Askeaton, Co. Limerick'.

— XXVII (1907): Westropp, T.J., 'The Principal Ancient Castles of the County Limerick'.

— XXXIX (1909).

— LVII (1927): 'History of Ballymote Castle'.

Index